The Effects of Social Health Insurance Reform on People's Out-of-Pocket Health Expenditure in China

Kai Liu

The Effects of Social Health Insurance Reform on People's Out-of-Pocket Health Expenditure in China

The Mediating Role of the Institutional Arrangement

Springer

Kai Liu
School of Labor and Human Resources
Renmin University of China
Beijing
China

ISBN 978-981-10-9445-3 ISBN 978-981-10-1777-3 (eBook)
DOI 10.1007/978-981-10-1777-3

Softcover reprint of the hardcover 1st edition 2016

Printed on acid-free paper

This Springer imprint is published by Springer Nature
The registered company is Springer Nature Singapore Pte Ltd.

Foreword

The new healthcare reform in China has entered its seventh year. Despite the earlier debate on the direction of healthcare reform towards marketization or public welfare, social health insurance (SHI) has become a central measure in response to the plight of "difficult access to and unaffordable cost of healthcare". With the coverage of social health insurance gradually expanding to include almost the entire population, research in recent years has attempted to evaluate the effectiveness and efficiency of the health insurance scheme as a key strategy of reform. However, systematic research with rigorous data and theoretical discussion about the operation and implementation of social health insurance are still rare.

This book distinguishes itself among all researches of China's healthcare reform with four prominent strengths. First, it asks an important but insufficiently studied question: Why does the application of social health insurance in China turn out to work against its original will to reduce the cost of healthcare, but instead lead to the inflation of medical expenditure, especially individuals' out-of-pocket spending (OOPS)? The book is devoted to deciphering this paradox through comprehensive analyses and thoughtful interpretation of empirical data. Second, it attempts to understand the mechanism of the actual operation of social health insurance via a unique angle, the theoretical perspective of institutional arrangements. Through investigation of the mediating role of reimbursement, behavior management and purchasing mechanism of the social health insurance, the book clearly demonstrates the paths by which participation in social health insurance leads to increased out-of-pocket spending of patients. Third, it employs a mixed-methods design to delineate the full picture of the operation of social health insurance. In addition to the sophisticated quantitative analyses using the nationally representative data, China Health and Retirement Longitudinal Study (CHARLS), what makes this book outstanding is the rich qualitative data collected from the author's immersion in the daily practice of health facilities for four months of intensive fieldwork. The observation of everyday administration of social health insurance agencies and health facilities, as well as the communications with multiple stakeholders with regard to their various experiences in the process, provides convincing explanations of why this unintended cost-inflating effect of social health insurance actually happens as a result of malfunctioned purchasing mechanism. Last, the book proposes a single payer model which provides valuable insights to the next stage of healthcare reform in China. Given the complicated interactions among multiple stakeholders revealed in the study, it suggests establishing a strong and unified social health insurance purchaser to overcome the drawbacks of fragmented small-scale social health insurance agencies and to mobilize greater resources for raising the benefits of reimbursement. Eventually, the reform shall lead to a healthy and active social health insurance governance system.

As the supervisor of Mr. Kai Liu's doctoral study, I had the privilege to witness the entire process of this research. I can say with definite confidence that this is a work that condenses the author's original thoughts, strong commitment, and full dedication to the field of health policy research. It is with great enthusiasm that I recommend this book to you, and believe that you will learn a lot from it, be you a researcher, educator, student, health practitioner, policy maker, or just anyone who is interested in what is going on with our healthcare system and reform.

August 2016

Qiaobing Wu
Associate Professor
Department of Social Work &
Jockey Club School of Public Health and Primary Care
The Chinese University of Hong Kong
Hong Kong

Acknowledgements

What makes me be me? I have been thinking of this bizarre but stimulating question throughout my academic career. In the toughest moments of my doctoral study, I built a mental kingdom in my mind where I decided my future growth. I called it "the awakening of self-consciousness." However, the expansion of this kingdom smashed numerous invaluable things, including friendship, sympathy, happiness, and life. I began to revisit the question. What indeed makes a better self? I found an answer that I firmly believe cannot be wrong any longer—it is people. I am indebted to people around me who talk to me, make friends with me, and give me my second life.

This book was developed using a revised version of my doctoral dissertation. First and foremost, I thank my dissertation supervisors, Prof. Wu Qiaobing and Prof. Wong Chack-Kie. It is interesting that I am the last doctoral student of Prof. Wong and the first of Prof. Wu. It is very fortunate for me to act as the connection between their academic lives. Prof. Wu must be the first person to whom I have to give all my thanks. She is either my supervisor, or one of my best friends. Her never-ending support helps me find my path onto the broad academic road. She and her outstanding work have introduced me to the world of genuine scientific research. Professor Wong, my former supervisor, acted as both a most learned theorist and a strict father. He inspired me with a great interest in social welfare theories as well as their application. His challenging comments always pushed me to constantly rethink my ideas and research framework. My habit of critical thinking must be bestowed to him.

I also want to thank my dissertation committee chair, Prof. Wong Hung, and the committee members, Prof. Dai Haijing and Prof. Xiong Yuegen, for their outstanding guidance, careful review, and considerate kindness. I received academic training by Prof. Wong even as a master's student. He is a role model for applying theoretical studies to practice. In fact, I learned a lot from his admirable achievements in the social movement, and with poverty and labor issues. Professor Dai surprised me with both her academic works and teaching. I was once the teaching assistant in her course Fundamentals of Social Welfare. Her innovative teaching style encouraged me to revisit many theories and to find the real interesting points. Professor Xiong met with me in California. Despite such a short meeting, I was convinced by his academic and humanistic feelings.

Thanks must also be extended to the Department of Social Work at The Chinese University of Hong Kong, where I grew from beginner to academic researcher. The Department is like a mother ship, in which I am deeply rooted. I am indebted to all the professors, lecturers, as well as staff there, especially Prof. Ngai Ngan-Phum, Prof. Chen Ji-Kang, Prof. Mok Bong-Ho, Prof. Lam Ching-Man, Prof. Joyce Ma, Prof. Steven Ngai, Prof. To Siu Ming, Prof. Xu Ying, Stephanie, Heman, Joey, and Carol. I also thank the School of Social Welfare, University of California, Berkeley and Harvard Medical School, both in the United States, where I spent over one year as a visiting student under the supervision of Prof. Julian Chow and Prof. Chunling Lu. Prof. Chow generously offered to help admit me to UC Berkeley, which was my first time visiting another country. Moreover, he was tolerant, nice, and inspiring, which created a comfortable surrounding for my research. Professor Lu opened my eyes to health economics and the healthcare systems worldwide. She offered me most valuable multidisciplinary training.

My gratitude must also go to all my dear friends. Professor Wu Fan, Liao Mingxi, Wang Yazhen, Wang Zhilong, Hou Diankun, Ma Yi, Zhang Kai and Ayi Guli, Zheng Feng, Wang Xile, and Zhang Guangqiang provided generous support for my study, either financially or emotionally. Without this support, I could not even survive physically. In particular, Prof. Wu Fan is just like an older sister to me. All my academic and personal growth owes much to her. I want to express my heartfelt thanks to Dr. Liu Xiaoting, Prof. Liu Junqiang, Prof. Su Yang, Liang Yan, Zhao Ruiling, Luan Hui, Li Mengting, Guo Rui, Lin Chuan, Li Chunkai, Ma Gaoming, Carol Peng, Wang Miao, Ge Lisha, Sun Qian, Yu Miao, Xia Lili, Bai Xiao, Yuan Rui, and Liu Ying. Most of the guys without a "Prof." title are my dear classmates in the doctoral program. Without their intellectual and emotional support, I really could not travel such a long journey. I have firm confidence that they will become an excellent group of scholars with the "Prof." title in future.

I have had a notion in mind for a long time. If translated directly from Chinese, it reads that "I own the earth with my parents and the sky with my wife." I grew up in a poor peasant family. My parents, Liu Fuyuan and Guo Jingrong, fed the hungry family by relying on farming. It has been them who gave me the greatest courage to discover the world. My wife, Danni, opened a new and colorful world for me. The unexpected meeting with her is the sweetest thing. I hope that the next sweet thing is growing old with her by my side. I also thank my younger brother, my mother-in-law, and my father-in-law. I am never alone in the company of them.

Finally, I would like to gratefully acknowledge financial support from the National Social Science Foundation of China (Youth Project, 16CSH032).

Kai Liu

Contents

About the Author

Dr. Kai Liu is an Assistant Professor of the Department of Social Security, School of Labor and Human Resources, Renmin University of China. His areas of expertise lie in health policy, social policy in China, and the comparative social security system. He obtained his Ph.D. degree from The Chinese University of Hong Kong. In 2013, he visited the University of California, Berkeley in the United States to study health policy and health economics. He won a Fulbright Scholarship and from 2014 to 2015 visited Harvard University in the United States to conduct a comparative study of catastrophic health spending.

Abbreviations

BHRSS	Bureau of Human Resources and Social Security
BoH	Bureau of Health
CHARLS	China Health and Retirement Longitudinal Study
CHC	Community Health Center
DHRSS	Department of Human Resources and Social Security
DoH	Department of Health
DRGs	Diagnosis-Related Groups
GMI	Government Medical Insurance
NCMS	New Cooperative Medical Scheme
OOPS	Out-of-Pocket Health Spending
SEM	Structural Equation Modeling
SHI	Social Health Insurance
THC	Township Health Center
UEBMI	Urban Employee Basic Medical Insurance
URBMI	Urban Resident Basic Medical Insurance

List of Figures

List of Tables

Summary

This study examines and explains the relationship between social health insurance (SHI) participation and out-of-pocket spending (OOPS), as well as the mediating role that the institutional arrangement of SHI plays in this relationship, in China.

Accordingly, this study embraces a new institutionalist approach and develops a theoretical framework that involves two perspectives: of determination and of strategic interaction. From the perspective of determination, we identify three mechanisms of SHI; that is, reimbursement, behavior management, and purchasing. From the perspective of strategic interaction, we adopt a calculus approach to explore the interaction between SHI agencies, healthcare providers, and patients, and the role that SHI and other institutions play in shaping that interaction.

This study uses a mixed-method design. The quantitative analysis draws data from a nationally representative dataset. It employs regression analysis using the instrumental variables method to test the impact of SHI participation on a series of medical expenditure indicators, and uses structural equation modeling to examine the performance of the three mechanisms of SHI. The qualitative analysis uses semistructured interviews to trace the interaction among stakeholders and between stakeholders and institutions in the healthcare sector. We conduct fieldwork in a Chinese province. We adopt thematic analysis to facilitate the data analysis.

The quantitative analysis finds that SHI schemes have a statistically positive effect on the rise of medical expenditures by increasing the use of treatment items, prolonging days of hospitalization, and increasing total medical expenditures. Structural equation modelling reveals that the reimbursement mechanism offers considerable benefits to insured patients; however, the behavior management and purchasing mechanisms perform poorly. SHI participants prefer to go to higher-level hospitals, use more medical items, and have a longer hospital stay compared with uninsured patients. As a result, SHI participation has a weak or no significant association with OOPS. It indicates that the malfunction of the behavior management and purchasing mechanisms undermines the performance of the reimbursement mechanism.

The qualitative analysis of the behavior management mechanism reveals that SHI agencies use the referral system and tiered copayment and deductibles to guide patients' choices of health facilities. However, the magnitude of these strategies is offset by the inequitable allocation of healthcare resources and the benefits concern of patients. In addition, the reimbursement provided by SHI may stimulate patients to go to high-level health facilities.

Furthermore, the qualitative analysis of the purchasing mechanism reveals that SHI agencies use similar strategies of purchasing to restrain the improper prescription behaviors of doctors and the excessive demands of patients, including payment methods reform, and indicator management. However, these strategies are undermined by the strategic interaction between SHI agencies, doctors, and patients, which is further shaped by larger disenabling institutional surroundings. The inequitable allocation of healthcare resources, the poor compensation system of health facilities, the distorted price schedule, and the fragmented design of the SHI system induce SHI agencies to be weak purchasers, propel healthcare providers to be profit-driven, and are responsible for the moral hazard of patients.

This study is expected to contribute to theory and policy practice in the following ways. It implies that the institutional arrangement plays a mediating role in the relationship between welfare institutions and social outcomes; it also suggests that welfare institutions may be shaped and undermined by the larger institutional surroundings through the strategic interaction among actors. Finally, this study proposes a single payer model, profiling the process of establishing a strong and unified SHI purchaser.

Chapter 1
Understanding a Paradox in the Social Health Insurance Reform in China

For developing nations, there is a crucial issue of concern for health policy development: how to mobilize and manage financial resources for health systems. Among the major designs of health schemes, two stand out as competing options: social health insurance (SHI) and a tax-based system (e.g., the National Health Service in the United Kingdom). Nevertheless, a wave of SHI initiatives has swept across many developing countries in recent years (Hsiao and Shaw 2007; Wagstaff 2007). SHI, as an approach to financing the mobilizing of funds and the pooling of risk, is seen by many health planners as a "magic" solution to health financing and delivery problems (Hsiao and Shaw 2007).

1.1 Social Health Insurance in China

SHI has made remarkable progress in China from the end of the 1990s to the beginning of the 2010s, alongside the restoration of Chinese social security systems under economic transition from a planned to a market economy. The main efforts of SHI reform focus on replacing the traditional with new types of insurance schemes and expanding the new schemes to the population nationwide (Wong et al. 2006).

The SHI system has undergone a major transition since the foundation of the People's Republic of China in 1949. Before the large-scale health insurance reform starting at the end of 20th century, China implemented the Government Medical Insurance (GMI) for employees in government and public institutions, the Labor Insurance for workers in state-owned enterprises, and the Cooperative Medical Scheme for rural residents. These former schemes were established in accordance with collectivism and the planned economy that was implemented from 1949 to around 1978. As the emerging marketization reform ruined the political, social, and economic basis of these schemes, they gradually collapsed, leaving 47 % of all residents and 87 % of rural residents with no health insurance in 1998 (Wang 2005).

K. Liu, *The Effects of Social Health Insurance Reform on People's Out-of-Pocket Health Expenditure in China*, DOI 10.1007/978-981-10-1777-3_1

As a developing country with the largest population in the world, China's healthcare system was under tremendous pressure. To protect people's financial risks due to serious health cost inflation, the Chinese government chose the SHI model to reinvent healthcare financing. In 1998, the state established the Urban Employee Basic Medical Insurance (UEBMI) for employees with formal relationships with employers in urban areas, replacing the traditional Labor Medical Insurance (State Council 1998). In 2003, the New Cooperative Medical Scheme (NCMS) was enacted by the state to cover rural residents, replacing the traditional Cooperative Medical Scheme (General Office of State Council 2003). In 2007, the state piloted the Urban Resident Basic Medical Insurance (URBMI) for urban residents without employment, such as the elderly, children, and the disabled (State Council 2007), and expanded it to other cities gradually. Now, the SHI system in China is composed of these three schemes, UEBMI, URBMI and NCMS, together with GMI for employees in governments and public institutions in a few places, and the Medical Financial Assistance scheme for low-income households in urban and rural areas. During the first decade of the 21st century, under the guidance of the expedient policy principle *Universal Coverage with Shallow Benefits* proposed by the central government (Yip et al. 2012), coverage expansion became a policy priority through which almost all people in China were recruited into SHI schemes within a short period of time. The number of enrollees of UEBMI in urban China rose from 18 million in 1997 to 237 million in 2010, with a 13.47 times increase; the number of URBMI in urban China grew 4.54 times from 43 million in 2007 to 195 million in 2010; and NCMS in rural China witnessed the most considerable development with the number of enrollees rising 12.11 times, from 69 million in 2004 to 836 million in 2010. The development of various SHI schemes in China is demonstrated in Fig. 1.1.

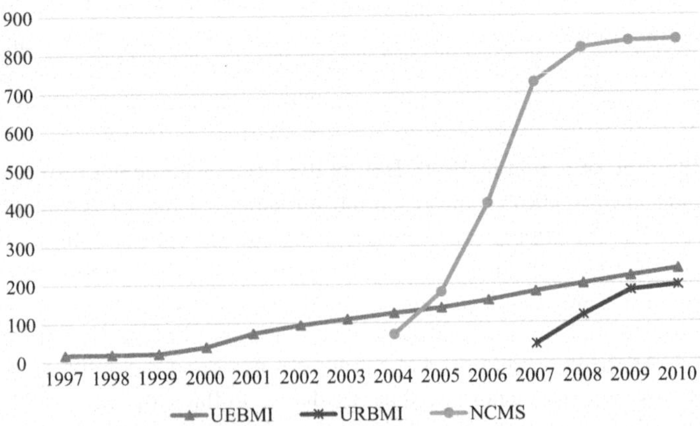

Fig. 1.1 The coverage of SHI schemes: 1997–2010. *Note* Unit = 1 million people. *Source* China Health Statistical Yearbook, 2000–2011; China Labor Statistical Yearbook, 2000–2011

However, the development of SHI has not actually gained consensus from both policy makers and scholars to be used as a major measure of China's national healthcare reform, which started in about 2005. There are basically two debates about the reform: the so-called "government-oriented opinion" and the "market-oriented opinion." The essence of the former opinion is to subsidize healthcare providers, arguing that the main problem of China's healthcare system lies in the retrenchment of government subsidies to healthcare providers, which indulges the healthcare market with excessive development. It advocates that the government should take the role of a major healthcare provider, replacing the dominant role of doctors in the market (Li 2009). According to the views of some scholars (Gu et al. 2006), the arguments favoring government provision are prone to advocate, in essence, the return of the traditional public health service model of the Maoist era. On the contrary, the essence of the market-oriented opinion is to subsidize demand side of healthcare; that is, to support enrollment into SHI schemes. Although it also attributes the major cause of Chinese healthcare problems to the retrenchment of government subsidies, it is opposed to the restoration of the public health service model of the Maoist era, which it argues conflicts with the global trend of public–private cooperation in the public service realm. The opinion advocates the establishment of a national SHI system through which public interests in the healthcare sector are represented by SHI agencies instead of by individuals themselves. SHI agencies are believed to possess great bargaining power, which enable them to negotiate with healthcare providers to improve the efficiency, quality, and utilization of health services (Gu 2010). In the new round of healthcare reform enacted in 2009, the government invested an additional fund of ¥800 billion to assist the reform, of which about two thirds were used to subsidize the demand side (Yip et al. 2012). This indicates the significance of SHI reform in healthcare system reform in China.

As China's healthcare reform continues to pave its way, many practical problems and their corresponding debates have emerged. One of the debates is whether and how SHI reform affects medical expenditures, especially out-of-pocket health spending (OOPS), the protection of which is the initial aim of SHI.

1.2 An Emerging Paradox

The slogan favored by those who advocate SHI is that it decreases patients' OOPS and hence reduces health-related financial problems. However, the problem of the affordability of healthcare seems to be unmitigated by the development of SHI, even though such schemes now cover almost the whole population in China.

Before the new round of healthcare reform in 2009, coverage expansion of SHI was given significant priority, through which the government aimed to reach universal coverage to ensure health security for everyone (Gu 2008; Yip et al. 2012). However, a 2010 survey showed that public complaints about the problems of healthcare reform and affordability in urban areas increased from 21.1 % in 2007 to

34.8 % in 2009 (Horizon China Research and Consultation Group 2010). In more recent years, a few studies have emerged that investigated the effect of SHI participation on the health status of, access to healthcare of, affordability of and financial protection to citizens (Chen et al. 2011 ; Chen and Jin 2012; Jiang et al. 2011; Jung and Liu 2012; Lei and Lin 2009; Liu and Zhao 2006; Liu et al. 2002, 2012; Long et al. 2010; Lu et al. 2011; Shi et al. 2010, 2011; Sun et al. 2009, 2010; Wagstaff and Lindelow 2008; Wagstaff et al. 2009; Wang et al. 2005, 2009; Xiao et al. 2010; Yi et al. 2009; Yip and Hsiao 2009; You and Kobayashi 2009; Zhang et al. 2010; Zhou et al. 2008, 2012). Some of these studies found there to be an adverse effect of SHI schemes on enrollees' affordability of medical access and medical expenditure. The studies recognized that the SHI schemes may not reduce medical expenditures, but may even increase them. Using the China Health and Nutrition Survey data, together with two other household surveys, Wagstaff and Lindelow (2008) suggested that SHI increases the risk of high and catastrophic spending, which is due to SHI encouraging individuals to seek care when they are sick and also, to seek it from higher-level providers. Zhou et al. (2012) conducted a study to evaluate the benefit equity that insured residents with different economic levels obtained from UEBMI, URBMI, and NCMS, respectively, using data from a household survey in Mei County, Shannxi Province. They found that the number of rich people who could obtain benefits from UEBMI, URBMI, and NCMS was more than that of the poor; meanwhile, the rich could obtain more compensation from UEBMI and NCMS than the poor could. In addition, most studies noted no measurable effect of NCMS on the reduction of financial risk (Lei and Lin 2009; Liu and Tsegao 2011; Long et al. 2010; Sun et al. 2009; Wagstaff et al. 2009; Yip and Hsiao 2009). A study examining the differential effects of NCMS across eastern, central, and western regions employed data prior to 2008 and showed that while NCMS significantly increased outpatient use in the east and west, it had no effect on hospital admissions or the incidence of catastrophic expenditure (defined as OOPS greater than 10 or 20 % of a household's total consumption expenditure). In fact, the NCMS increased the incidence of catastrophic expenditure among households in the western region (Liu and Tsegao 2011). A study with trend data from 2008 to 2010 from one city showed that the inpatient use rate for NCMS enrollees increased from 5.8 to 7.0 %. During the same period, NCMS reimbursement per admission increased by 4 % on average. However, the total expenditure and OOPS per admission increased even faster at 11 and 18 %, respectively (Shi et al. 2011).

However, other studies arrive at the opposite conclusion, arguing that different SHI schemes reduce medical expenses and increase affordability. Liu and Zhao (2006) analyzed the effect of UEBMI on OOPS using data from a pilot experiment conducted in Zhenjiang and concluded that the post-reform insurance model did not compromise equity in cost sharing, while at the same time containing cost inflation and increasing insurance coverage for the urban population. Although OOPS increased for all groups after the reform, the redistributions of OOPS appear to have been in favor of the disadvantaged groups, suggesting a more equitable change led by the reform. Results of one study using data from nine cities show that URBMI has some success in reducing participants' financial risk. OOPS for inpatient admissions for URBMI enrollees are 26 % ($p < 0.01$) lower than those uninsured urban residents, despite no significant difference in per-admission expenditure. Meanwhile, URBMI enrollees have moderately higher rates of medical utilization than their uninsured counterparts (Liu et al. 2011). Similarly, Jung and Liu (2012), using the China Health and Nutrition Survey data between 1991 and 2006, found that although the probability of positive OOPS increased with the availability of health insurance, the actual level of OOPS decreased. More specifically, for a person with positive OOPS, having health insurance significantly reduced the level of OOPS by 11.4–13.6 %. If, on the other hand, the level of OOPS was a priori unknown, they did not find a significant relationship between health insurance and OOPS levels.

At the same time, this study notes this mismatch from the official statistics, which indicates the positive relationship between the development of SHI and the level of OOPS. According to the political propaganda and official statistics, the indicator of the share of OOPS (individual) of the total health expenditure (government + social + individual) has always been used as a significant indicator of the importance of government spending (Central Committee of Communist Party of China and State Council 2009; Gu 2009, 2010). As Fig. 1.2 shows, the share of OOPS decreased from 52.84 % in 1997 to 35.30 % in 2010, which is associated with the increasing role of government and SHI in healthcare financing. However, this indicator is misleading because the decrease of the share of OOPS does not imply the decrease of the absolute OOPS, which is more related to people's affordability of service access.

Figure 1.3 shows that the share of annual OOPS in the consumption expenditure per person (OOPS/consumption) increased in the recent decade, coinciding with the

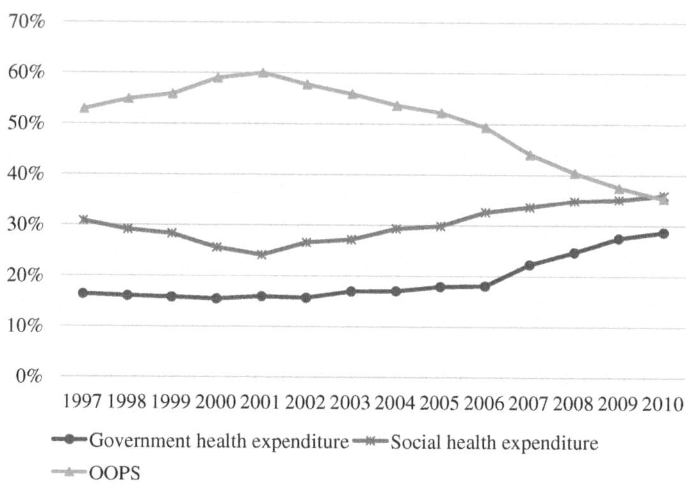

Fig. 1.2 The composition of total health expenditure: 1997–2010. *Note* Total health expenditure = government health expenditure + social health expenditure + OOPS. Social health expenditure is composed mainly of SHI funds expenditure. *Source* China Statistical Yearbook 2011

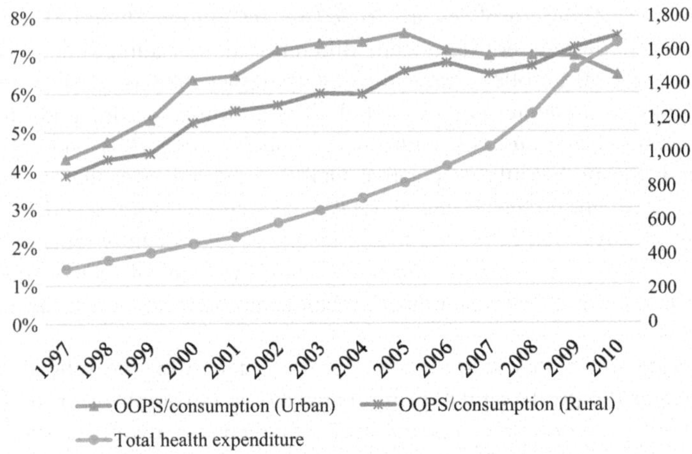

Fig. 1.3 The share of OOPS in consumption expenditure per person and total health expenditure: 1997–2010. *Note* OOPS/consumption = the share of annual OOPS in the annual consumption expenditure per person. Unit: OOPS/consumption (%); total health expenditure (1 billion yuan, calculated at constant price with price of year 1997 as 100 yuan). *Source* China Health Statistical Yearbook, 2000–2011; China Statistical Yearbook 2011

increase of SHI coverage shown in Fig. 1.1. OOPS/consumption in urban China increased from 4.29 % in 1997 to 6.47 % in 2010, although it has decreased a little since 2005. The more serious situation happens in rural areas, because OOPS/consumption in rural areas demonstrates an almost continuous increase from 3.86 % in 1997 to 7.50 % in 2010, even though the coverage of the NCMS rose sharply from 2005. This is mainly because total health expenditure increased even faster, with the amount in 2010 being 5.15 times larger than that in 1997. The escalating health costs seem to be uncurbed by the remarkable development of SHI and these new efforts.

Why is the impact of SHI participation on the problem of affordability and medical expenses so controversial? This paradox is rather frustrating and inevitably leads us to doubt the efficiency and results of SHI reform. Moreover, attention should be paid to the potential positive relationship between SHI coverage and OOPS, which calls for scientific research to explore the relationship between SHI participation and individuals' ultimate affordability.

It should be noted that health expenditure inflation is prevalent in nearly all the countries in the world. The past decade has seen severe worldwide healthcare cost inflation, which exceeds the average growth in GDP (Hagist and Kotlikoff 2009; Stabile and Thomson 2012). The inflation of health expenditures derives from multiple factors, such as economic development, the improvement of living conditions, the development of healthcare technology, the changing healthcare financing system, and so on. Why do we define health cost inflation in China as a problematic phenomenon compared with other countries?

This is mainly because the trend of health cost inflation in China is too radical compared with the other countries. Total health expenditure increased by 13.30 % annually from 2000 to 2012, which is almost three times faster than the average global level (see Table 1.1). The radical health cost inflation will devour the limited resources of the people and society in the future, despite the decreasing share of OOPS in total health expenditures. In addition, the decreasing share of OOPS is mainly owing to the substantial infusion of government finance and SHI expenditures. Without a cost-effective institutional arrangement, a huge amount of these infusions are more likely to be wasted. It is highly doubtful whether the decreasing share of OOPS is sustainable in a poor health governance system.

1.3 A Call for Investigating the Mediating Mechanisms of the Institutional Arrangement

Although there are a large number of studies on China's healthcare reform, most of them focus on arguing the importance of establishing the SHI system or the problems without SHI, such as poor equity, high level of OOPS, and catastrophic expenses (e.g., Liu 2011; Gu and Fang 2004; Wang 2005).

Previous studies investigating the problem of affordability and health cost inflation attribute the sources of the problem to serious malfunctions in its healthcare systems, including passive purchasing performance and fee-for-service payments, perverse incentives for providers and supplier-induced demand for unnecessary care, distorted price schedules, nonevidence-based benefit packages, and so on. According to these studies, a predominantly fee-for-services payment system coupled with the overuse of tests and drugs of unclear clinical indication, a distorted fee schedule, and drug markups are the core culprits of the rapid inflation of health expenditure. These studies can be further categorized into four themes: SHI and its agencies, health providers, patients, and the institutional surroundings.

Studies of SHI and its agencies. SHI in China as seen as an inefficient financing program and a passive purchasing mechanism (Xu and Van de Ven 2009). An effective financing program could limit unreasonable fee-charging behaviors, while an ineffective one was likely to encourage providers to induce overconsumption. In China, a fee-for-services payment method rather than methods such as capitation, diagnosis-related groups (DRGs), prospective payments, global budgets, and so on, remained dominant. The inefficiency of the fee-for-services method could distort further the incentive structure for doctors and encourage their unreasonable fee-charging behaviors, which would inevitably induce an unreasonable increase of total healthcare expenditure (Wagstaff and Lindelow 2008; Yip et al. 2012). In addition, the third-party purchasing of SHI was criticized for being inefficient. SHI agencies lacked incentives, resources, and bargaining and contracting skills to conduct negotiation of medical prices with healthcare providers and pharmaceutical suppliers. Some scholars attributed the generally dysfunctional third-party

Table 1.1 Per capita total expenditure on health at purchasing power parity

	2000	2001	2002	2003	2004	2005	2006	2007	2008	2009	2010	2011	2012	Annual growth rate (%)
China	107	117	136	152	168	189	213	238	282	343	367	423	480	13.30
Low-income nations	40	41	43	43	47	52	57	59	63	69	72	74	78	5.80
Lower-middle-income nations	121	125	131	142	150	161	172	188	201	213	223	227	247	6.10
Upper-middle-income nations	379	453	416	444	472	502	642	602	652	688	695	730	767	6.00
High-income nations	1605	1716	1855	1964	2077	2168	2323	2446	2595	2754	2743	2807	2926	5.10
Global	615	670	701	744	787	826	917	945	1007	1068	1069	1095	1151	5.40

Note National currency unit per US$. *Source* World Health Organization (2014)

purchasing of SHI to the inefficient fee-for-services payment method, low purchasing incentives for SHI agencies, and the distorted price schedule of drugs and healthcare services (Gu 2010; Meng 2008; Xu and Van de Ven 2009; Yip and Hanson 2009). SHI agencies had very poor purchasing and supervision abilities, and simply worked as reimbursement channels. The result was that most insurance premiums led to the profits of providers instead of quality health services. Moreover, there was insufficient room for municipal and county SHI agencies to negotiate the prices of drugs and healthcare services whose regulation was left to provincial price bureaus (Xu and Van de Ven 2009).

Studies of healthcare providers. Healthcare providers in China have always been criticized for inducing unnecessary demands and propelling medical expenditure (Eggleston et al. 2008; Liu and Mills 1999; Yip and Hsiao 2008, 2009; Yip et al. 2012). Doctors may take advantage of the reimbursement of SHI to provide unnecessary services. In many areas of China, doctors inquire about patients' SHI status before conducting diagnosis and treatment. If patients are enrolled into SHI, these doctors will prescribe expensive medicines and tests (Wagstaff and Lindelow 2008). However, Chinese doctors also suffer from many dilemmas, which propel them to overtreatment. They are employees of hospitals rather than independent professionals, with hospital administrative control replacing professional self-regulation ethics, they receive low levels of basic salaries and have to compromise to earn bonuses by altering their prescribing behaviors, and they suffer from heavy workloads as they have to compete to attract and hold on to patients to generate earnings for hospitals (Yip et al. 2010). Further, the government uses increasingly strict supervision to control drug profit, and even worse, doctors are suffering from deteriorating reputations as both government and social media are suggesting a decrease in the social morality of the medical profession (Bloom et al. 2000; Yang et al. 2008). Last, the relationship between doctors and patients is deteriorating, with doctors often becoming victims of terrible violence (The Lancet 2010).

Studies of patients. Patients suffer from income risks due to catastrophic healthcare spending. Some researchers argue that individuals are willing to go to large-scale hospitals where medical services are expensive. This is because they are not satisfied with the healthcare quality in primary health facilities, such as the number of qualified physicians, beds, and other related facilities (Yip et al. 2012). Other researchers attribute the problem of the affordability of healthcare to the human tendency to prioritize health over wealth/costs. The healthcare market is distinguished from other markets in that the supply–demand curve in the healthcare market does not fit the general law of value. Individuals regard health as more important than wealth. Although the prices in tertiary hospitals are high, individuals are still willing to seek treatment there (Li 2009).

Studies of the institutional surroundings. Studies attributing the problem of affordability and health cost inflation to institutional surroundings focus on two institutions. One is the poor compensation system. China has been experiencing serious health cost inflation since the 1990s. Retrenching public finance is criticized as being one of the most salient risk factors because it stimulates perverse incentives for doctors. Without adequate public finance, the hospital has to rely on user charges to survive, which exacerbate supplier-induced demands (Wang 2005; Yip et al. 2010). In addition, the poor compensation system does not render doctors satisfied with their income because both the wage structure of doctors and the governance of the healthcare system are distorted. Many doctors suffer from poor living conditions. Their basic salary is comparably lower than those in other sectors (Bloom et al. 2000). As a result, their financial pursuits triumph over their professional ethical responsibility. The demand for bonuses and off-the-book income incentivizes them to prescribe excessive medical items and drugs (Hsiao 2008). The other institution is the distorted price schedule. The government sets the price of basic services below cost and that of high-tech interventions above cost. It generates strong incentives for doctors to overprescribe more profitable tests and treatments (Bloom et al. 2000; Eggleston et al. 2008). In addition, the unsound drug tender and procurement system expands the potential for corruption for both pharmaceutical suppliers and doctors, causing drug kickbacks paid to doctors by pharmaceutical suppliers that pervaded hospitals (Xu and Van de Ven 2009).

Although these studies have made great contributions to profiling the various parts of the healthcare system and its reform, they fail to consider the role these parts play in operating the relationship between SHI participation and medical expenditures. Few studies have investigated the mediating mechanisms of the institutional arrangement of SHI in linking SHI participation to outcomes. Given the rapid development of SHI in China, an emerging question is whether its development can improve the performance of various parts of the healthcare system and, in turn, improve individuals' affordability of healthcare.

Specific effort should be devoted to investigating in more depth the mechanisms by which SHI participation affects patients' OOPS. SHI is, theoretically, not only a financial intermediary that aims to reimburse its enrollees, but also a policy instrument to regulate care-seeking behaviors and an active purchaser involved in regulating and inspecting the perverse incentives for healthcare providers (Eggleston et al. 2008; Hsiao 2007; Yip and Hanson 2009).

In practice, the development of SHI is one of the major methods used to improve the performance of the healthcare system in China (Central Committee of Communist Party of China and State Council 2009; Ministry of Human Resource and Social Security 2011). At the end of the 1990s, policy priority in the early stages was given to SHI coverage enlargement and reimbursed benefits enhancement, with the third-party purchasing reform being piloted in only a few areas. However, the new round of healthcare system reform in 2009 took the reform of third-party purchasing into consideration (Central Committee of Communist Party of China & State Council 2009), which was undoubtedly a milestone for China's SHI reform. Nevertheless, since then, local governments have been piloting many new prospective payment methods, such as capitation, DRG payments, global budgets, and so on (Meng 2008; Yip and Hanson 2009). Until 2011, over 80 % of rural areas had launched various kinds of payment methods reform for the NCMS (Ministry of Health 2012). In addition, China was experimenting with new programs to reform its health governance, including increasing the infusion of government health spending, piloting an essential medicines system with a zero-drug-markup policy, disconnecting the income and budgets of primary care providers from drug revenues, motivating primary care providers to increase the provision of prevention and primary care, reforming the governance of public hospitals, and so on (Yip et al. 2010).

Furthermore, China invested over ¥1.5 trillion in the health system from 2009 to 2011, of which about half was invested in the extension of SHI schemes. However, the lion's share of the investment was criticized for being wasted and becoming the profits of providers rather than becoming real benefits for patients (Yip and Hsiao 2014; Yip et al. 2012). As long as inappropriate healthcare and healthcare expenditure escalation are not controlled, no insurance scheme will be sustainable and patients will continue to bear the heavy costs of medical care.

Therefore, it is an urgent matter to evaluate the mediating role of the institutional arrangement of SHI in cost containment. Such a study is significant to unveil whether the substantial investments in SHI can be translated into better risk protection, health outcomes, and public satisfaction. Moreover, in the largest middle- and low-income country in the world, the government and SHI administrators face far more complexity than that of other countries. Therefore, by examining China's case, we wish to provide valuable insights for those fledging SHI schemes in developing countries.

1.4 The Purpose of the Study

This study, arguing a mismatch between SHI participation, the mediating institutional arrangement, and the ultimate outcomes (OOPS), aims to conduct an evaluation of the efficiency of the institutional arrangement in the process from participation to outcome. To be specific, this study aims to investigate the mediating role of the institutional arrangement of SHI operating on the relationship between SHI participation and patients' OOPS. The initial puzzle of this study is reflected in the following three questions.

1. What is the effect of the expanding SHI participation on individuals' OOPS in China's healthcare reform?
2. Through what kind of institutional arrangement does the effect take place?
3. How does the institutional arrangement take effect?

It is expected to fill the knowledge gap of previous studies, which have overlooked the mediating role of the institutional arrangement of SHI. Moreover, to date, most performance measurement targets in Chinese healthcare reform have been criticized as being input-based (such as finance, enrollment, training sessions, and buildings) rather than outcome-based (Yip et al. 2012). Without cost-effective institutional arrangements, the lion's share of health investment in China is likely to be wasted and captured by healthcare providers as higher income and profits, rather than producing benefits and improved well-being for patients. This serious potential problem, along with the commendable development of SHI, makes it both necessary and urgent to investigate the performance of the institutional arrangement of SHI and to assess its role in transforming benefits and input into cost-effective services and the well-being of the people.

Two sets of fundamental principles are highlighted in the study. One is the importance of the institutional arrangement. Welfare participation may not equate with ultimate well-being, as the more detailed mediating institutional arrangement may generate unexpected ineffectiveness and inefficiency. Therefore, the efficiency and effectiveness of the institutional arrangement of the welfare system should be considered specifically and should have equal importance to the provision of welfare benefits and the establishment of welfare institutions. The other is the importance of individual well-being. Individual well-being, as one of the ultimate pursuits for human society, should have the most important status in welfare institutions compared with welfare participation and the corresponding institutional arrangement. This implies that welfare participation is only the first step, and is not an end in itself.

Chapter 2
A New Institutionalist Approach of Healthcare Reform

Institutions matter in the determination of social and political outcomes. When we investigate the relationship between SHI participation and OOPS, we are actually probing into the effect of welfare institutions, and participation in them, on social outcomes. If welfare participation is to be effective in providing benefits, we shall require effective political institutions (Twine 1994). Specialized mediating institutional arrangements could be enacted to maintain a sound process from policy inputs to policy outputs.

In addition, the optimal functioning of institutional arrangements is realized through the actions of individuals. According to the new institutionalism, on the one hand, institutions structure and shape the behavior of individuals by providing a calculus or cultural arena. On the other hand, human beings acting collectively can, in principle, change and mold the frameworks of a number of economic, political, and social constraints within which we make our choices. The relationship between institutions and the actions of individuals have to be construed when elucidating the effects of institutions on social and political outcomes.

The importance of institutions in determining social outcomes was neglected half a century ago. In postwar Western society, the social sciences have been gradually dominated by a behavioral and a rational revolution (Peters 1999). Both movements have fundamentally transformed the discipline of political science by portraying politics as a reflection of society, political phenomena as the aggregate consequences of individual behavior, and human action as the result of choices based on calculated self-interest, and so on (March and Olsen 1984). However, since the 1970s, the new institutionalism has emerged through the rediscovery of the autonomy of institutions and the importance of symbolic action to an understanding of politics. The role that institutions play in the determination of social outcomes is emphasized by understanding the relationship between institutions and behavior and the process whereby institutions originate and change.

However, the new institutionalism does not constitute a unified body of thought. Instead, at least three diverse theoretical approaches have been identified; that is, historical institutionalism, rational choice institutionalism, and sociological

K. Liu, *The Effects of Social Health Insurance Reform on People's Out-of-Pocket Health Expenditure in China*, DOI 10.1007/978-981-10-1777-3_2

institutionalism (Hall and Taylor 1996). They provide quite different accounts of the nature of institutions as well as the relationship between institutions and behaviors.

First, rational choice institutionalists still employ the assumptions of behaviorism. The actors are said to have fixed preferences and to behave in a way that maximizes the attainment of these preferences (Elster and Hylland 1986; Shepsle and Weingast 1987). Institutions serve to structure the interactions among actors by affecting the range and sequence of the choices made by the actors or by formulating mechanisms in reducing uncertainty of the reacting behaviors of others.

Second, sociological institutionalists take a broad view of institutions by involving not only formal rules, procedures, or norms, but the symbol systems, cognitive scripts, and moral templates that formulate the "frames of meaning" affecting the nature and choices of human action (Campbell 1998; Scott 1994). Institutions, then, do not just influence the strategic calculations of individuals, as rational choice institutionalists claim, but also their underlying preferences or identities as well as the cognitive scripts, categories, and models that are indispensable for action (Berger and Luckmann 1966; DiMaggio and Powell 1983; Wendt 1987).

Third, historical institutionalists associate institutions with organizations and the rules or conventions promulgated by formal organization. They are quite eclectic toward the relationship between institutions and action in that they may accept the opinions of both rational choice institutionalists and sociological institutionalists. In addition, they focus on the role of historical development and the path dependence of social causation. Institutions are deemed persistent features of the historical landscape (Hall and Taylor 1996).

This study embraces the new institutionalism to understand the relationship between SHI participation and OOPS. In theory, we focus on two fundamental issues: (1) how to examine the effects of welfare institutions on social outcomes; and (2) how to construe the relationship between institutions and behavior. The two issues are the two different perspectives for answering the same question about the relationship between institutions and outcomes: the first is a perspective of determination, while the second is of strategic interaction.

The first perspective is related to the linear relationship between welfare institutions and social outcomes. We also try to find the mechanisms of the relationship between institutions and social outcomes by considering the mediating role of the institutional arrangement. By and large, we try to find a determinative model of the effects of welfare institutions on social outcomes. Correspondingly, we first devise a hypothesized model by proposing the relationships between SHI participation, the institutional arrangement, and OOPS.

The second perspective focuses on the strategic interaction between welfare institutions and actors, and among different actors. The dimension is necessary in that it reveals the specific actions of key stakeholders and their interactions and, therefore, facilitates explanation of the determinative relationship investigated in the first dimension. As a result, we formulate a framework of the relationship between welfare institutions and the behaviors of actors to explain the determinative hypothesized model.

In addition, the two different perspectives shed light on what kind of methodology we should use to explore the three research questions proposed in Chap. 1. The perspective of determination and that of strategic determination are just two sides of a coin, with the former focusing on the observable attributes of the truth, and the latter on the complicated attributes of the truth. The dual theoretical perspectives used in the study guide us to adopt a paradigm of postpositivism and a mixed-methods design.

2.1 Effects of Welfare Institutions on Social Outcomes: The Perspective of Determination

Welfare institutions are designed to achieve social outcomes through the redistribution of resources, both horizontally across a life course and vertically across income hierarchies. As economic growth is questioned as the route to improve well-being, issues of distribution and redistribution become central to political debate, and social rights to obtain resources for human development evolves to be the focus of policy priority (Twine 1994).

However, due to the various risks that exist in the attributes of welfare institutions and the corresponding institutional arrangement, the function of social rights is debated in terms of being an effect on social outcomes.

From the perspective of social democrats, the provision of welfare benefits is seen as effective and necessary to enhance individuals' well-being (Marshall, 1963; Titmuss, 1963). Turner (1993) suggests that citizenship—mainly social rights, once inscribed in the institutions of the welfare state—is a buffer against the vagaries of the marketplace and the inequalities of the class system. Welfare institutions are thus seen as effective and necessary to manage social problems and to meet individuals' basic needs.

However, scholars from the New Right argue that social rights may not increase people's well-being, but rather reduce it in the long run (Mead 1986; Murray 1996). New Right scholars devote their attention to outlining why a proliferation of welfare provision may be damaging to individuals and the wider society. In Western society, the state provision of welfare services and the gradual expansion of the state's role from the 1950s onward are argued to have driven up public expenditure to a point where the costs of state welfare have interfered with the successful operation of a free market economy. Allied to this is the belief that permissive welfare provision undermines individual/familial responsibility and nurtures the development of a welfare-dependent "underclass" (Alcock 1989; Mead 1986; Murray 1996).

New communitarian writers, emphasizing the importance of community over individual, are also opposed to unconditional universal benefit provision (Etzioni 1997). They believe universal provision ruins the establishment of a good society. Access to collectively provided welfare benefits should be conditional on individuals accepting communally defined obligations. Social policy should seek to promote a particular moral framework and judge the actions of individual citizens (Deacon 2002). Etzioni (1997) approves that the state should provide only a minimal safety net of welfare via the provision of the "social basics," which is targeted selectively at those unemployed, disabled, and so on.

Correspondingly, we are unable to identify the effects of welfare institutions on social outcomes if we only evaluate the direct effects of welfare participation on outcomes. To be specific, the focus from the outset on welfare provision, the extent of welfare spending, the nature of social rights, and so on, provides little information for investigating the mechanisms of the effects of welfare institutions. Welfare reform is more a process of pragmatic choices than ideological debates in many countries. Policy makers always consider "how to provide welfare benefits" after deciding "whether or not to provide." An increasing number of scholars deemphasize the nature of welfare rights per se, focusing instead on the rationality and efficiency of the mediating institutional arrangement of social policies (Gilbert and Terrell 2013; Le Grand 1993).

Institutional arrangements denote the mechanisms in the policy process from welfare input to outcomes. The conceptual framework of social policy has evolved through a process that flows from welfare input to institutional arrangement, then to policy output, and ultimately to outcomes (Wong and Walker 1998). This study formulates an analytical framework of the institutional arrangement to elaborate on the relationship between welfare participation and outcomes. Meanwhile, it is aware of various ideological debates on the attributes of social rights and the appropriateness of the corresponding institutional arrangement.

This study, taking SHI reform in China as an example, sets out to combine the theoretical studies of institutional arrangements, from social policy and empirical studies of SHI, to develop a systematic insight into the effects of SHI participation (welfare participation) on patients' OOPS (outcome). This initiative is in response to the debates raised by different theories of institutional arrangement and to the design of SHI schemes.

2.1.1 A Conceptual Framework of Institutional Arrangements

From the outset, we employ actual participation in SHI schemes (SHI participation) to represent welfare participation in the domain of SHI. In theory, welfare participation is regarded by many as a centrally important aspect of "effective citizenship" and helps to define the extent and quality of a citizen's substantive welfare entitlement (Dwyer 2010). Harrison (1995, p. 20–21) argues that "effective citizenship certainly means being included in the systems of rights and welfare provisions that are mediated or managed by state agencies, and having one's needs met through mainstream political intermediation." Meanwhile, the welfare system of most nations embraces a combination of "means-tested" and "as of right" benefits. The latter may be further divided into those depending on a contribution record and those that are tax-financed (Twine 1994). SHI is a sort of welfare institution by which benefits are payable "as of right" in contingent situations of unemployment, sickness, or retirement when the necessary contribution conditions have been met. Thus, SHI enrolls those who make contributions to it and then spreads the income risks of those enrollees with illness or diseases. The term "social" means SHI is established and implemented by the state rather than by private or voluntary organizations.

Furthermore, this study employs a resource allocation perspective proposed by Dwyer (2000) and Gilbert and Terrell (2013) to explore the mechanisms of institutional arrangement under the discourse of social rights. In this perspective, a critical question for the institutional arrangement is: how are resources going to be allocated in order to best meet people's various needs that occur? Questions of "who gets what, how they get it, and why they are seen as being entitled to it" are very much part and parcel of institutional arrangement debates (Dwyer 2000). Just as Dean (2001) points out, the reason and appropriateness for taking this perspective are that the essential character of social rights is "distributional in the sense that they relate to the social redistribution of resources." Similarly, Gilbert and Terrell (2013) use a benefit-allocation framework to interpret social welfare policies as choices among principles determining "what benefits are offered, to whom they are offered, how they are delivered, and how they are financed."

Following these insights, five institutional components of a welfare institution can be detected: the target of welfare benefits (who gets welfare benefits), benefits provision (what benefits are offered), provision rationale (why beneficiaries are seen as being entitled), provision mode (how benefits are delivered), and financing (how benefits are financed). This study considers the target of benefits to be in itself an institutional component, reflecting welfare participation, and SHI as an approach to health financing. Therefore, the study excludes the components of target and financing, and constructs a conceptual framework of institutional arrangements that involves benefits provision, provision rationale, and provision mode to explore the vehicles for the delivery of SHI.

First, benefits provision and the reimbursement mechanism of SHI. Social democrats see welfare institutions as necessary to realize social solidarity (Titmuss 1963). From the state planning perspective of the traditional welfare state period, uniform, mass-produced, and centrally distributed benefits were seen as efficient in eliminating many of the wasteful and duplicative aspects of competition in the open marketplace (Gilbert and Terrell 2002). However, the New Right sees human nature as individualistic, self-interested and rational. Individuals, as actors within a market economy, should decide on how to meet their welfare needs. Therefore, the New Right is hostile towards the intervention of government into the free market to provide welfare benefits (Burch 1999; Gilbert and Terrell 2002). At the same time, Marxists, ignoring the discussion of the forms of welfare benefits, argue that the substantial and increasing welfare expenditure is ineffective and inefficient. It merely acts to compensate certain individuals for some of the negative consequences of capitalism but fails to address the causes of their problems and/or adequately meet the needs of many citizens (Offe 1982). Despite these debates, the universal social rights to participate in welfare institutions, as with any kind of benefit, will inevitably increase such benefits in the total related societal expenditure.

With regard to SHI, the reimbursement mechanism is the initial and most important institutional arrangement of SHI to provide welfare benefits and to generate a risk-spreading function. SHI agencies, established by the state, collect premiums and pool them. Enrollees are reimbursed benefits from the pooling account when they spend in the designated health facilities. Speaking from the macro level, as not all enrollees are ill and thus spend at one fixed period, those with medical spending transfer their income risk horizontally across the population, potentially avoiding the risk of poverty due to catastrophic illness spending (Ron et al. 1990). The form of welfare benefits of SHI is actually a kind of reimbursement where its immediate result is the acquirement of the reimbursement fee obtained. The increase of the reimbursement fee level is indicative of the reimbursement mechanism, and it is expected to reduce patients' OOPS.

Second, provision rationale and the behavior management mechanism of SHI. Social democrats see inequality and poverty as being caused by structural dysfunctions such as unemployment and industrialization. Thus, they advocate that the state should confer social rights unconditionally to its members since these are their rights based on prior agreement and social contract. However, the issue of why individuals are seen as entitled to welfare benefits is argued to be redefined considering the conditionality of social rights and the balance between rights and duties (Lister 2003). Therefore, individuals must take greater responsibility for their well-being by working, exercising more, and reducing consumption of tobacco and alcohol (Redden 2002). Furthermore, many critiques of the welfare state are to do with welfare dependency and the behavioral dysfunctions of the underclass, caused by the dutiless rights to welfare benefits. The New Right regards universal entitlement to welfare benefits as socially damaging. It believes that it is not structural dysfunction but the unconditional social rights conferred by the state that create the underclass and their welfare dependency (George and Wilding 1994; Mead 1986; Murray 1996). As a result, the systems of welfare are concerned with not only making welfare services available to citizens or other individuals, but utilizing welfare policy in an instrumental way to advance particular outcomes or to promote certain attitudes or types of behavior (Deacon 2002). The associated duties, therefore, refer to either the contribution to welfare participation or management of problematic behaviors. Sustaining welfare systems necessitates personal responsibility, without which dysfunctional behaviors and welfare dependency would result.

In the SHI realm, the behavior management mechanism of SHI corresponds to the provision rationale of welfare benefits. The behavior management mechanism actually includes two more detailed processes. First, the SHI agency formally cooperates with designated providers. Individuals must seek treatment from these providers if they want to obtain reimbursement; otherwise, they will not be reimbursed. Second, the SHI agency sets a higher rate of reimbursement for treatments in primary health facilities, and a lower rate for those in tertiary hospitals. The aim of the various payment levels is to encourage individuals to seek treatment in primary health facilities and thus, to improve the allocation of medical resources. The efficient running of this mechanism could mitigate the unaffordable access to healthcare and major financial risks related to OOPS expenses (Li 2009).

Third, provision mode and the purchasing mechanism of SHI. Social democrats see direct government provision as efficient and necessary to embrace social solidarity. This state-centered model is criticized seriously by scholars from the New Right, who advocate the power of the free market in providing services. However, a free market without state intervention has little public accountability and is therefore vulnerable to risks. Moreover, the free market is accompanied by some devastating externalities to bring social costs (Baldock et al. 2003). As a result, a free market is also not a perfect solution to provide welfare benefits.

In the public welfare realm, a balance between state intervention and the market has been gradually reached. Since the 1980s, new managerialism, a reform including privatization, contracting out, setting precise targets, and rewarding the achievement in public services, has dominated the social policy of governments, resulting in a greater mixed economy of welfare (Baldock et al. 2003). More and more countries have replaced direct provision by the state with indirect provision under the "contract model." In this model, the role of government changes from provider to purchaser of welfare services with the aim of enhancing the efficiency and effectiveness of provision.

With regard to SHI, the purchasing mechanism emerges in accordance with the transforming role of government from benefits provider to purchaser. SHI reimbursement flows not only between SHI agencies and enrollees, but between SHI agencies and health facilities. The reimbursement mechanism alone cannot dissolve the risks of enrollees' expenses as it is the healthcare providers that charge fees to enrollees. It can only try to reduce the income risks of enrollees due to catastrophic spending, but cannot stop providers from charging unreasonable fees and patients from abusing medical services. So, the purchasing mechanism emerges to monitor the efficiency and quality of healthcare delivery (Yip and Hanson 2009; Yip et al. 2012). With the aim of ensuring the affordability of health services, the SHI agency actually acts not only as payer for the enrollee, but also as purchaser of health services collectively from healthcare providers. Individuals who do not participate in SHI must deal with healthcare providers independently, while those who participate transfer their purchasing power to the SHI agency, which represents their interests and thus has collective bargaining power with healthcare providers. With the expansion of SHI coverage and the increase of SHI funds, the SHI agency would have a strong bargaining power to restrict the improper fee-charging behaviors of healthcare providers, as well as to reduce the moral hazard of patients. The effective working of the purchasing mechanism is expected to moderate the behaviors of healthcare providers and patients, which would inevitably reduce healthcare fee-charging levels, enrollees' medical expenditures, as well as OOPS (Gu 2010).

2.1.2 Developing a Hypothesized Model

According to the propositions derived from our analytical framework, we develop a hypothesized model and formulate three major hypotheses. We also generate several key variables for measurement. The hypothetical model of the study is presented in Fig. 2.1.

First, the reimbursement mechanism. Social democracy theory sees welfare benefits as necessary to realize social solidarity. Structural inequality is seen as a major threat to freedom, and the provision of welfare benefits by government as an effective means of creating and increasing individual freedom (Titmuss 1963). Thus, the logic of social democracy theory seems to be straightforward: one obtains welfare benefits through enrolling in welfare programs, and as a result, enhances one's well-being. That is, the performance of benefits provision mediates the effect of participation in welfare programs on beneficiaries' well-being.

The reimbursement mechanism is the first and most important institutional arrangement of SHI to generate a risk-spreading function and to provide benefits. An SHI agency collects premiums and pools them into a shared account. Enrollees can have the lion's share of their medical expenses reimbursed by the pooled funds when they spend with the designated health facilities (Hsiao and Shaw 2007). The increase in the reimbursed fee indicates the improved performance of the reimbursement mechanism. Therefore, this study uses the variable *reimbursement rate* to represent such performance.

We thus develop the first hypothesis, namely, that individuals enrolled in SHI schemes, whether GMI, UEBMI, URBMI, or NCMS, will enjoy a higher reimbursement rate than those who are uninsured, and further, that the reimbursement rate has a negative association with OOPS (**Hypothesis 1**).

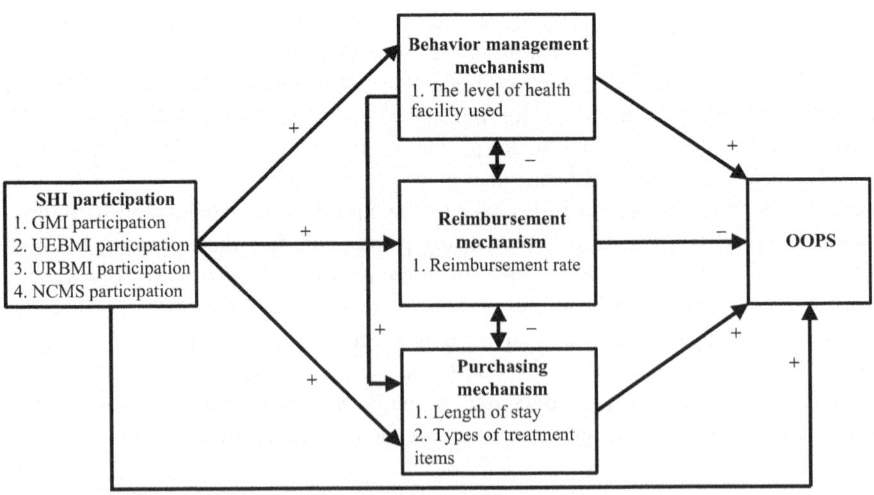

Fig. 2.1 Hypothetical model

Second, the behavior management mechanism. Many neo-liberal and New Right scholars critique social democracy theory as focusing too much on the extent but not the nature of social policy (George and Wilding 1994; Mead 1986; Taylor 2007). Universal welfare rights are regarded as socially damaging and the cause of many social problems such as welfare dependency and the behavioral dysfunction of the underclass. Mead (1986) argues that the fundamental cause of these problems is the permissiveness of welfare programs rather than their size. If social programs are unavoidable, beneficiaries must take on some responsibilities, such as enrollment contribution and behavior management, before or after they enjoy the welfare rights offered. Welfare systems should therefore be concerned, not only with making services available, but utilizing welfare policy in an instrumental way to promote certain types of behavior (Deacon 2002). The performance of a behavior management mechanism may thus have a mediating effect on the relationship between participation in welfare programs and beneficiaries' well-being. The behavior management mechanism of SHI lies with the agency trying to guide patients to be admitted to lower-level rather than higher-level hospitals. In this study, we use the variable *level of health facility* used by patients to denote the performance of the behavior management mechanism.

However, things are different in China where there is extreme inequity in health resource allocation. Personnel in rural health facilities are less qualified, small health facilities and hospitals have limited kinds of equipment and drugs, and some township health centers (THCs) and community health centers (CHCs) are poorly managed (Zhang and Kanbur 2005). Despite resources being limited overall, they are overallocated to tertiary hospitals in cities due to the special political and economic priorities that emphasize urban development. Furthermore, consumer information about either health insurance or the restricted choice of healthcare providers in China is limited (Xu and Van de Ven 2012). The amount of equipment and drugs, and the scale of health facilities, are among the most important factors that attract the attention of patients (Xiong et al. 2012). Against this backdrop, insured patients may be more willing than the uninsured to choose secondary or tertiary hospitals with good-quality resources but higher fees and copayments. This is because the reimbursements provided by SHI may encourage insured patients to use higher-level facilities.

We thus develop the second hypothesis, that patients who participate in SHI (that is, GMI, UEBMI, URBMI, or NCMS) are more likely to go to higher-level health facilities for treatment than the uninsured, and that such facilities will require patients to pay higher OOPS (**Hypothesis 2**).

Third, the purchasing mechanism. Social democracy, neo-liberalism, and New Right theories propose two different approaches to providing welfare: social democracy, which advocates for direct government provision, and neo-liberalism and the New Right, which emphasize the role of the free market (Dwyer 2010; George and Wilding 1994; Taylor 2007). However, both approaches have been criticized as being too extreme to deliver welfare efficiently (Baldock et al. 2003). Since the 1970s, the new managerialism movement, a reform supporting the privatization and contracting out of public services, has dominated the social policy of many governments, resulting in a mixed economy of welfare. The introduction of a third-party purchaser changes the nature of power and politics in the welfare system, transforming the role of government from direct provider to monitor or regulator (Baldock et al. 2003). The performance of the purchasing mechanism is expected to play a salient mediating role in the relationship between welfare rights and individuals' well-being.

A purchasing mechanism was first introduced into health insurance reforms in the United States in the 1970s to restrict the cost inflation of healthcare and to enhance the efficiency and quality of delivery (Enthoven 1988). In terms of SHI, the agency acts not only as a payer for enrollees, but also a purchaser in terms of purchasing health services collectively from providers. Such an SHI agency must be able to control fraudulent claims and supplier-induced demand for unnecessary services through developing and implementing adequate inspection and auditing mechanisms (Figueras et al. 2005; Hsiao 2007). An active purchasing mechanism is expected to play a cost-containment function in terms of payments. This study thus uses the variable *cost-containment level* to represent the performance of the purchasing mechanism in terms of medical costs. Specifically, we use two indicators, length of stay in hospital and type of treatment items (medication, tests involving high-tech equipment, surgery, and so on), to represent the cost-containment level of the purchasing mechanism.

Studies indicate that the purchasing mechanism in China is generally dysfunctional due to inefficient fee-for-service payment schemes and the lack of bargaining and contracting skills of SHI agencies (Gu 2010; Meng 2008; Xu and Van de Ven 2009; Yip and Hanson 2009). Therefore, the passive purchasing of SHI agencies may not deliver the cost-containment function, but rather stimulate perverse incentives for healthcare providers to take advantage of the reimbursement and risk-pooling of the arrangements of SHI schemes to charge more for insured patients. Additionally, we also test for the association between health facility level and the performance of the purchasing mechanism. Higher-level health facilities are even harder to inspect and monitor than their lower-level counterparts, because the former have advanced status in terms of either information asymmetry or bargaining power. If, as we hypothesize, SHI participation makes patients move up the provider ladder from lower- to higher-level health facilities, this may accentuate the informational asymmetry between healthcare provider and patient and cause healthcare providers to prescribe more high-tech and expensive care (Wagstaff and Lindelow 2008).

Therefore, we develop the third hypothesis, that patients participating in SHI schemes (that is, GMI, UEBMI, URBMI, or NCMS) will have longer hospital stays and receive more types of treatment items than the uninsured, a longer stay will increase the number of types of treatment items, a longer stay and more types of treatment items will raise patients' OOPS, and the level of health facilities that patients use will have a positive relationship with the length of stay and type of treatment item (**Hypothesis 3**).

2.2 The Relationship Between Institutions and Actors: The Perspective of Strategic Interaction

Institutions generate their effects on social outcomes through the actions of individuals. Investigating the mechanisms of the institutional arrangement may help to answer the second question of this study, that is: through which kinds of institutional arrangement does SHI participation have an effect on OOPS? In order to answer the third question, that is, how the institutional arrangement takes effect, we have to explore the interaction among actors, and between actors and welfare institutions.

By and large, new institutionalists use two approaches to respond to the question about the effects of institutions on the behavior of individuals; that is, a calculus approach and a cultural approach (Hall and Taylor 1996). Basically, the rational choice institutionalists may advocate the calculus approach, and the sociological institutionalists the cultural approach. Historical institutionalists are eclectic as they may use both calculus and cultural approach. The question of how institutions affect the behavior of individuals can be further dismantled into three subquestions: how do actors behave, what do institutions do, and why do institutions persist over time? The two approaches provide different answers to the three questions.

First, the behavior of actors. The calculus approach assumes that human behavior is instrumental and based on strategic calculation. It takes further the actor's preferences as being given exogenously to institutions. However, the cultural approach deems human behavior not fully strategic but bounded by an individual's value system. Established routines, cognitive scripts, and fixed patterns of behavior influence individuals to attain their preferences. Individual preferences are therefore endogenous to institutions. Human actions depend on the interpretation of a situation rather than purely on calculation (Hall and Taylor 1996).

Second, the role of institutions. The advocators of the calculus approach argue that institutions provide actors with certain degrees of certainty about the behavior of other actors. Institutions also provide enforcement mechanisms for agreements, penalties for defection, and so on. They affect the actions of individuals by changing the expectations of individuals about the actions that others may take in response to their own actions. Differing from these opinions, the cultural approach sees that institutions affect individual behavior by providing moral or cognitive templates for interpretation and action. It deems the individual deeply embedded in a world of institutions. Institutions are composed of symbols, scripts, and routines, and provide the filters for individual interpretation (Hall and Taylor 1996).

Third, the persistence of institutions. Those who adopt the calculus approach explain the persistence of institutions over time in terms of the benefits provided by institutions. Through providing benefits, institutions embody an equilibrium. Individuals behave in certain patterns because behavior deviation will make the individual worse off than they would follow these patterns. The more gains an institution brings to individuals, the more robust it will be. The cultural approach uses the existence of the conventions related with institutions to explain the persistence of the latter. The conventions cannot readily be the explicit objects of individual choice. Instead, the routines, symbols, and cognitive templates of some institutions are so conventional or taken for granted that they escape direct scrutiny. Moreover, they are constructed collectively by individuals and cannot, therefore, be readily transformed by the actions of any one individual (Hall and Taylor 1996).

This study uses the calculus approach to structure the relationship between welfare institutions and individual behavior. We appreciate the role that human intentionality plays in the determination of social outcomes in the form of strategic calculation. We try to integrate the role of strategic calculation with the role of structural variables associated primarily with the determinative dimension of institutions, with the purpose of casting a full map of the relationship between institutions and outcomes. The reason we do not use a cultural approach is because of our distinctive focus on formal institutions and the postpositivism research paradigm we hold. We study the formal functions, procedures, and institutional arrangement of SHI schemes and investigate the role they play in the determination of OOPS. Our focus is not on the cognitive and normative dimension of institutional impact. In addition, there is an apparent influence of social constructivism on sociological institutionalism. Institutions are seen to provide the very terms through which meaning is assigned in social life and the self-images and identities of actors are constructed (Berger and Luckmann 1966; Wendt 1987). However, we hold firmly a postpositivism paradigm and focus on the discovery of objective truth rather than the construction of meaning.

Accordingly, we have three primary assumptions. First, the behavior of an actor in SHI reform is likely to be driven by a strategic calculus. Second, the calculus is deeply affected by the expectations of the actor on how others in the healthcare sector may behave. Third, institutions including SHI and other healthcare institutions structure the strategic interaction among actors through affecting the range of alternative choices of actors, altering the expectations of an actor toward the corresponding behaviors of others, and guiding actors toward particular calculations.

We focus on the interaction of different stakeholders and the way in which institutions structure the interaction. The operation of the institutional arrangement of SHI involves many kinds of stakeholders. These stakeholders play quite different roles in the three mechanisms of the institutional arrangement, that is, the reimbursement, the behavior management, and the purchasing. From the aspect of the reimbursement mechanism of SHI, SHI collects premiums contributed by individuals, employers, and the government into a pooling account to spread enrollees' income risk due to illness or disease. When individuals pay for medical expenses, they could obtain some reimbursements from the pooling account of SHI. In addition, SHI provides not only financial reimbursement to enrollees, but also manages their healthcare-seeking behaviors; that is, their choices of healthcare providers. Moreover, unlike other social insurance such as a pension, SHI refers not only to money, but also in-kind health services. As the executive organization of SHI schemes, the SHI agency plays a major role in cost containment. It represents enrollees to purchase medical services from providers. Except for SHI agencies, healthcare providers, and patients, the operation of the institutional arrangement also involves the government in policy making, implementing, monitoring, and financial processing, as well as the pharmaceutical manufacturer and representatives in the production and logistics process of medicine and medical devices.

Therefore, SHI involves the interaction of multiple stakeholders, including the government, SHI agencies, health facilities, pharmaceutical manufacturers and representatives, and enrollees. If the quantitative analysis in this study reveals poor performance on the part of SHI schemes in behavior management and cost containment, it does not mean that SHI agencies alone are responsible. Rather, poor performance might be a result of complicated interactions among different stakeholders. Therefore, we must involve multiple participants to reveal these interactions.

In this study, we focus mainly on the interactions between SHI agencies, health facilities, and enrollees, as these stakeholders are directly associated with the flow of medical expenditures and reimbursements of SHI. We devote our attention to interpreting the operation of the three mechanisms of the institutional arrangement of SHI, portraying the strategic interaction between different stakeholders in the operation process, and understanding the institutional surroundings where the interaction between these stakeholders was structured and shaped.

2.3 Methodology: Postpositivism and a Mixed-Methods Design

Scientific research is conducted within a certain paradigm framework, under the guidance of certain ontology, epistemology, and axiology, and with the assistance of methodology and specific methods. It is not just a process of using some strategies of datacollection and analysis to probe into certain questions, but is a recurrent inquiry based on the researchers' world values and cognition of social facts, knowledge, their own social and academic positions, and so on.

Based on such a reflection, this study chooses an appropriate methodology that is suitable to elaborate on the dual theoretical perspectives of both determination and strategic interaction. The dual perspectives follow the deterministic laws of probability and uncertainty (Cook and Campbell 1979). To be specific, the determinative relationship between welfare institutions and social outcomes sees social fact or truth as observable and measurable, while the interactive relationship between institutions and actors sees social fact or truth as complicated and hard to discover with one-time observation.

Accordingly, this study holds a postpositivist paradigm by recognizing the objective existence of truth that can be hardly knowable and is theory-laden. It tries to use multiple strategies to assist in finding evidence of truth. Correspondingly, it uses a mixed-methods design by combining both quantitative and qualitative methods to explore the institutional arrangement of SHI in China.

2.3.1 Paradigm Shift and Postpositivism

Scientific research, especially in natural science, had been governed by a positivism philosophy of science before the introduction of the conception of paradigm. Naïve realism was held to deem truth to exist objectively and to be knowable for human beings. In social science, the mathematical and statistical methods used commonly in the natural science field were introduced to explain and predict complicated social facts that were often seen as a series of statistical relationships between variables (Clark 1998; Schumacher and Gortner 1992).

The dominance of positivism in scientific research has been challenged with the emergence of the conception of paradigm. Tomas Kuhn (1962) argues that scientific researchers work not value-free, but within the context of a paradigm—a conceptual framework that is shared by inquirers in a science community, determines the concepts used, and models inquiries through previous exemplars. Paradigms may guide scientific research through regulating key topics and formulating research hypotheses, as well as introducing the most suitable empirical methods to explore these topics. The paradigm shared in a science community often divides problems into essential and trivial issues, by which researchers being trapped within the paradigm would devote themselves to the investigation of the valuable issues while neglecting others. Researchers in one paradigm may judge certain issues as being true, while those in other paradigms may judge them as false. Furthermore, a certain paradigm will be confronted with anomalies. Correspondingly, some researchers may abandon this paradigm and adopt some alternative challenging paradigms. These competing paradigms coexist until the challenging paradigms are consolidated and replace the traditional paradigm. A paradigm shift will then happen.

The postpositivist paradigm emerged with such a paradigm shift. It was proposed by reflecting on the problems of the dominating positivism. It is devoted to replacing naïve realism with a critical realism, the justificationist account of knowledge with a critical rationalism, and the deterministic laws with laws of probability and uncertainty (Cook and Campbell 1979; Guba and Lincoln 2005; Phillips 1990). Most postpositivists draw their standpoints from the philosophy of science of Karl Popper, especially his two well-known monographs *The Logic of Scientific Discovery* (1959) and *Conjectures and Refutations* (1962).

Popper (1962) considers truth as an essential regulative ideal. He suggests abandoning the assurance that researchers are able to know when they reach the truth, although they do not have to abandon the notion of objective truth. He uses a metaphor of climbing mountains to illustrate his view of truth:

> The status of truth in the objective sense, as correspondence to the facts, and its role as a regulative principle, may be compared to that of a mountain peak which is permanently, or almost permanently, wrapped in clouds. The climber may not merely have difficulties in getting there—he may not know when he gets there, because he may be unable to distinguish, in the clouds, between the main summit and some subsidiary peak. Yet this does not affect the objective existence of the summit … The very idea of error, or of doubt … implies the idea of an objective truth which we may fail to reach. (Popper 1962, p. 226)

Furthermore, Popper argues that there is neither confirmative knowledge (Popper 1959) nor solid foundation for knowledge (Popper 1962). On the one hand, Popper is hostile to the empiricist monism of the positivists who usually use induction to generalize from particular observations to general scientific propositions. On the other hand, he is also prudent to deduction from a scientific proposition. Although the data may fit the deducted pattern being tested, Popper deems such corroboration to be supporting the theory to the provisional extent but never proving it to be true. The corroboration only achieves the status of "not yet disconfirmed" but is far from the status of "being true" (Popper 1959). Furthermore, traditional rationalists (like Descartes) and empiricists (such as Locke, Berkeley, and Hume) regard knowledge as being built upon some solid and unchallengeable foundation and therefore, a starting point for knowledge should be sought (Phillips 1990). However, Popper denies the existence of such ideal sources of knowledge. He deems all such "sources" liable to lead us into errors at times. He uses an entirely different question to replace the question about the sources of knowledge: "How can we hope to detect and eliminate error?" (Popper 1962, p. 25)

Except for the complicated nature of truth and knowledge, observation is believed to be theory-laden rather than theoretically neutral to discover truth and knowledge. In his well-known work *Patterns of Discovery*, Hanson (1958) argues that there is a distinction between "seeing as" and "seeing that," which means that all observations are presumptive and are impregnated with a "thematic framework" of our existing preconceptions. Observation is, therefore, theory-laden. In the field of scientific research, in the same way, all data are theory-, method-, and measurement-dependent (Ratcliffe 1983). Therefore, the values, experiences, and subjectivity of researchers have to be taken into consideration in the process of scientific research.

Because truth, knowledge, and observation are all full of uncertainty, Popper (1959, 1962) argues that scientific theory cannot be tested directly. He holds that scientific theory is irreducibly conjectural and falsifiable and cannot be proved. He further develops a perspective of falsification and a trail-and-error method by arguing that scientific theories cannot be verified, but can only be falsified by scientific testing. A scientific theory has to be falsifiable; that is, if it is false, it could be shown by observation or experiment. Besides, a scientific theory has to be devoted to error elimination before it advances toward future problems. This interplay between tentative theories (conjectures) and error elimination (refutation) determines whether the theories can or cannot withstand falsification.

2.3.2 A Mixed-Methods Design

The paradigm shift from positivism to postpositivism makes it possible to conduct mixed-methods research. Popper emphasizes tests with multiple validation criteria that renders a theory to be preferred over another. Therefore, postpositivists might collect data from multiple sources and conduct a variety of strong tests to generate multiple disconfirmations. The disconfirmation from any one refutation test is not objective in the sense of being free of all theoretical assumptions. Multiple disconfirmations would render theory under test convincing (Cook and Campbell 1979). As a result, postpositivists might use a modified experimental/manipulative method and include qualitative methods to falsify hypotheses (Guba and Lincoln 2005). The multiple methods might be used to consolidate the "not yet disproven" status of theory and to eliminate plausible rival hypotheses.

Among these multiple methods, mixed-methods research has become increasingly popular as it breaks through the conventional methodological boundaries between quantitative and qualitative methods to avoid methodological biases. It is argued to be one of the three major methodological paradigms, which include quantitative research, qualitative research, and mixed-methods research (Johnson et al. 2007). Its emergence was also derived from the shift from the so-called paradigm wars of the 1980s to the paradigm dialogue of the 1990s (Denzin and Lincoln 2011; Guba 1990). It is used to avoid the apparent drawbacks of using only a quantitative or qualitative research method. On the one hand, quantitative research is used to test hypotheses and to generalize results obtained from sampling the population through measurement and statistical inference. However, it could direct attention to the results rather than process through the presentation of statistical relationships between variables. On the other hand, qualitative research intends to represent the meaning constructed by informants, to interpret the process of social problems, and to establish a complicated and holistic scene in a natural setting. However, it lacks the capability to generalize results to a more representative scope (Guba and Lincoln 2005). Mixed-methods research emphasizes the corroboration of both quantitative and qualitative elements, such as viewpoints, data collection and analysis, inference techniques, and so on (Johnson et al. 2007). It owns multiple purposes including triangulation, complementarity, development, initiation, and expansion (Greene et al. 1989). It has become increasingly popular in the studies of health systems (Ozawa and Pongpirul 2014).

This study adopts a sequential mixed-methods design, which exploits the ability to understand the mechanisms behind newly discovered associations or to test emergent hypotheses (Creswell 1994; Small 2011). The quantitative study serves as the primary and main design to test the theoretical model, while the qualitative study is used to confirm and explain in further depth the quantitative findings through illustrations generated by qualitative data (Morse 2010).

2.4 Summary

This study embraces a new institutionalist perspective to investigate the effects of welfare institutions on social outcomes. It uses both a determinative and an interactive perspective to construe the relationship.

It first summarizes the theoretical arguments of the relationship between welfare institutions and outcomes. It further argues that the mediating role of the institutional arrangement must be taken into consideration to elaborate on the concrete mechanisms of the process from welfare participation to outcomes. Based on these efforts, this study formulates an analytical framework of the institutional arrangement. Meanwhile, considering the policy design of SHI schemes, it combines the theoretical studies of the institutional arrangement and the empirical studies of SHI to adapt the framework to the study of SHI schemes. We also formulate three major hypotheses according to the propositions derived from the newly established analytical framework. The hypothetical model establishes a pathway from welfare entitlement, to the mediating institutional arrangement, and then to outcomes.

Apart from the perspective of determination, we also adopt a perspective of strategic interaction to explore the relationship between welfare institutions and the behavior of actors. We adopt a calculus approach to probe into the role SHI and its institutional arrangement play in structuring the interaction of stakeholders in the healthcare sector. We focus on the interaction of three kinds of stakeholders, that is, SHI agencies, healthcare providers, and patients.

In addition, the dual theoretical perspectives of determination and strategic interaction determine the methodology used in this study. We adopt a postpositivist paradigm and a sequential mixed-methods design to facilitate the statistical tests and the explanation of the relationship between welfare institutions, the behavior of actors, and social outcomes. We use a quantitative study to examine the role of the institutional arrangement of SHI operating on the relationship between SHI participation and individuals' OOPS in China. Furthermore, we use a qualitative study to explain the mechanisms of the institutional arrangement tested in the quantitative study.

Chapter 3
Effects of Social Health Insurance Participation on Patients' Out-of-Pocket Spending

The slogan of SHI advocates a decrease in patients' OOPS and a reduction in their health-related impoverishment. However, the problem of the affordability of healthcare seems not to be mitigated by the development of SHI, even though SHI schemes have covered almost the whole population of China. Why does the impact of SHI participation on mitigating the problem of affordability and medical expenses seem controversial? We explored this issue by investigating the mediating role that the institutional arrangement of SHI plays in the relationship between SHI participation and patients' OOPS. We first conducted a quantitative study in order to answer the first two research questions proposed in Chap. 1; that is, "What is the effect of the expanding SHI participation on people's medical expenditures?" and "Through what kind of institutional arrangement does SHI participation affect people's OOPS?"

To answer the first question, we examined the effect of SHI participation on a series of indicators of medical expenditures, including the usage of treatment items (device test, lab test, drip infusion, injection, and surgery), the share of out-of-pocket drug costs of total medical expenditures, the length of stay in hospital, total medical expenditures, and OOPS.

To probe the second question, we used structural equation modeling to test the hypothetical model proposed in Chap. 2. We conducted a confirmatory factor analysis to test our measurement model, which was followed by a test of the hypothesized structural model. Lastly, we discussed our findings from the quantitative analysis at the end of this chapter.

K. Liu, *The Effects of Social Health Insurance Reform on People's Out-of-Pocket Health Expenditure in China*, DOI 10.1007/978-981-10-1777-3_3

3.1 Method 1: Testing the Effect of SHI Participation on Patients' Medical Expenditure

3.1.1 Data

The data used in this study were drawn from the latest wave of the China Health and Retirement Longitudinal Study (CHARLS), which was administered in 28 out of the 31 provinces (Tibet, Ningxia, and Hainan were not included) of China, in 2011. The sample is representative of people aged 40 and over. All samples were collected over four stages using a multistage cluster sampling method, at county, neighborhood, household, and respondent level, with probability proportional to size sampling used in the former two stages. At the first stage, 150 counties/districts were selected randomly by region from over 2000 counties/urban districts/county-level cities in 28 provinces, according to the population size of each county/district. At the second stage, three administrative villages (*cun*) in rural areas or neighborhoods (*shequ*) in urban areas were selected randomly from each selected county/district, and adjusted for the population size of villages and neighborhoods. At the third stage, 80 households from each village/neighborhood were selected randomly with the assistance of a specialized geographical information system software program. Finally, at the fourth stage, one person aged 45 or older and his/her spouse were randomly selected from each eligible household, while one person aged between 40–44 was also selected for future rounds of the survey. A total of 17,587 participants were finally selected from 10,257 households, with a response rate of 80.51 % (Zhao et al. 2013).

The data used in this study were obtained from the available information of 1475 inpatients who had been hospitalized in the past year and 1271 outpatients who had received outpatient services in the past month. Missing data were excluded from the analysis. It must be noted that the original number of outpatient cases was 3294; however, this study excluded 2023 outpatients in communities where the SHI benefit package for outpatient services had not yet been launched. The insured patients in these places, like those who were uninsured, had to pay for their outpatient services completely out-of-pocket. This meant that SHI participation would be uncorrelated with medical expenditures, therefore generating selection bias for our coefficient estimates. Thus, in order to focus on the effects of the real and substantial benefits of SHI schemes, it was necessary to exclude outpatient cases in these communities.

We further divided each of these two samples into three subsamples according to different insurance status, resulting in a total of six subsamples, that is, UEBMI outpatient and inpatient samples, URBMI outpatient and inpatient samples, and NCMS outpatient and inpatient samples. Each subsample placed uninsured people as the reference group, and then compared them with participants in one corresponding SHI scheme.

3.1.2 Measures

Measures of variables used in this analysis are displayed in Table 3.1. Participation in different SHI schemes was recoded into three dummy variables: *UEBMI participation* (1 = yes; 0 = no insurance), *URBMI participation* (1 = yes; 0 = no insurance), and *NCMS participation* (1 = yes; 0 = no insurance), with uninsured patients as the reference group.

We also measured dependent variables. Participants were asked if they used a device test, lab test, drip infusion, injection, and/or surgery during their last outpatient, as well as inpatient, service. The usage of these medical items was recoded into dummy variables respectively: *device test usage* (1 = yes; 0 = no), *lab test usage* (1 = yes; 0 = no), *drip infusion usage* (1 = yes; 0 = no), *injection usage* (1 = yes; 0 = no), and *surgery usage* (1 = yes; 0 = no; not applicable for the outpatient samples). Participants were also asked to report their *out-of-pocket drug costs*. We obtained the *share of out-of-pocket drug costs* of total medical expenditures by dividing the cost of drugs paid out-of-pocket by the total medical expenditures during their last outpatient or inpatient service. The CHARLS also asked patients who received inpatient services to report their *length of stay in hospital* or the dates starting hospitalization and ending hospitalization (not applicable for outpatient samples). If participants reported the dates, we obtained their length of stay in hospital by subtracting the date they ended hospitalization from the date they started hospitalization. Participants were asked to report their *total medical expenditures* and *OOPS* during their last inpatient or outpatient service.

In addition, several variables were controlled for to avoid spurious effects, including age, gender, education, place of residence, facility location, self-reported health status, chronic conditions, functional limitations, per capita household income, and per capita household wealth. Participants were asked to report their *age, gender* (1 = male; 0 = female), *educational level* (1 = no education; 2 = elementary school; 3 = middle school; 4 = high or vocational school; 5 = bachelor's or associate degree; 6 = master's or doctoral degree), *place of residence* (1 = urban area; 0 = rural area), and the *location of the facilities* they visited during their last hospitalization (1 = this street/village; 2 = this district/township; 3 = this city/county; 4 = this province; 5 = other province). *Self-reported health status* was measured by one question: "Would you say your health is excellent, very good, good, fair, poor, or very poor?" The response category of "excellent" was scored as 1, "very good" as 2, "good" as 3, "fair" as 4, "poor" as 5, and "very poor" as 6. *Chronic conditions* were assessed by asking participants the number of chronic diseases from which they suffered. *Functional limitations* were measured by the 11-item adjusted version of the Instrumental Activities of Daily Living Scale (IADLS; Lawton and Brody 1969). Participants were asked to use a 4-point response scale ranging from "I don't have any difficulty (1)" to "I cannot do it (4)" to indicate whether they had difficulty performing any of the following activities: dressing, bathing, eating, getting into or out of bed, using the toilet, controlling urination and defecation, doing household chores, preparing hot meals,

Table 3.1 Variables and measures used in the regression analysis of the effect of SHI participation on patients' medical expenditure

Variables	Measurements
Independent variables	
UEBMI participation	1 = yes; 0 = no insurance
URBMI participation	1 = yes; 0 = no insurance
NCMS participation	1 = yes; 0 = no insurance
Dependent variables	
Device test usage	Whether X-ray, CT, B-ultrasonic, or MRI was used during the last medical treatment (1 = yes; 0 = no)
Lab test usage	Whether a laboratory test was used during the last medical treatment (1 = yes; 0 = no)
Drip infusion usage	Whether drip infusion was used during the last medical treatment (1 = yes; 0 = no)
Injection usage	Whether injection was used during the last medical treatment (1 = yes; 0 = no)
Surgery usage	Whether surgery was used during the last medical treatment (1 = yes; 0 = no)
Proportion of out-of-pocket drug costs	Cost of drugs paid out-of-pocket divided by total medical expenditures during the last medical treatment
Length of stay in hospital	The date ending hospitalization minus the date starting hospitalization during the last hospitalization
Total medical expenditures	Total medical expenditures during the last medical treatment
OOPS	Out-of-pocket spending during the last medical treatment
Control variables	
Age	Age
Gender	1 = male; 0 = female
Education	1 = no education; 2 = elementary school; 3 = middle school; 4 = high or vocational school; 5 = bachelor's or associate degree; 6 = master's or doctoral degree
Place of residence	1 = urban areas; 0 = rural areas
Facility location	The location of the facilities in which participants visited during their last medical treatment (1 = this street/village; 2 = this district/township; 3 = this city/county; 4 = this province; 5 = other province)
Self-reported health status	1 = excellent; 2 = very good; 3 = good; 4 = fair; 5 = poor; 6 = very poor
Chronic conditions	Number of chronic diseases from which participants suffered
Functional limitations	Measured using an adjusted version of the Instrumental Activities of Daily Living Scale (Lawton and Brody 1969). A 4-point Likert-type scale ranging from "I don't have any difficulty (1)" to "I cannot do it (4)" was used. Eleven items were identified to indicate whether participants had difficulty in dressing, bathing, eating, getting into or out of bed, using the toilet, controlling urination and defecation, doing household chores, preparing hot meals, shopping for groceries, managing

(continued)

Table 3.1 (continued)

Variables	Measurements
	money, and taking medications. Cronbach's alpha of the scale was 0.912 for the inpatient sample and 0.903 for the outpatient sample. The standardized sum score of the scales was used to measure the functional limitations of participants
Per capita income	Sum of incomes received by all household members divided by family size
Per capita wealth	(Total value of household houses, land, equipment, and financial assets minus total value of household debts) divided by family size
Instrumental variables	
Employment status	Including the following five categories: unemployed, employed, self-employed, retired, and farming. These were recoded into four dummy variables, including employed (1 = employed; 0 = unemployed), self-employed (1 = self-employed; 0 = unemployed), retired (1 = retired; 0 = unemployed), and farming (1 = farming; 0 = unemployed), with unemployed participants as the reference group
hukou type	1 = nonagriculture *hukou*; 0 = agriculture *hukou*
hukou location	1 = this village/neighborhood; 2 = another village/neighborhood in this county/city; 3 = another county/city in this province; 4 = another province
Amount of households in local community	Amount of households in the community in which participant lived

shopping for groceries, managing money, and taking medications. Cronbach's alpha of the scale in this sample was 0.912. In this study, the standardized sum score of the scale was used as an observed indicator to assess the functional limitations of participants. Per capita household income was calculated by dividing household income by household size, where household income was obtained by summing all types of income received by all household members. Per capita household wealth was assessed by dividing household wealth by household size, where household wealth was obtained by evaluating the total value of all types of asset possessed by all household members, including houses, land, equipment, and financial assets less debt.

We also designed and measured several instrumental variables, including *employment status*, *hukou type* (*hukou* meant the household registration system which classified residents into those with agriculture *hukou* and with nonagriculture *hukou* in China), *hukou location*, and *amount of households in the local community*. *Employment status* included five categories: unemployed, employed, self-employed, retired, and farming. These were then recoded into four dummy variables, including employed (1 = employed; 0 = unemployed), self-employed (1 = self-employed; 0 = unemployed), retired (1 = retired; 0 = unemployed), and farming (1 = farming; 0 = unemployed), with unemployed participants as the reference group. *Hukou type* was recoded into a dummy variable (1 = nonagriculture *hukou*; 0 = agriculture *hukou*). *Hukou location* was measured as the regional location of participants' hukou (1 = this village/neighborhood; 2 = another village/neighborhood in this county/city; 3 = another county/city in this province; 4 = another province). Lastly, *amount of households in the local community* was drawn from the community survey of the CHARLS, and was measured by the amount of households in the community in which participants lived.

3.1.3 Statistical Analysis

We constructed two sets of regression models for analysis: a probit regression model for the five binary dependent variables (device test usage, lab test usage, drip infusion usage, injection usage, and surgery usage), and an ordinary least squares (OLS) regression model for the four continuous dependent variables (the share of out-of-pocket drug costs, length of stay in hospital, total medical expenditures, and OOPS).

Although we controlled for as many of the variables that had the potential to affect both SHI participation and indicators of medical expenditures as possible, the confounding variables could not all be observed and measured. Unobservable variables, such as the type and severity of diseases, might still affect simultaneously SHI participation and medical expenditures, making a correlation between SHI participation and the error term in our estimating equations (Wagstaff and Lindelow 2008). We took into account this endogeneity problem through the method of instrumental variables (IV). We first found instruments that were correlated with SHI participation but uncorrelated with the error term in our estimating equation. After that, we conducted an overidentification test, the null hypothesis of which is that the instruments were uncorrelated with the error term and therefore valid. We also ran an endogeneity test to examine whether there was a significant difference between the OLS/probit models and IV regression/probit models systematically, where a significant difference denotes SHI participation to be endogenous.

There is a distinctive difference of entitlement between UEBMI participation and URBMI participation, as well as NCMS participation. The former is based on employment status and targeted at those working in formal organizations, while the latter two are linked with the *hukou* system. Usually, only residents that have corresponding local urban or rural *hukou* can be enrolled in URBMI (urban) or NCMS (rural). Therefore, we used the *employment status* of participants as instrumental variables for the UEBMI subsamples. For the URBMI subsamples, we used the *type of hukou* of participants and the *amount of households in the community* where participants live as instrumental variables. In addition, we used *the type and the location of hukou* of participants for the NCMS subsamples.

3.2 Method 2: Testing the Mediating Effect of Institutional Arrangement in the Relationship Between SHI Participation and Hospitalized Patients' OOPS

3.2.1 Data

The data for the analysis of the mediating role of the institutional arrangement of SHI were also obtained from the CHARLS in 2011–2012. In this study, we selected those participants from the original sample who had been hospitalized in the past year, giving a sample of 1645. In addition, we included patients enrolled in the GMI. We also used regression imputation to deal with missing data. Therefore, the sample was slightly larger than that used above in the regression analysis of the relationship between SHI participation and medical expenditures.

3.2.2 Measures

The measures of all the variables shown in our hypothetical model (Fig. 2.1) are summarized in Table 3.2. We first measured the key independent and dependent variables. Participants reported their OOPS for their last hospitalization. In this study, we measured OOPS using ¥1000 as the unit. Participants were asked if they participated in any of the SHI schemes, including GMI, UEBMI, URBMI, and NCMS. In the analysis, SHI participation was recoded into four dummy variables: *GMI participation* (1 = yes; 0 = no insurance), *UEBMI participation* (1 = yes; 0 = no insurance), *URBMI participation* (1 = yes; 0 = no insurance), and *NCMS participation* (1 = yes; 0 = no insurance), with uninsured patients as the reference group.

We also measured a series of mediating variables related to the institutional arrangement of SHI. *Reimbursement rate* of SHI was measured by reimbursed fees divided by the total medical cost of the last hospitalization. *Facility level* was assessed by the level of the healthcare agencies visited by patients during their last inpatient care, with a value of 1 indicating "healthcare post/village clinic/private clinic," 2 indicating "township/community health center," 3 indicating "county/district hospital," 4 indicating "city/regional hospital," and 5 indicating "provincial/ministry/military hospital." *Length of stay in hospital* was measured by the number of inpatient days during the last hospitalization. Participants were also asked to report the *types of treatment items* provided by doctors during their last hospitalization, using a multiple-choice question, including five main categories: medications, tests involving high-tech equipment (X-ray, CT, B-ultrasonic, and MRI), surgery, injections, and laboratory tests.

Several variables were controlled for when testing the hypothesized model, including age, gender, place of residence, education, employment, facility location, health status, and economic status. Participants were asked to report their *age*, *gender* (1 = male; 0 = female), *place of residence* (1 = urban area; 0 = rural area),

Table 3.2 Variables and measures used in the structural equation modeling when testing the mediating role of institutional arrangement

Concepts	Variables	Measurements
OOPS	OOPS	Out-of-pocket medical spending for the last hospitalization (¥1000)
SHI participation	GMI participation	1 = yes; 0 = no insurance
	UEBMI participation	1 = yes; 0 = no insurance
	URBMI participation	1 = yes; 0 = no insurance
	NCMS participation	1 = yes; 0 = no insurance
Reimbursement mechanism	Reimbursement rate	Reimbursed fees divided by total medical cost for the last hospitalization
Behavior management mechanism	Facility level	1 = healthcare post/village clinic/private clinic; 2 = THC/CHC; 3 = county/district hospital; 4 = city/regional hospital; 5 = provincial/ministry/military hospital
Purchasing mechanism	Length of stay	The dates ending hospitalization minus the dates starting hospitalization during the last hospitalization
	Types of treatment items	No. of types of treatment items for the last hospitalization
Control variables	Age	Age
	Gender	1 = male; 0 = female
	Place of residence	1 = urban areas; 0 = rural areas
	Facility location	The location of the facilities which participants visited during their last medical treatment (1 = this street/village; 2 = this district/township; 3 = this city/county; 4 = this province; 5 = other province)
	Education	1 = no education; 2 = elementary school; 3 = middle school; 4 = high or vocational school; 5 = bachelor's or associate degree; 6 = master's or doctoral degree
	Employment status	
	Employed	1 = yes; 0 = unemployed or never worked
	Self-employed	1 = yes; 0 = unemployed or never worked
	Farming	1 = yes; 0 = unemployed or never worked
	Retired	1 = yes; 0 = unemployed or never worked
	Health status	
	Self-reported health status	1 = excellent; 2 = very good; 3 = good; 4 = fair; 5 = poor; 6 = very poor
	Chronic conditions	Number of chronic diseases from which participants suffered
	Functional limitations	Instrumental activities of daily living scale (11 items)
	Economic status	
	Household income	Amount of income received by all household members (¥10,000)
	Household wealth	Total value of household houses, land, equipment, and financial assets minus total value of household debts (¥10,000)

educational level (1 = no education; 2 = elementary school; 3 = middle school; 4 = high or vocational school; 5 = bachelor's or associate degree; 6 = master's or doctoral degree), and the *location of the facilities* they visited during their last hospitalization (1 = this street/village; 2 = this district/township; 3 = this city/county; 4 = this province; 5 = other province). They were also asked to report their *employment status,* including unemployed or never worked, employed, self-employed, farming, and retired. We recoded employment status into four dummy variables: employed (1 = yes; 0 = unemployed or never worked), self-employed (1 = yes; 0 = unemployed or never worked), farming (1 = yes; 0 = unemployed or never worked), and retired (1 = yes; 0 = unemployed or never worked), with the unemployed or those who had never worked as the reference group. Health status and economic status were assessed as two latent constructs. The observed indicators forming the latent construct of *health status* included *self-reported health status, chronic conditions, and functional limitations*, which have been reported to be good indicators (Gu et al. 2009; Idler and Benyamini 1997). Self-reported health status was measured by one question: "Would you say your health is excellent, very good, good, fair, poor, or very poor?" The response category of "excellent" was scored as 1, "very good" as 2, "good" as 3, "fair" as 4, "poor" as 5, and "very poor" as 6. Chronic conditions were assessed by asking participants the number of chronic diseases from which they suffered. Functional limitations were measured by the 11-item adjusted version of the IADLS (Lawton and Brody 1969). Participants were asked to use a 4-point Likert-type scale ranging from "I don't have any difficulty (1)" to "I cannot do it (4)" to indicate whether they had difficulty performing any of the following activities: dressing, bathing, eating, getting into or out of bed, using the toilet, controlling urination and defecation, doing household chores, preparing hot meals, shopping for groceries, managing money, and taking medications. Cronbach's alpha of the scale in this sample was 0.912. In this study, the standardized sum score of the scale was used as an observed indicator to assess the functional limitations of participants. Finally, two variables, *household income* and *household wealth*, were used to form the latent construct of *economic status* (Stewart 2009). Household income was calculated by asking participants to indicate all types of income received by members. Household wealth was assessed by asking participants to evaluate the total value of all types of asset possessed by household members, including houses, land, equipment, and financial assets less debt. In this study, we measured the two indicator variables using ¥10,000 as the unit.

3.2.3 *Statistical Analysis*

We used structural equation modeling (SEM) with maximum likelihood estimation, conducted using AMOS 20 (Arbuckle 2011), to test the hypothesized model. Confirmatory factor analysis was first conducted to ensure that the measurement model of the two latent constructs, that is, health status and economic status, had a good fit. Next, the final SEM model, including the full dataset of all hospitalized patients, was tested. Missing data in this sample were imputed using AMOS regression imputation.

Three indicators of goodness-of-fit were used. The chi-square coefficient (χ^2), where a nonsignificant χ^2 represents a closer fit of the hypothesized model to the perfect fit (Bollen 1989), was used. However, due to the sensitivity of χ^2 to sample size, it was common for a well-fitting hypothesized model to yield a significant χ^2 if the sample size was large. Indeed, researchers have addressed the chi-square limitation by developing another two indictors of goodness-of-fit indices as follows, which take a more pragmatic approach to the evaluation process. To be specific, we used the comparative fit index (CFI), where values above 0.90 represent a good fit (Bentler 1990), and the root mean square error of approximation (RMSEA), where a value of less than 0.05 indicates a close fit, between 0.05 and 0.08 indicates a reasonable fit, and above 0.10 indicates a poor fit (Steiger 1990; Kline 2005).

3.3 Result 1: The Effect of SHI Participation on Patients' Medical Expenditure

3.3.1 Descriptive Statistics

The descriptive statistics of variables used in Method 1 are shown in Table 3.3.

SHI participation. In the outpatient sample, 15 % were UEBMI enrollees, 4 % URBMI enrollees, 65 % NCMS enrollees, and 16 % uninsured. In the inpatient sample, 15 % were UEBMI enrollees, 4 % URBMI enrollees, 67 % NCMS enrollees, and 14 % uninsured.

Medical expenditure indicators. For participants who received outpatient services in the past 2 weeks, 20 % of them received a device test, 38 % received a lab test, 50 % received drip infusion, and 44 % received an injection. The average share of the cost spent on drugs of the total medical expenditures was 49 %. The average total medical expenditures and OOPS were ¥1299 and ¥812, respectively. For patients who received inpatient services in the past year, 56 % received a device test, 51 % received a lab test, 88 % received drip infusion, 47 % received an injection, and 25 % received surgery. Thirty-eight percent of their total medical expenditures was spent on drugs. Their average length of stay in hospital was 13 days. Their total medical expenditures and OOPS for inpatient services were ¥7024 and ¥4670, respectively.

Sociodemographic characteristics. The average ages of the participants in the outpatient and inpatient samples were 61 years and 62 years, respectively. Among them, 43 % of the outpatients and 48 % of the inpatients were male. Forty-nine percent of the outpatients and 50 % of the inpatients had no education. Forty-one percent of the outpatients and 42 % of the inpatients came from urban areas. Forty-four percent of the outpatients chose health facilities located in a local street

Table 3.3 Descriptive statistics of samples: method 1

	Outpatient sample			Inpatient sample		
	N	*Mean*	*SD*	*N*	*Mean*	*SD*
UEBMI insured	1270	0.15	0.35	1475	0.15	0.36
URBMI insured	1270	0.04	0.20	1475	0.04	0.20
NCMS insured	1270	0.65	0.48	1475	0.67	0.47
Uninsured	1270	0.16	0.37	1475	0.14	0.34
Device test usage	1121	0.20	0.40	1473	0.56	0.50
Lab test usage	0.17	0.38	0.17	1473	0.51	0.50
Drip infusion usage	0.51	0.50	0.51	1473	0.88	0.32
Injection usage	0.26	0.44	0.26	1473	0.47	0.50
Surgery usage	–			1473	0.25	0.43
Share of out-of-pocket drug costs	884	0.49	0.39	906	0.38	0.34
Length of stay in hospital		–	–	1468	12.99	10.81
Total medical expenditures	1159	1298.63	6857.15	1416	7024.40	12252.29
OOPS	1151	812.21	5507.06	1398	4670.27	10952.90
Age	1269	61.17	10.57	1475	61.98	10.38
Male	1270	0.43	0.49	1475	0.48	0.50
Education						
No education	1266	0.49	0.50	1469	0.50	0.50
Elementary school	1266	0.22	0.41	1469	0.21	0.41
Middle school	1266	0.18	0.39	1469	0.19	0.39
High/vocational school	1266	0.09	0.28	1469	0.08	0.27
Bachelor's/associate degree and above	1266	0.02	0.14	1469	0.02	0.14
Urban	1270	0.41	0.49	1475	0.42	0.49
Facility location						
This street/village	1201	0.44	0.50	1461	0.13	0.34
This district/township	1201	0.26	0.44	1461	0.28	0.45
This city/county	1201	0.26	0.44	1461	0.48	0.50
This province	1201	0.03	0.18	1461	0.08	0.27
Other province	1201	0.01	0.11	1461	0.03	0.17
Self-reported health status	1269	4.38	0.78	1474	4.46	0.77
Chronic conditions	1221	1.96	1.56	1421	2.19	1.67
Functional limitations	1229	4.17	4.42	1428	4.83	4.75
Per capita household income (¥1000)	1191	8.44	13.26	1396	7.32	9.75
Per capita household wealth (¥1000)	1254	62.69	183.49	1459	44.22	90.01

(continued)

Table 3.3 (continued)

	Outpatient sample			Inpatient sample		
	N	*Mean*	*SD*	*N*	*Mean*	*SD*
Employment						
Unemployed or never worked	1174	0.32	0.47	1395	0.37	0.48
Employed	1174	0.11	0.32	1395	0.09	0.29
Self-employed	1174	0.08	0.27	1395	0.06	0.23
Farming	1174	0.35	0.48	1395	0.32	0.47
Retired	1174	0.14	0.35	1395	0.17	0.38
Hukou type						
Agriculture *hukou*	1263	0.78	0.42	1466	0.77	0.42
Nonagriculture *hukou*	1263	0.22	0.42	1466	0.23	0.42
Hukou location						
This village/neighborhood	1267	0.87	0.34	1475	0.87	0.33
Another village/neighborhood in this county/city	1267	0.11	0.31	1475	0.11	0.31
Another county/city in this province	1267	0.02	0.13	1475	0.01	0.10
Another province	1267	0.01	0.08	1475	0.01	0.08
Amount of households in local community	1200	970.80	1466.71	1392	934.23	1283.36

Note N sample size; *SD* standard deviation; *OOPS* out-of-pocket spending

or village, while 48 % of the inpatients chose those located in a local city or county. Self-reported health status had an average sum score of 4.38 for the outpatient sample, and of 4.46 for the inpatient sample; chronic conditions indicated that the outpatients had 1.96 types of chronic disease on average, and that inpatients had 2.19; functional limitations had an average sum score of 4.17 for the outpatients and 4.83 for the inpatients. One member of a household on average earned ¥8440 in the past year and owned ¥62,690 of wealth in the outpatient sample, and earned ¥7320 in the past year and owned ¥44,220 of wealth in the inpatient sample.

3.3.2 *Effects of SHI Participation on Medical Expenditure Indicators*

The results of regression analysis for the outpatient and inpatient subsamples are displayed in Tables 3.4, 3.5, respectively. Due to limited space, we have reported coefficients of estimates only for the SHI participation variables. Coefficients of estimates for covariates are presented in Appendix A.

Table 3.4 Results of regression analysis for the outpatient subsamples: method 1

	OLS/Probit		Overidentification test (*p*)	Endogeneity test (*p*)	IV regression/probit	
	Coefficient	*p*			Coefficient	*p*
UEBMI participation						
Device test usage	1.175	0.000	0.538	0.822	0.986	0.014
Lab test usage	0.815	0.003	0.049	0.394	1.024	0.018
Drip infusion usage	0.243	0.276	0.226	0.185	−0.118	0.731
Injection usage	−0.494	0.027	0.223	0.574	−0.349	0.328
Share of out-of-pocket drug costs	−0.384	0.000	0.464	0.005	−0.154	0.129
Total medical expenditures	2498.885	0.001	0.827	0.421	3170.531	0.008
OOPS	678.215	0.079	0.985	0.517	941.526	0.116
URBMI participation						
Device test usage	1.046	0.001	0.912	0.443	0.553	0.583
Lab test usage	0.675	0.038	0.717	0.793	0.458	0.640
Drip infusion usage	0.341	0.197	0.974	0.531	−0.012	0.987
Injection usage	−0.412	0.154	0.137	0.635	−0.724	0.325
Share of out-of-pocket drug costs	−0.465	0.000	0.807	0.543	−0.652	0.011
Total medical expenditures	718.018	0.022	0.150	0.278	−171.538	0.850
OOPS	117.633	0.643	0.232	0.151	−828.346	0.282
NCMS participation						
Device test usage	0.381	0.017	0.273	0.648	0.603	0.256
Lab test usage	0.375	0.028	0.784	0.825	0.470	0.347
Drip infusion usage	0.482	0.000	0.944	0.785	0.388	0.331
Injection usage	−0.216	0.081	0.033	0.632	−0.063	0.879
Share of out-of-pocket drug costs	−0.272	0.000	0.497	0.660	−0.232	0.017
Total medical expenditures	854.697	0.200	0.916	0.642	1717.295	0.378
OOPS	519.160	0.361	0.983	0.638	1265.283	0.446

Note OLS ordinary least squares; *IV* instrumental variables; *OOPS* out-of-pocket spending

Table 3.5 Results of regression analysis for the inpatient subsamples: method 1

	OLS/Probit		Overidentification test (p value)	Endogeneity test (p value)	IV regression/probit	
	Coefficient	p value			Coefficient	p value
UEBMI participation						
Device test usage	0.442	0.021	0.998	0.263	0.812	0.038
Lab test usage	0.653	0.001	0.279	0.005	1.627	0.000
Drip infusion usage	−0.233	0.294	0.141	0.779	−0.097	0.839
Injection usage	0.509	0.007	0.314	0.708	0.618	0.113
Surgery usage	0.001	0.996	0.625	0.492	0.216	0.612
Share of out-of-pocket drug costs	−0.344	0.000	0.218	0.143	−0.177	0.179
Days of hospitalization	3.094	0.072	0.067	0.266	6.594	0.056
Total medical expenditures	2734.531	0.123	0.339	0.031	9550.248	0.009
OOPS	−3106.187	0.018	0.379	0.009	3064.248	0.262
URBMI participation						
Device test usage	0.410	0.059	0.560	0.082	1.599	0.025
Lab test usage	0.544	0.015	0.075	0.052	1.852	0.012
Drip infusion usage	−0.186	0.478	0.069	0.851	−0.446	0.606
Injection usage	0.126	0.557	0.107	0.030	1.583	0.024
Surgery usage	−0.216	0.385	0.724	0.080	0.986	0.189
Share of out-of-pocket drug costs	−0.166	0.038	0.221	0.882	−0.180	0.473
Days of hospitalization	1.034	0.619	0.981	0.727	3.108	0.608
Total medical expenditures	−515.081	0.759	0.552	0.221	5660.527	0.253
OOPS	−3925.806	0.017	0.390	0.090	3665.752	0.446
NCMS participation						
Device test usage	0.160	0.123	0.078	0.021	−0.614	0.093
Lab test usage	0.253	0.015	0.079	0.012	−0.608	0.103
Drip infusion usage	0.227	0.072	0.395	0.638	0.443	0.338
Injection usage	0.189	0.069	0.718	0.196	−0.232	0.508
Surgery usage	0.113	0.326	0.252	0.051	−0.606	0.117

(continued)

Table 3.5 (continued)

	OLS/Probit		Overidentification test (*p* value)	Endogeneity test (*p* value)	IV regression/probit	
	Coefficient	*p* value			Coefficient	*p* value
Share of out-of-pocket drug costs	−0.226	0.000	0.401	0.786	−0.199	0.048
Days of hospitalization	0.094	0.907	0.073	0.633	−1.160	0.676
Total medical expenditures	2236.331	0.022	0.137	0.351	−634.649	0.846
OOPS	268.552	0.780	0.140	0.429	−2200.932	0.503

Note OLS ordinary least squares; *IV* instrumental variables; *OOPS* out-of-pocket spending

We discussed first the validity of our instruments and the endogeneity of SHI participation. Generally speaking, our instruments were valid at a 0.05 significance level, except for usage of lab test in the UEBMI outpatient subsample and for usage of injection in the NCMS outpatient subsample. However, there were some differences between the outpatient and inpatient subsamples in terms of endogeneity. The endogeneity of SHI participation did not exist in the outpatient subsamples, except for the share of out-of-pocket drug costs in the UEBMI outpatient subsample. With regard to the inpatient subsamples, the endogeneity of SHI participation was revealed for use of a lab test, total medical expenditures, and OOPS in the UEBMI inpatient subsample, use of an injection in the URBMI inpatient subsample, and use of a device test and lab test in the NCMS subsample. This might be because hospitalization was more expensive and was more likely to induce catastrophic health expenditures. As a result, people gave priority to the reimbursement of inpatient over outpatient services.

After that, we focused on the effect of SHI participation on the outcome variables. In the outpatient subsamples, compared with their uninsured counterparts, all of the UEBMI, URBMI, and NCMS outpatients were more likely to receive a device test and a lab test. In addition, the NCMS outpatients might use more drip infusion. As a result, both the UEBMI and URBMI outpatients might have higher total medial expenditures. No significant differences in OOPS were found between any of the UEBMI, URBMI, and NCMS outpatients and uninsured outpatients. Similarly, in the inpatientsubsamples, compared with those who were uninsured, the UEBMI inpatients were more likely to receive a device test, lab test, and injection, and the URBMI inpatients a lab test and injection. The total medical expenditures of the UEBMI and NCMS inpatients, respectively, was significantly higher than that of their uninsured counterparts. As a result, the OOPS of both the UEBMI and NCMS inpatients had no significant difference to that of those who were uninsured. Only the OOPS of the URBMI inpatients was significantly lower than that of the uninsured.

There were several exceptions to the statistically positive relationship between SHI participation and medical expenditures. Except for that of the UEBMI outpatients, the proportions of out-of-pocket drug costs of all the other five groups, including the URBMI and NCMS outpatients and the UEBMI, URBMI, and NCMS inpatients, were significantly lower than those of the uninsured patients. In addition, the UEBMI outpatients were less likely to use injections than the uninsured outpatients.

3.4 Result 2: The Mediating Effect of Institutional Arrangement in the Relationship Between SHI Participation and OOPS

3.4.1 Descriptive Statistics

We first describe the basic characteristics of the sample. As mentioned above, the sample for this quantitative analysis was 1645 patients who had been hospitalized in the past year. The results of the descriptive analysis are presented in Table 3.6.

SHI participation and OOPS. The participants of various SHI schemes, as well as the uninsured patients, were unequally distributed. Among the cases, 2.6 % were GMI participants, 13.3 % UEBMI, 3.7 % URBMI, 57.8 % NCMS, and 15 % uninsured patients at the time of survey from 2011 to 2012. The proportion of patients with no insurance was higher than that in the official report. According to a summary report of the Healthcare Reform Office of the State Council, over 95 % of people had been enrolled into various SHI schemes (The Healthcare Reform Office of the State Council 2012), which indicated that the uninsured people should be less than 5 %. The gap cast a doubt on the authenticity of the official report. In addition, patients being hospitalized spent ¥4640 on average.

Medicating variables. Reimbursement rates for GMI, UEBMI, URBMI, and NCMS participants were 58, 58, 45, and 33 %, respectively, which indicated that urban insurance schemes provided more benefits than rural insurance schemes. Meanwhile, people being hospitalized in primary healthcare organizations including THCs, CHCs, healthcare posts, and village and private clinics accounted for 24.2 % out of the sample. Over half of the patients (52.3 %) were admitted to county hospitals in rural areas and district hospitals in urban areas. The remaining 18.2 % of patients were hospitalized in city, provincial, regional, ministry, and military hospitals. It should be noted that most of the county and district hospitals were secondary hospitals, while most of the provincial, regional, ministry, and military hospitals and some city hospitals were tertiary hospitals. The results above indicated that about 70 % of patients flew to secondary and tertiary hospitals. Furthermore, the average length of stay in hospitals was 13.25 days, while the average number of types of treatment items was 2.86 out of the five main types.

Sociodemographic characteristics. The average age of the participants was 62.32. Among them, 49.2 % were male and 43.6 % were from urban areas. The participants who had no education accounted for 29.2 %; most of them (59.5 %) had attended elementary or middle schools, and only 11 % of them had obtained diploma of high or vocational school and above. A total of 36.3 % of the participants were unemployed or had never worked, 14.3 % were employed and self-employed, 28.7 % were farmers, and the remaining 18.5 % were retirees. With regard to the location of facilities where patients were hospitalized, 40.7 % of the participants were admitted to hospitals within their districts or townships including their streets or villages, 46.5 % in their cities or counties, 7.7 % in their provinces, and 2.6 % in other provinces. In terms of the two latent variables, health status and economic status, each included some observed variables. Health status included a self-reported health status with an average sum score of 4.44, chronic conditions that indicated that the participants had 2.20 types of chronic diseases on average, and functional limitations with an average sum score of 15.69. Economic status included household income, which indicated that the households of the participants earned ¥25,600 in the past year, and household wealth had an average value of ¥141,300.

3.4.2 Test of Measurement Model

The measurement model of the two latent constructs, namely health and economic status, was examined before testing the hypothesized structural model.

As indicated by the analysis result, the measurement model offered a good fit to the data ($\chi^2 = 20.043$, $df = 4$, $p < 0.001$; CFI = 0.982; RMSEA = 0.049) with a CFI greater than 0.90 and RMSEA smaller than 0.05.

A confirmatory factor analysis indicated that all the observed variables were significantly loaded on the corresponding latent constructs in the expected directions. It suggested that the observed variables represented the underlying constructs reasonably and in a statistically reliable manner. As Table 3.7 shows, the standardized factor loadings of the indicators for each latent construct were all greater than 0.30, which is the rule of thumb of acceptable factor loadings (Agnew 1991). In addition, the correlation between the two latent constructs was also tested and was found to be statistically significant.

3.4.3 Test of Structural Model

A test of the hypothesized structural model showed that it provided a good fit to the data ($\chi^2 = 251.098$, $df = 58$, $p < 0.001$; CFI = 0.977; RMSEA = 0.045) with a CFI greater than 0.90 and RMSEA smaller than 0.05. A total of 24.6 % of the variance in the OOPS of hospitalized patients was explained by this model.

Before we reported the solution for the test of the structural model, we first established a set of criteria for testing the significance of mediation effects (Baron and Kenny 1986; Holmbeck 1997; MacKinnon et al. 2000, 2002). First, both the direct effects of the independent variable on the mediator, and of the mediator on

Table 3.6 Descriptive statistics: method 2

	Frequency	Percent	*Mean*	*SD*
SHI participation				
GMI	43	2.6		
UEBMI	218	13.3		
URBMI	61	3.7		
NCMS	950	57.8		
No insurance	246	15.0		
Facility level				
Healthcare post/village clinic/private clinic	34	2.1		
THC/CHC	364	22.1		
County/district hospital	860	52.3		
City/regional hospital	222	13.5		
Provincial/ministry/military hospital	78	4.7		
Length of stay (days)			13.25	11.21
Types of treatment items			2.86	1.60
Reimbursement rate				
GMI			0.58	0.37
UEBMI			0.58	0.28
URBMI			0.45	0.31
NCMS			0.33	0.29
No insurance			0.00	0.00
OOPS (¥1000)			4.64	10.42
Age			62.32	10.59
Gender				
Male	810	49.2		
Female	835	50.8		
Place of residence				
Urban	717	43.6		
Rural	928	56.4		
Education				
No education	480	29.2		
Elementary school	669	40.7		
Middle school	309	18.8		
High or vocational school	144	8.8		
Bachelor's or associate degree	37	2.2		
Master's or doctoral degree	0	0		
Employment				
Unemployed or never worked	548	36.3		
Employed	149	9.1		
Self-employed	86	5.2		
Farming	472	28.7		

(continued)

Table 3.6 (continued)

	Frequency	Percent	*Mean*	*SD*
Retried	305	18.5		
Facility location				
This street/village	223	13.6		
This district/township	446	27.1		
This city/county	765	46.5		
This province	126	7.7		
Other province	43	2.6		
Health status				
Self-reported health status			4.44	0.77
Chronic conditions			2.20	1.67
Functional limitations			15.69	6.63
Economic status				
Household income (¥10,000)			2.56	3.28
Household wealth (¥10,000)			14.13	25.43

Note SHI social health insurance; *OOPS* out-of-pocket spending; *GMI* government medical insurance; *UEBMI* urban employee basic medical insurance; *URBMI* urban resident basic medical insurance; *NCMS* new cooperative medical scheme

Table 3.7 Standardized factor loadings of observed variables on latent constructs: method 2

	Standardized factor loading
Health status	
Self-reported health status	0.788
Chronic conditions	0.468
Functional limitations	0.486
Economic status	
Household income	0.727
Household wealth	0.578

the dependent variable or another mediator, should be statistically significant. Second, the mediation effects, calculated as the product of the two regression coefficients indicated in the first criterion, must also be statistically significant using the procedure indicated by Sobel (1987). It should be noted that the total effect of the independent variable on the dependent variable was not required to be significant. If there were several medication paths between the independent and the dependent variables, the direction of these paths might be different, with some being positive and others negative. As a result, their combined effects might be offset mutually or by the direct effect of the independent variable on the dependent variable. MacKinnon et al. (2000) called this effect the "suppression effect". In addition, we used bootstrapping methods to test the significance of the indirect effects hypothesized in the model.

The unstandardized and standardized direct, indirect, and total effects are presented in Table 3.8. The standardized solution for the test of the structural model is

Table 3.8 Direct, indirect, and total effects: method 2

	Facility level	Length of stay			Types of treatment items			Reimbursement Rate	OOPS		
	Direct	Direct	Indirect	Total	Direct	Indirect	Total	Direct	Direct	Indirect	Total
GMI	0.459*** (0.092)	5.952** (0.086)	1.161*** (0.017)	7.113** (0.103)	0.107 (0.011)	0.298*** (0.030)	0.405 (0.041)	0.510*** (0.264)	−2.529 (−0.039)	−0.331 (−0.005)	−2.860 (−0.044)
UEBMI	0.613*** (0.261)	1.551 (0.048)	1.551*** (0.048)	3.101** (0.096)	0.321* (0.069)	0.292*** (0.063)	0.613*** (0.131)	0.529*** (0.586)	−1.776 (−0.058)	−1.358* (−0.045)	−3.135** (−0.103)
URBMI	0.547*** (0.129)	0.310 (0.005)	1.384*** (0.024)	1.695 (0.029)	0.291 (0.034)	0.243*** (0.029)	0.534* (0.063)	0.437*** (0.267)	−1.765 (−0.032)	−1.309* (−0.024)	−3.074*** (−0.056)
NCMS	0.143** (0.084)	−0.172 (−0.007)	0.361** (0.015)	0.188 (0.008)	0.318** (0.093)	0.059* (0.017)	0.377*** (0.111)	0.300*** (0.456)	1.921** (0.086)	−1.570*** (−0.071)	0.351 (0.016)
Facility level		2.531*** (0.183)		2.531*** (0.183)	0.393*** (0.197)	0.042*** (0.021)	0.435*** (0.218)		1.593*** (0.122)	1.010*** (0.078)	2.602*** (0.200)
Length of stay					0.016*** (0.114)		0.016*** (0.114)		0.311*** (0.330)	0.008* (0.009)	0.319*** (0.339)
Types of treatment items									0.512* (0.078)		0.512* (0.078)
Reimbursement rate									−6.828*** (−0.202)		−6.828*** (−0.202)
Age	−0.003 (−0.042)	−0.074* (−0.071)	−0.008 (−0.008)	−0.082* (−0.079)	−0.009* (−0.057)	−0.003** (−0.017)	−0.011* (−0.075)	0.004*** (0.121)	−0.059* (−0.060)	−0.060*** (−0.061)	−0.120*** (−0.121)
Gender	0.034 (0.021)	2.372*** (0.107)	0.086 (0.004)	2.458*** (0.111)	0.106 (0.033)	0.054** (0.017)	0.160 (0.050)	−0.011 (−0.018)	0.511 (0.025)	0.975*** (0.047)	1.486** (0.071)
Place of residence	0.113** (0.070)	0.595 (0.027)	0.286** (0.013)	0.881 (0.039)	−0.069 (−0.021)	0.059** (0.018)	−0.010 (−0.003)	−0.025 (−0.040)	1.252* (0.060)	0.618* (0.029)	1.870*** (0.089)
Education	0.020 (0.025)	−1.070** (−0.097)	0.049 (0.004)	−1.021** (−0.093)	−0.076 (−0.048)	−0.009 (−0.006)	−0.085 (−0.053)	−0.014 (−0.046)	0.366 (0.035)	−0.233 (−0.023)	0.133 (0.013)
Employed	−0.115	−2.446*	−0.292	−2.737*	−0.136	−0.091*	0.226	0.091**	−2.377*	−1.775***	−4.152***

(continued)

Table 3.8 (continued)

	Facility level	Length of stay			Types of treatment items			Reimbursement Rate	OOPS		
	Direct	Direct	Indirect	Total	Direct	Indirect	Total	Direct	Direct	Indirect	Total
	(−0.041)	(−0.064)	(−0.008)	(−0.071)	(−0.024)	(−0.016)	(−0.041)	(0.085)	(−0.066)	(−0.049)	(−0.114)
Self-employed	−0.004 (−0.001)	−2.181 (−0.044)	−0.009 (0.000)	−2.189* (−0.044)	0.065 (0.009)	−0.037 (−0.005)	0.028 (0.004)	0.034 (0.024)	−1.669 (−0.036)	−0.903 (−0.019)	−2.572* (−0.055)
Farming	−0.143** (−0.080)	−1.270 (−0.052)	−0.361** (−0.015)	−1.630 (−0.066)	−0.029 (−0.008)	−0.083*** (0.023)	−0.112 (−0.031)	0.057** (0.082)	−1.356* (−0.058)	−1.178*** (−0.051)	−2.533*** (−0.109)
Retired	0.081 (0.039)	0.953 (0.033)	0.205 (0.007)	1.158 (0.041)	0.348* (0.085)	0.051 (0.012)	0.398* (0.097)	0.007 (0.009)	−0.329 (−0.012)	0.642 (0.024)	0.314 (0.012)
Health status	−0.002 (−0.001)	3.373*** (0.156)	−0.006 (0.000)	3.367*** (0.156)	−0.149 (−0.048)	0.055* (0.018)	−0.094 (−0.030)	0.019 (0.031)	0.775 (0.038)	0.867* (0.043)	1.641* (0.081)
Economic status	0.004* (0.088)	0.037 (0.056)	0.011 (0.016)	0.048 (0.072)	0.006 (0.063)	0.002* (0.026)	0.009 (0.088)	0.003** (0.136)	0.031 (0.048)	0.009 (0.014)	0.039 (0.062)
Facility location	0.399*** (0.452)	0.792* (0.065)	1.010*** (0.083)	1.802*** (0.148)	0.156** (0.088)	0.187*** (0.106)	0.342** (0.194)	−0.022*** (−0.066)	0.805** (0.070)	1.524*** (0.133)	2.329*** (0.203)

*$p < 0.05$; **$p < 0.01$; ***$p < 0.001$

Note Unstandardized regression coefficients are shown by numbers without brackets; standardized regression coefficients are shown by numbers within brackets

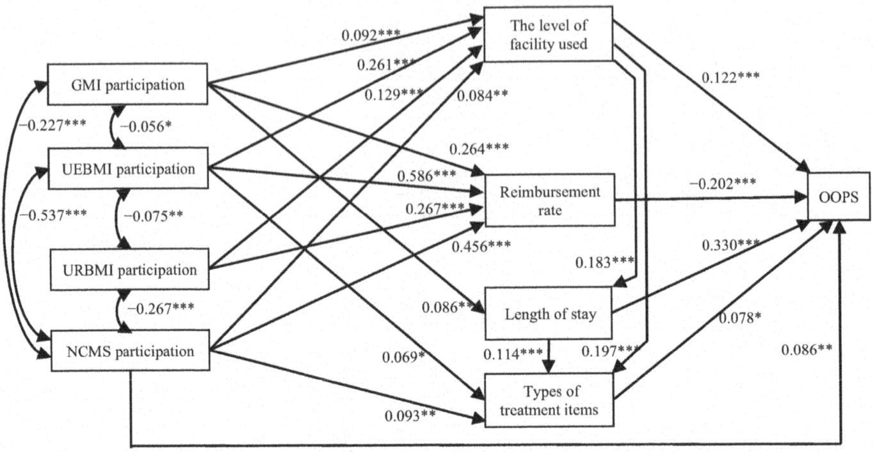

Fig. 3.1 Standardized solutions for the structural model. *Note* * = $p < 0.05$; ** = $p < 0.01$; *** = $p < 0.001$

presented in Fig. 3.1. For the sake of parsimony, only the significant paths are displayed. In addition, we used β to represent the unstandardized regression coefficient.

Performance of the behavior management mechanism. The behavior management mechanism of all four SHI schemes (the GMI, the UEBMI, the URBMI, and the NCMS) demonstrated effects as hypothesized. Patients enrolled in the GMI (β = 0.459, $p < 0.001$), the UEBMI (β = 0.613, $p < 0.001$), the URBMI (β = 0.547, $p < 0.001$), and the NCMS (β = 0.143, $p < 0.01$) were significantly more likely to seek healthcare from higher-level hospitals than the uninsured. Meanwhile, the level of facility used (β = 1.593, $p < 0.001$) had a significant positive association with OOPS, with a one-unit increase matched by an increase of ¥2602 in the OOPS.

Performance of the purchasing mechanism. Our analysis of the purchasing mechanism of SHI demonstrated similar effects. Patients who participated in the GMI (β = 5.952, $p < 0.01$) were more likely to extend their length of stay in hospital than the uninsured. On average, a GMI patient stayed 5.952 days longer than a patient with no insurance. Patients enrolled in the UEBMI (β = 0.321, $p < 0.05$) and the NCMS (β = 0.318, $p < 0.01$) were more likely to receive more types of treatment items than the uninsured. All three direct effects were statistically significant. In addition, taking the mediation of the level of facility and length of stay into consideration, participation in the GMI (β = 1.161, $p < 0.001$), the UEBMI (β = 1.551, $p < 0.001$), the URBMI (β = 1.384, $p < 0.001$), and the NCMS (β = 0.361, $p < 0.01$) had a significant and positive indirect relationship with length of stay, and participation in the GMI (β = 0.298, $p < 0.001$), the UEBMI (β = 0.292, $p < 0.001$), the URBMI (β = 0.243, $p < 0.001$), and the NCMS (β = 0.059, $p < 0.05$) also had a significant and positive indirect relationship with the types of treatment items. Finally, length of stay in hospital had a significant positive direct ($\beta = 0.311$, $p < 0.001$) and indirect ($\beta = 0.008$, $p < 0.05$) association with OOPS, with one more day of stay increasing total OOPS by ¥319. Type of treatment items ($\beta = 0.512$, $p < 0.05$) also had a significant and positive direct association with OOPS, with the provision of one more type of treatment item raising OOPS by an average of ¥512.

Performance of the reimbursement mechanism. The reimbursement mechanism of SHI played a significant role in reducing OOPS. Participation in the GMI ($\beta = 0.510$, $p < 0.001$), the UEBMI ($\beta = 0.529$, $p < 0.001$), the URBMI ($\beta = 0.437$, $p < 0.001$), and the NCMS ($\beta = 0.300$, $p < 0.001$) had a significant and positive association with the reimbursement rate of medical expenses. Reimbursement rate ($\beta = -6.828$, $p < 0.001$), in turn, had a significant negative association with OOPS. Compared with an insured patient who received total reimbursement of all of his/her medical expenses (reimbursement rate = 1, OOPS = ¥0), the average uninsured patient was a further ¥6828 out-of-pocket.

Interplay between the reimbursement and the behavior management and purchasing mechanisms. The association between the reimbursement mechanism and OOPS was seriously undermined by malfunctions in the behavior management and purchasing mechanisms. Although the OOPS of patients enrolled in the GMI, the UEBMI, the URBMI, and the NCMS was reduced by ¥3482 (= 0.510 * ¥6828), ¥3612 (= 0.529 * ¥6828), ¥2984 (= 0.437 * ¥6828), and ¥3114 (= 0.456 * ¥6828), respectively, through the mediation of reimbursed rate, at the same time it increased by ¥3151 (= ¥3482 − ¥331), ¥2254 (= ¥3612 − ¥1358), ¥1675 (= ¥2984 − ¥1309), and ¥1544 (¥3114 − ¥1570), respectively, by means of the level of facility used, length of stay, and types of treatment items. In terms of total effect, the OOPS of patients participating in the UEBMI ($\beta = -3.135$, $p < 0.01$) and the URBMI ($\beta = -3.074$, $p < 0.001$) was significantly reduced by ¥3135 and ¥3074, respectively. Although participation in the GMI also exerted a negative total effect on OOPS, this was statistically insignificant. Finally, the role of participation in the NCMS was controversial. It had a significant positive direct association ($\beta = 1.921$, $p < 0.01$) with OOPS despite its negative indirect association ($\beta = -1.570$, $p < 0.001$), with patients enrolled in the NCMS paying ¥1921 more than the uninsured. Therefore, taking the direct and indirect effects together, patients enrolled in the NCMS were ¥351 more out of pocket than the uninsured, although this total effect was statistically insignificant.

Role of the sociodemographic variables. Firstly, place of residence ($\beta = 0.113$, $p < 0.01$), economic status ($\beta = 0.004$, $p < 0.05$), and facility location ($\beta = 0.399$, $p < 0.001$) had positive and significant effects with the level of facility. This indicated that urban residents were more likely than rural to flow to higher-level hospitals, that patients with better household economic status were more likely to go to higher-level hospitals than those with worse status, and that a hospital being located farther from a patient was more likely to be a higher-level hospital. Farming ($\beta = -0.143$, $p < 0.01$) had a significant negative association with the level of facility, indicating that farmers were less likely to be hospitalized at higher-level hospitals than the unemployed or patients who had never worked. Secondly, gender ($\beta = 2.372$, $p < 0.001$), health status ($\beta = 3.373$, $p < 0.001$), and facility location ($\beta = 0.792$, $p < 0.05$) had significant positive associations with length of stay in health facilities. Age ($\beta = -0.074$, $p < 0.05$), education ($\beta = -1.070$, $p < 0.01$), and employed ($\beta = -2.446$, $p < 0.05$) had significant negative association with length of stay. In addition, place of residence ($\beta = 0.286$, $p < 0.01$), farming ($\beta = -0.361$, $p < 0.01$), and facility location ($\beta = 1.010$, $p < 0.001$) had significant indirect association with length of stay through the mediating role of level of facility. Taking direct and indirect effects together, age ($\beta = -0.082$, $p < 0.05$), gender ($\beta = 2.458$, $p < 0.001$), education ($\beta = -1.021$, $p < 0.01$), employed ($\beta = -2.737$, $p < 0.05$), self-employed ($\beta = -2.189$, $p < 0.05$), health status ($\beta = 3.367$, $p < 0.001$), and facility location ($\beta = 1.802$, $p < 0.001$) generated significant total effects on length of stay. An older or highly educated patient was more likely to stay for a shorter time than a younger or lowly educated one; on average, a male patient might stay 2.458 days longer than a female; an employed or self-employed patient might stay shorter than an unemployed one; an unhealthy patient might stay longer than a healthy one; and a patient with poorer health status or living farther from the hospital where he/she had been hospitalized was more likely to stay longer than a patient with better health status or who was living closer to the hospital. Thirdly, age ($\beta = -0.009$, $p < 0.05$), retired ($\beta = 0.348$, $p < 0.05$), and facility location had significant direct association with types of treatment items. Taking the mediating role of level of facility and length of stay into consideration, age ($\beta = -0.003$, $p < 0.01$), gender ($\beta = 0.054$, $p < 0.01$), place of residence ($\beta = 0.059$, $p < 0.01$), employed ($\beta = -0.091$, $p < 0.05$), farming ($\beta = -0.083$, $p < 0.001$), health status ($\beta = 0.055$, $p < 0.05$), economic status ($\beta = 0.002$, $p < 0.05$), and facility location ($\beta = 0.187$, $p < 0.001$) had significant indirect association with types of treatment items. In terms of total effect, age ($\beta = -0.011$, $p < 0.05$), retired ($\beta = 0.398$, $p < 0.05$), and facility location ($\beta = 0.342$, $p < 0.01$) had significant association with types of treatment items. An older patient was more likely to use fewer types of treatment items than a younger one; a retired patient was more likely to use more types of treatment items than an unemployed one; and a patient living farther from the hospital where he/she had been hospitalized was more likely to use more types of treatment items than one living closer. Fourthly, age ($\beta = 0.004$, $p < 0.001$), employed ($\beta = 0.091$, $p < 0.01$), farming ($\beta = 0.057$, $p < 0.01$), and economic status ($\beta = 0.003$, $p < 0.01$) had positive association with reimbursement rate. A one-year increase in age might raise the reimbursement rate by 0.4 %, the employed patients or farmers were more likely to enjoy a higher reimbursement rate than the unemployed ones, and patients with better economic status might enjoy a higher reimbursement rate than those with poor economic status. Facility location ($\beta = -0.022$, $p < 0.001$) had a significant negative association with reimbursement rate. A patient living farther from the hospital where he/she had been hospitalized might receive a lower reimbursement rate than one living closer. Finally, age ($\beta = -0.059$, $p < 0.05$), place of residence ($\beta = 1.252$, $p < 0.05$), employed ($\beta = -2.377$, $p < 0.05$), farming ($\beta = -1.356$, $p < 0.05$), and facility location ($\beta = 0.805$, $p < 0.01$) had significant direct association with OOPS.

Age (β = −0.060, $p < 0.001$), gender (β = 0.975, $p < 0.001$), place of residence (β = 0.618, $p < 0.05$), employed (β = −1.775, $p < 0.001$), farming (β = −1.178, $p < 0.001$), health status (β = 0.867, $p < 0.05$), and facility location (β = 1.524, $p < 0.001$) generated significant indirect association with OOPS through the mediating role of level of facility, length of stay, types of treatment items, and reimbursement rate. In terms of total effect, age (β = −0.120, $p < 0.001$), gender (β = 1.486, $p < 0.01$), place of residence (β = 1.870, $p < 0.001$), employed (β = −4.152, $p < 0.001$), self-employed (β = −2.572, $p < 0.05$), farming (β = −2.533, $p < 0.001$), health status (β = 1.641, $p < 0.05$), and facility location (β = 2.329, $p < 0.001$) had significant association with OOPS. An older patient might spend less out of pocket than a younger one; a male patient might spend ¥1486 more out of pocket than a female one; an urban patient might spend ¥1870 more out of pocket than a rural one; an employed patient might spend ¥4152 less, a self-employed one might spend ¥2572 less, and a farmer might spend ¥2533 less out of pocket than an unemployed one; a patient with poorer health status might spend more out of pocket than one with better health status; and a patient living farther from the hospital where he/she had been hospitalized might have to pay more out of pocket than a patient living closer.

3.5 Summary of Findings

The regression analysis of the effect of SHI participation showed that SHI schemes had positive effects on the rise of medical expenditures by increasing the usage of treatment items, prolonging days of hospitalization, and therefore increasing total medical expenditures.

The statistical evidence showing the mediating role of institutional arrangement presented above supported most of our hypotheses about how the reimbursement, behavior management, and purchasing mechanisms of SHI mediated the relationship between SHI participation and OOPS. As a result, SHI participation has a weak negative association (for UEBMI and URBMI) or no significant association (for GMI and NCMS) with the OOPS of hospitalized patients.

The reimbursement mechanism of the SHI. The findings indicated that the reimbursement mechanism offered considerable benefit to insured patients. As the essence of SHI, in terms of protecting enrollees from health-related financial problems, reimbursement was a policy priority for the Chinese government, alongside expanding SHI coverage. Although the reimbursement mechanism of SHI had been criticized for its high co-payment rate, unreasonable reimbursement formularies of drug, health service, and medical technology, inadequate ceiling amount, and so on (Gu 2010), it still played a salient role in reducing the likelihood of sustaining catastrophic medical expenses. Compared with the collapse of the health security system in the previous three decades, this "zero-to-one" change marked a remarkable milestone in the restoration of the health security system in China.

Looking at the mixed-premium contribution system, that is, the premium of UEBMI paid by the employer and the individual and of GMI, URBMI, and NCMS paid by the government and the individual, the policy implication of this study is that these contributors, especially the government, should act together to raise the reimbursement rate still further. This could be done either by paying higher premiums or by adjusting the reimbursement formularies to incorporate more cost-effective drugs and services. However, we must be cautious of the allocation of responsibility for this process. The contribution rate of employer and employee to social insurance (old age, medical, unemployment, workers' compensation and maternity), which accounts for about 40 % of wages in China, is thought to be too high (Zhou 2012). Therefore, further scientific and rigorous investigation of this issue is warranted.

The behavior management mechanism of the SHI. Although the reimbursement mechanism benefited enrollees, the malfunction of the behavior management and purchasing mechanism undermined this effect. The SHI regulations, in terms of requiring either a referral or tiered co-payment, failed to guide enrollees to utilize primary health facilities efficiently. On the contrary, the reimbursement benefits provided by SHI might stimulate them to access higher-level facilities.

Previous investigations have attributed this anomaly to the extreme inequity of health resource allocation and the lack of information for consumers in China (Xu and Van de Ven 2012; Zhang and Kanbur 2005). Therefore, relying on the regulation of referral mechanisms and the tiered co-payment requirement to guide people's care-seeking behavior is not enough. More efforts should be devoted to reforming the allocation of limited health resources between rural and urban areas, between different levels of facilities, and across regions, to promote greater equity. Meanwhile, strategic promotion should be conducted to guide consumer choice of healthcare services. These efforts, emphasizing the broader reform of China's healthcare system, call for joint actions among various government departments and between the state and its people.

The purchasing mechanism of the SHI. This study also provides helpful evidence of the malfunction of the purchasing mechanism of SHI in China. SHI participants were inclined to stay longer in hospital and to receive more types of treatment items than the uninsured, either directly or through the mediating effect of facility level. This reflected an unsolved but prevalent problem with the purchasing mechanism in China.

Studies have attributed this problem to the inefficient fee-for-services payment method, low purchasing incentives for SHI agencies, and the distorted price schedule of drugs and healthcare services. The lagged payment method for SHI agencies is gradually being replaced with different kinds of prospective methods such as capitation, diagnosis-related group payment, global budgets, and so on (Meng 2008; Yip and Hanson 2009). However, local SHI agencies still lack either the incentive to be prudent purchasers or attain the tools this requires, such as actuarial cost estimates, strong negotiating skills, and a consolidated information platform for inspection. Moreover, SHI agencies are also constrained by the larger political economy. For instance, there is insufficient room for municipal and county

SHI agencies to negotiate the prices of drugs and healthcare services whose regulation is left to provincial price bureaus (Xu and Van de Ven 2009). It is widely claimed, however, that the distorted price schedule, whereby the government sets the price of basic services below cost and of high-tech interventions above cost, gives providers strong incentives to overprescribe more profitable tests and treatments (Eggleston et al. 2008).

Against this backdrop, this study provides evidence of a unique phenomenon in China; that is, the collective purchasing power of SHI agencies may not be more efficient than individual purchasing, due to either the perverse incentives for providers or the low bargaining incentives of SHI agencies. More efficient investment in improving SHI agencies' contracting incentives and skills, establishing an inspection information platform, and further reforming the distorted price schedule are thus proposed to enhance the collective purchasing power of SHI agencies.

It should be noted that it might not be unreasonable for insured persons to spend more than the uninsured to enjoy good-quality health services. However, it was hard to judge whether this was the preference of patients themselves or was induced by doctors, and whether this was necessary. This must be investigated further, based on more microlevel data. Meanwhile, the malfunction of the behavior management mechanism also contributed to the high medical costs borne by insured patients. This should be adjusted as it was unfavorable to the equitable distribution of healthcare resources. Correspondingly, we would explore the behavior management and purchasing mechanisms and probe the interplay between the two mechanisms and the reimbursement mechanism.

To conclude, taking SHI reform in China as an example, this study has set out to combine theoretical studies of the institutional arrangements from social policy and empirical studies of SHI to develop a systematic insight into the association between SHI participation and patients' OOPS in China. This initiative is in response to the debates raised by different theories of institutional arrangement and provides specific evidence of the malfunctions of SHI in China. The behavior management and purchasing mechanisms have been shown to offer relatively poorer performance, which undermines the function of the reimbursement mechanism, thus mitigating the association between SHI participation and OOPS. These findings are expected to provide valuable insights into the ongoing healthcare reform in China.

Chapter 4
Why Did Social Health Insurance Become a Care-Seeking Behavior Booster?

This study followed a postpositivist paradigm and employed a mixed-methods design to both test the hypothetical model and explain the results of the tests. In Chap. 3, the quantitative analysis drew data from a nationally representative dataset CHARLS and found that SHI participation stimulated patients to seek care at high-level health facilities, increased the use of medical treatment items, prolonged length of stay in hospital and, in turn, increased patients' OOPS. It revealed that the poor performance of the behavior management and purchasing mechanisms of SHI offset the effect of its reimbursement mechanism on OOPS in China.

Why did SHI have a poor behavior management and purchasing mechanism in terms of curbing OOPS in China? To explain and interpret the poor performance of these two mechanisms, in this chapter, I probe into the behavior management mechanism of SHI, and in Chap. 5, I explore the purchasing mechanism of SHI. Before demonstrating the findings of the fieldwork, however, I will first introduce the methods of the qualitative study.

4.1 Methods of the Qualitative Study

The qualitative study aimed to confirm and explain the results of the quantitative study and answer the third research question: "How do these institutional arrangements take effect?" I conducted four months of fieldwork in three cities and one county, in a province in central China. I used semistructured interviews to collect as much data as possible from essential stakeholders in the healthcare sector. A total of 70 stakeholders participated in the research, including officers in urban and rural SHI agencies, doctors and SHI reimbursement managers in urban and rural health facilities at different levels, patients enrolled in various SHI schemes, and so on. A thematic analysis was used to develop useful themes and to explain the quantitative findings. Meanwhile, reflexivity was used to ensure the trustworthiness of this study.

K. Liu, *The Effects of Social Health Insurance Reform on People's Out-of-Pocket Health Expenditure in China*, DOI 10.1007/978-981-10-1777-3_4

4.1.1 Data Collection

I conducted fieldwork in a province of central China, "ProvCentral (I am calling ProvCentral to maintain anonymity)," from August to December 2012. As the participants in my fieldwork, I selected officers in county NCMS management offices, municipal and county SHI agencies, SHI reimbursement managers, doctors in health facilities at different levels in urban and rural areas, and patients enrolling in different SHI schemes. In addition, I collected the voices of others such as government officials and pharmaceutical sales representatives. For the sake of ethical consideration, I did not report the names and the detailed socioeconomic characteristics of our research sites and participants. I discuss in detail this consideration in the section regarding data collection. The basic information of interviewees is presented in Table B.1.

Before I introduce the detailed procedures of sampling and data collection, and in order to facilitate understanding of healthcare reform, I will first explain the basic structure of health facilities and SHI agencies in China. Health facilities in China are characterized by a hierarchical structure that designates the level of these facilities in both urban and rural areas. Health facilities consist of hospitals, grassroots healthcare institutions, and other health institutions such as centers for disease control and pharmacies. Hospitals are classified as tertiary, secondary, and primary according to their infrastructure, technical and management competence, quality of services, and so on. Grassroots healthcare institutions include CHCs and health posts in urban areas, THCs and village clinics in rural areas, as well as private clinics. SHI agencies, set up in accordance with the structure of SHI programs, were responsible for premium collection, contract formulation of designated health facilities, settlement of SHI funding, and so on. These can be divided into UEBMI agencies, URBMI agencies, and NCMS agencies. However, because each of the three SHI programs, especially funds, was managed by the local authority, there were thousands of SHI agencies nationwide. For example, the NCMS was managed by county NCMS management offices, while there were over 2000 counties in the country. For my fieldwork, this fragmented design of SHI and its agencies led to a complicated choice of officers in SHI agencies and SHI reimbursement managers in health facilities. Generally speaking, there were three kinds of essential stakeholders in SHI reform in China: SHI agencies, healthcare providers, and patients. The detailed classification of these stakeholders is presented in Fig. 4.1.

I then selected the province ProvCentral as the field in which I would conduct my interviews. The province had a population of over 100 million, of which over 55 % were rural residents, and was one of the largest provincial populations in China. It was composed of tens of prefectural-level cities. Its economic development ranked middle-level compared with other provinces in China. The healthcare resources in the province were not quite as rich as developed regions such as Beijing and Shanghai. In 2014, ProvCentral had around 1400 hospitals and 67,000 primary healthcare facilities. There were about 190,000 registered physicians and

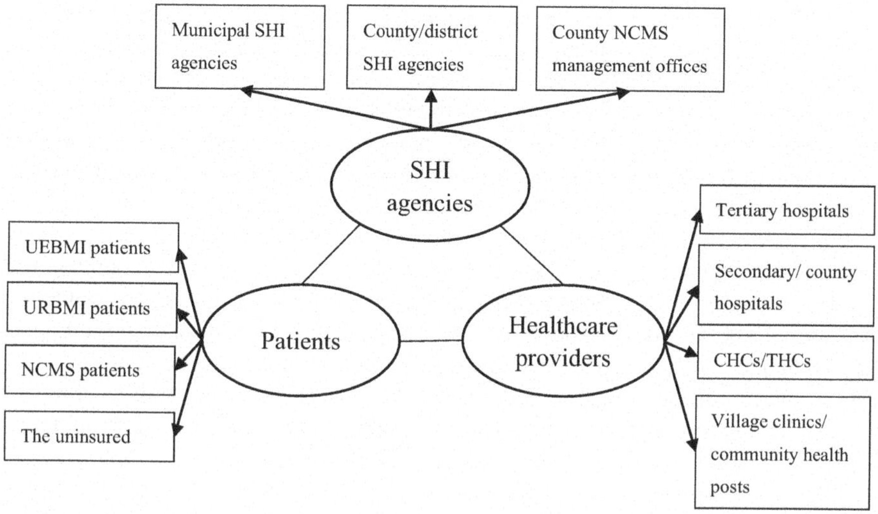

Fig. 4.1 Stakeholders in the SHI reform in China

191,000 registered nurses, rendering the ratio of registered physicians to the population and that of registered nurses to the population to be 2.01:1000 and 2.03:1000, respectively. In the same year, in Beijing the ratios were 3.72:1000 and 4.11:1000, respectively, and in Shanghai, the ratios were 2.52:1000 and 2.96:1000, respectively. In addition, healthcare costs were inflating rapidly in ProvCentral. For example, in hospitals, from 2013 to 2014 the average cost of outpatient services per admission increased by 6.7 %, and outpatient services per admission by 7.1 %. In THCs, the average cost of outpatient and inpatient services per admission increased by 10.9 and 10.4 %, respectively, and in CHCs by 18.3 and 19.0 %, respectively. With regard to SHI agencies, there were 159 urban SHI agencies in charge of the UEBMI and URBMI, and 106 county NCMS management offices in charge of the NCMS. Over 3600 staff members were employed at urban SHI agencies, with one urban SHI agency having only 18 employees. I found no information about the number of employees at NCMS management offices.

I chose three cities (City A, City B, and City C) and one county (County D) in ProvCentral in which to conduct my fieldwork. The cities were selected according to their population size and socioeconomic characteristics. City A, the capital city of the province, was a large city with a population of over 1 million in its urban districts. It was located in the central area of the province and had 12 urban districts, city-level counties, and counties. It had a long history compared with most cities in China. Most provincial-level hospitals were allocated to this city. In addition, it had thousands of health facilities at other levels. Therefore, it enjoyed the richest healthcare resources among the prefectural-level cities in the province. City B bordered City A in the south, and was a mid-sized city with a population between 0.5 million and 1 million in its urban districts. It had 12 urban districts, city-level counties, and counties. It had two tertiary Grade A hospitals, four tertiary Grade B and C hospitals, eight secondary hospitals, and thousands of health facilities at other levels. City C was located in the northeast of the province and was a small city with a population of under 0.5 million in its urban districts. It had one urban district and five counties. It was famous for its oil industry, which supported its economic development. It had three tertiary Grade A hospitals, hundreds of hospitals at other levels, and thousands of health facilities at other levels in total.

I also chose County D in City B to investigate SHI schemes, healthcare institutions, and patients in rural areas. County D was one of eight counties and city-level counties in City B. It had one county area, 11 townships, and a population of about 400,000. Its economic development lagged behind other counties in City B. In addition, it had a county hospital, a county Chinese medicine hospital, 11 THCs, and hundreds of health facilities at other levels, including village clinics.

Prior to my investigation, I had not thought about how to contact so many participants simultaneously. The research targets involved various stakeholders, including government officers, doctors, patients, and so on, which made a one-time contact list impossible. Therefore, I decided to use "snowball sampling," a method by which most participants were referred by other participants. The ensuing fieldwork investigation process was complex (see Fig. 4.2).

I started the fieldwork in a THC in County D in August 2012, which gave me an opportunity to learn about the NCMS and rural health facilities. I contacted the director of the THC via my personal relations, with whom I had no conflict of interest. The director was very nice to accept my investigation as he was a distant relative of my parents. Prior to the interviews, I promised anonymity and confidentiality. After giving an account of my study purpose, he introduced me to some

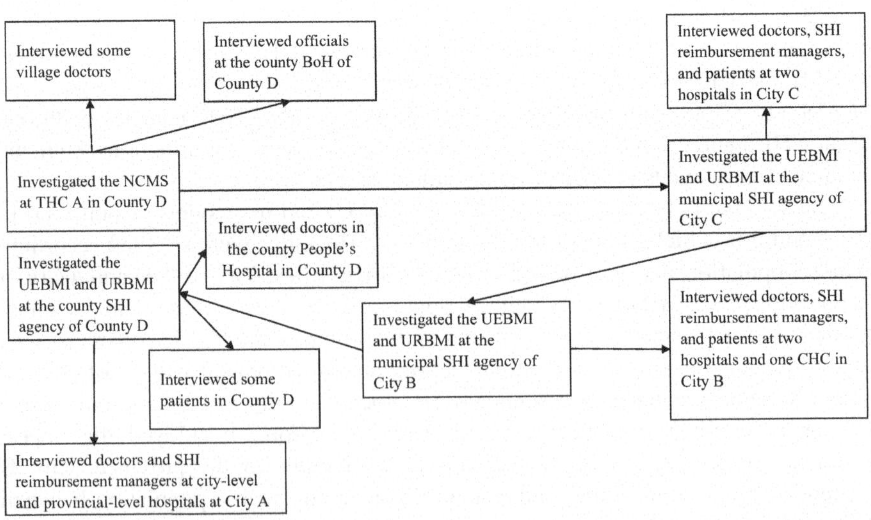

Fig. 4.2 Process of the fieldwork

of the doctors and SHI reimbursement managers, explaining that the study was to investigate the operations of the NCMS and that there would be no breaches of confidentiality. I also tried to develop personal relationships with them by sending small gifts such as water and cigarettes (note that in China, sending cigarettes is a sign of showing kindness and friendship, especially to men). They accepted my offer of interview, with some even telling me some secrets about this THC and the NCMS, permitting me to observe while the patients were present and to record their diagnoses of patients. During these times, I also interviewed a number of patients.

Two weeks after I started my fieldwork, the director of the THC dispatched a number of staff members to conduct health supervision in village clinics. He allowed me to accompany the staff to conduct interviews with village doctors. The staff of the THC conducted health supervision regularly, while supervising the work of the village doctors. As a result, the staff were quite familiar with the village doctors. With an introduction from the staff, the village doctors were willing to accept my offer of interview. I also interviewed a number of patients during the visit.

I stayed in the THC for almost one month before I was referred by the director of the THC to the county NCMS management office in County D. In early September, the director went to the county bureau of health (BoH) to attend a conference. He took me with him and introduced me to a deputy director of the NCMS management office. I investigated the operation and effects of the NCMS within the county with the deputy director during that afternoon. I had previously interviewed a deputy director of the county BoH when he visited the THC to supervise its work. I had also interviewed an NCMS inspector who was regularly dispatched by the county NCMS management office to inspect the reimbursement of the NCMS funds in the THC.

I then visited City C to investigate the operation of urban SHI schemes, including UEBMI and URBMI. I was referred by a relative working in the municipal court in City C to an officer in the municipal SHI agency in City C. However, this officer suffered from an ankle injury and applied for sick leave. But she was still able to refer me to the director and other officers in the agency personally on the first day. With the permission of the director of the municipal SHI agency, I contacted officers in the agency and located myself there for one week. I also visited a secondary hospital for mental health as well as a tertiary Grade A hospital to interview doctors and SHI reimbursement managers. I also met with a number of patients in the hospitals.

Following completion of my fieldwork in City C, I returned to City B to continue the study of urban SHI schemes. I was referred by a friend to the municipal SHI agency in City B. I spent one week interviewing the officers there, including a deputy director and other officers from various departments of the agency. I was referred by these officers to two city-level hospitals and one CHC to conduct interviews with doctors, SHI reimbursement managers, and patients.

I returned to County D after I finished my fieldwork in City B, where a friend introduced me to officers in the county SHI agency and doctors in the county People's Hospital. I conducted interviews with them to probe into the UEBMI and

URBMI at county level and the hospitals at county level. In addition, I found and interviewed a number of patients and their family members in County D, through personal relations.

In the final month, I was referred by a friend to two city-level and one provincial-level hospitals in City A. My friend had a former colleague who was a drug representative and sold some antitumor drugs who had worked in the provincial-level hospital and had therefore developed good personal relationships with a number of doctors, to whom I was introduced, as well as several SHI reimbursement managers. I spent three days in City A to conduct my fieldwork. It was noted that there was no conflict of interest between the drug representative and me. As a former doctor and a current drug representative, he was able to impart a considerable amount of information "under the table" about the hospitals, especially the drug kickbacks for doctors. My many questions were met with a positive response, and he talked about some matters that doctors were not willing to or did not dare to talk about. He became a key informant in my fieldwork in City A. My fieldwork ended following my visit to City A.

In total, I investigated 70 participants during my fieldwork, including 15 officers in urban and rural SHI agencies, seven SHI reimbursement managers, 33 doctors in urban and rural health facilities at different levels, 14 patients and/or their family members enrolled in various kinds of SHI schemes or having no insurance, and 1 drug representative. In addition, I interviewed a number of key informants repeatedly, which collected more information than was obtained from those interviewed only once. As a result, the 70 participants in this study were interviewed a total 90 times. The distribution of participants across districts and institutions is presented in Table 4.1.

I conducted semistructured in-depth interviews to collect the data. A consent form and interviewing guides were sent to the different stakeholders prior to my fieldwork. The interviewing guides comprised three versions, for officers in SHI agencies, for SHI reimbursement managers and doctors in health facilities at different levels, and for patients enrolled in different SHI schemes. The guides focused on the process of behavior management and cost containment of SHI, the performance of different mechanisms within the institutional arrangement and the interaction between these mechanisms, the concerns of the different stakeholders about these mechanisms, and the context in which these mechanisms were embedded. The interviews were conducted in Chinese. The English versions of the interviewing guides and content form are attached in Appendices C and D, respectively. Prior to my fieldwork, these were sent, along with my research proposal, to the Survey and Behavioral Research Ethics Committee of The Chinese University of Hong Kong for approval. Following this, I acquired a reference letter from the Department of Social Work at the University to facilitate entrance into my field.

I presented both the consent form and the reference letter to the participants to seek their agreement before being interviewed. Furthermore, I asked them whether I could audio record the interviews. If they did not permit it, I recorded the interviews by shorthand writing.

Table 4.1 The distribution of participants in the qualitative study

Category	Organizations/identity	City A	City B	City C	County D
SHI reimbursement managers in hospitals	SHI reimbursement managers in urban hospitals	2P/2T		2P/2T	
	SHI reimbursement managers in rural hospitals				3P/5T
SHI agencies	Officers in urban SHI agencies		4P/7T	6P/8T	2P/1T
	Officers in NCMS management office (rural SHI agency)				3P/3T
Urban health facilities	CHC		1P/3T		
	Secondary hospital		2P/2T	1P/1T	
	Tertiary hospital	9P/9T	1P/1T	1P/1T	
Rural health facilities	Village clinic				6P/6T
	THC				11P/22T
	County hospital				1P/1T
Patients and their family members	UEBMI		1P/1T		2P/3T
	URBMI			1P/1T	
	NCMS				9P/9T
	No insurance			1P/1T	
Others	Drug representative	1P/1T			
Total		70P/90T			

Note: P participant; *T* time. For example, 3P/5T means that 3 participants were interviewed 5 times

During the fieldwork, I complied rigorously with research ethics of anonymity and confidentiality. I avoided the disclosure of any information that may be used to identify the participants I interviewed and the organizations and places in which I conducted my fieldwork. Each city had only one municipal-level SHI agency despite many district- and county-level agencies. Similarly, each county had only one county NCMS management office and county SHI agency. Therefore, if the names and detailed socioeconomic characteristics of these places were presented, it would be easy to identify the information of the officers in those organizations. In addition, I concealed the actual name of the province in which I conducted my fieldwork, using an alias "ProvCentral." As City A was the capital city of the province, it would also be easy to identify the name of this city if the actual name of the province was revealed. To avoid the possibility of this information being disclosed, I have withheld the names of places, organizations, and participants.

To distinguish the participants in this study, I assigned a unique identification number to each. The identifier consisted of three parts. For instance, a participant with the number B20120921BJZ was investigated in City B (*B*20120921BJZ) in 2012 on September 21 (B*20120921*BJZ) with the abbreviated name BJZ (B20120921*BJZ*).

4.1.2 Thematic Analysis

Thematic analysis was adopted to analyze the data in this qualitative study. This was a reasonable choice to facilitate data reduction and to discover the patterns of interaction between the different mechanisms of the institutional arrangement of SHI.

Boyatzis (1998) defined thematic analysis as a process of encoding qualitative data and searching for themes within data. Thematic analysis serves as a major device to conduct reduction, organization, and interpretation of data. A theme is a pattern that is discovered in the data, which informs researchers of the description and organization of the possible observations at minimum, and of the interpretation of the phenomenon at maximum. Further, Braun and Clarke (2006) revealed that thematic analysis could be used to facilitate the summary of essential characteristics of a large data set and to provide thick descriptions.

In this study, data analysis was conducted in accordance with the procedures proposed by Boyatzis (1998) and Braun and Clarke (2006). I first transcribed the audio recordings of the interviews to document them verbatim. Following this, I imported the documents into NVivo 8.0, a software used for the analysis of qualitative data, in order to formulate a database for further analysis. Meanwhile, in Chap. 3, my quantitative analysis had tested a hypothetical model that demonstrated the primary performance of and interactions between the three mechanisms of the institutional arrangement of SHI. To explain these newly tested relationships, I identified relevant excerpts within the qualitative data and generated initial codes that could possibly be used to explain the findings in the quantitative study in Chap. 3. After a comprehensive coding process, I categorized codes with similar meanings into potential themes, repeating this method until no new themes emerged. During this process, I continued to relate different themes to each other, and kept refining the specifics of each theme and their mutual relations. By referring to the results of the quantitative analysis, I formulated a thematic map using these codes, themes, and relations.

For the purpose of presenting the findings of the qualitative analysis, I identified what I thought to be the most convincing and representative excerpts and categorized them according to the corresponding themes. I then translated the excerpts from Chinese to English. In this process, the most common problem was the asymmetry of meanings between Chinese and English characters, words, and sentences. I redressed this problem by maintaining the essential meanings expressed by the participants. To do this, it was sometimes necessary to replace a literal translation with a paraphrastic translation. In addition, the participants often used Chinese slang and proverbs, as well as incomplete words and sentences to express their opinions. I translated them using the same strategies of a paraphrastic translation.

4.1.3 Reflexivity as Trustworthiness

Qualitative studies can suffer from debates around their trustworthiness. This is because they focus on subjective meaning, using researchers but not standard scales and statistics as investigating instruments. In essence, such studies are value-laden. Nonetheless, researchers have developed many strategies to ensure trustworthiness in qualitative studies. For example, Guba (1981) developed a strategy of credibility, transferability, dependability, and confirmability to address the issue of trustworthiness in naturalistic or constructivist qualitative studies. The strategy is complex and is commonly used by constructivists, in which researchers and participants interact to construct meaning.

This study used reflexivity as an approach to ensure its trustworthiness. Bourdieu and Wacquant (1992) developed the concept of epistemic reflexivity to increase the reliability and validity of studies in the social sciences, emphasizing unification rather than the duality of objectivity and subjectivity. Researchers reflect on their social and academic positions and their own set of internalized structures in order to recognize themselves in the act of importing their own biases and prejudices into their work. Finlay (2002) identified five variants of reflexivity, including introspection, intersubjective reflection, mutual collaboration, social critique, and discursive deconstruction. She observed that reflexivity moved from the introspective toward critical realist and subjectivist accounts, and toward prioritizing the context via deconstructing the research encounter. She argued further that reflexivity could be used to evaluate the research process, to examine the influence of the researcher's position, perspective and presence, to open up unconscious motivations and implicit biases, to promote rich insight, to empower participants, and to enable public scrutiny of the integrity of the research.

Based on these strategies, I used reflexivity to examine my personal, social, and academic positions, accepting the critiques of my peers, to ensure the trustworthiness of this study.

First, I reflected on my personal experience and social position, which might affect my neutrality during the fieldwork. I grew up in a poor farmers' family. My parents hoped for a bright future for me and were demanding of my study when I was young. Therefore, I studied hard and engaged in academic research not only due to personal interest, but also due to responsibility toward my family. Later, I entered Nankai University as an undergraduate and chose social work as my major. This professional training led me to realize that I studied not only for my own future and my family, but also for the promotion of social justice. When I started my doctoral study at The Chinese University of Hong Kong, I chose health policy as my research field and engaged in the promotion of people's health-related well-being, expecting to take some responsibility for disadvantaged people, my family, and myself. This expectation generated a balance of my hopes for this study. To be specific, as a student I anticipated that I could finish my doctoral thesis and graduate on time. However, as a social work researcher I had to ensure the quality and significance of my study. During my fieldwork, I sometimes worried about the progress of my data collection and to mitigate this anxiety, I focused on the troubles faced by patients and told myself consistently that my research must be done responsibly as it had the potential to influence knowledge accumulation and policy reform.

Second, while in the field I continued to think about my academic preference and position. Different from constructivist qualitative studies, my study adopted a post-positivist paradigm and a mixed-methods design. On the one hand, I believe firmly in post-positivism. I hold a strong belief for the objective rather than the subjective existence of truth. I conducted a qualitative study mainly because I deem truth to be complicated and impossible to be fully discovered. As a result, as a researcher I have a strong curiosity in finding empirical evidence to examine whether the hypotheses tested in the quantitative study could be falsified. I deemed the participants in my fieldwork research targets rather than co-constructors and tried to find whether their real life was different from the statistical relationship. On the other hand, as a researcher I prefer to use mixed methods to conduct research. In this study, I conducted a quantitative analysis to test the hypotheses and to formulate new statistical relationships, prior to the qualitative study. The qualitative study then served to confirm and to explain in further depth these statistical relationships. Therefore, I was trying to ensure I was a neutral instrument, objectively collecting useful information from the participants. In the field, I tried to avoid suggestive questions, but used open questions to encourage the participants to talk about their stories, opinions, and attitudes. Meanwhile, I continued to think about whether participants' answers provided supporting or adverse evidence for my hypothetical model. In particular, when participants provided adverse evidence I would encourage them to talk more. I tried to examine whether the adverse evidence could falsify the quantitative findings.

Last, I accepted the supervision of my thesis supervisor and thesis committee members and listened to the critiques of fellow academics and research participants. My supervisor kept in regular contact with me during my fieldwork. She requested that I report on the progress of the fieldwork, my self-reflection and the problems I encountered, my plans for the next stage, and so on, every time I finished data collection at one research site. She provided useful advice to me when I had problems. Meanwhile, her supervision was consistent from the beginning of my doctoral study. Moreover, I discussed with fellow academics, such as classmates in the same doctoral program, the researcher whose courses I had audited, as well as the research collaborators with whom I collaborated to publish my work. The collaborators provided valuable insights for the design and implementation of my fieldwork. Most important of all, I listened to the participants and revised my studies according to their suggestions. As I had multiple kinds of participants, there were many different attitudes and opinions toward the same things. For example, some patients and doctors praised the effects of SHI schemes, while officers in SHI agencies complained that the former two stakeholders conspired to abuse healthcare services and the reimbursement of SHI. These officers suggested that I be suspicious of what patients and doctors said. This conflict of ideas played the role of triangulation, which was also helpful in increasing the trustworthiness of this study.

In summary, with the purpose of explaining the findings in the quantitative study, I conducted complicated fieldwork in a province in central China. I interviewed many officers in SHI agencies, doctors and SHI reimbursement managers in health facilities, and patients. I used thematic analysis to analyze data and used reflexivity to guarantee the trustworthiness of the qualitative study. In the next section, I will present the findings from the fieldwork.

4.2 Strategies for Adjusting Patients' Care-Seeking Behaviors

Welfare institutions, in theory, play a role not only as a mechanism of benefit provision, but as a policy instrument to manage dysfunctional behaviors and to formulate responsible behaviors of beneficiaries. This behavior management requirement corresponded with the regulation of the referral system to, and the tiered copayment and deductibles of SHI in many nations. That is, primary health facilities implementing SHI were treated as gatekeepers to the health service by referring patients to secondary and tertiary hospitals. Meanwhile, insurers set lower copayments and deductibles for treatments in primary health facilities, and higher ones in secondary and tertiary hospitals. The aim of these two regulations was to encourage people to seek treatment from primary health facilities and hence, to improve the equitable allocation of medical resources. The regulations were also designed to prevent patients from spilling over into higher-level hospitals and therefore, from abusing the pooled funds of SHI.

Although the regulations structured patients' choices of facilities, the effects depended on the possible benefits provided to patients and the interaction between patients, doctors, and SHI agencies. The interaction process was filled with strategic calculation by these stakeholders. As a result, the malfunctions of the behavior management mechanism needs to be explored by considering the benefit concerns of and the interaction between these stakeholders. The roles that key stakeholders played in shaping patients' care-seeking behaviors are presented in Fig. 4.3.

During the fieldwork, we found that the NCMS management office used a referral system to restrain rural patients from spilling into tertiary hospitals. Both the NCMS management office and urban SHI agency used tiered copayment and deductibles to guide patients to seek care at primary care facilities. In addition to these strategies, some other methods, such as tripartite negotiation and localized management of the SHI, were used either to change patients' care-seeking behaviors or to restrain patients from being excessively admitted as inpatients.

First, the referral system of the NCMS. The NCMS management office enforced a stepwise referral system. Rural patients who intended to go to hospitals at city level were required to obtain their referral certificates from the county hospitals to which they might not have been hospitalized. Those being admitted to hospitals at provincial level were required to obtain their referral certificates from

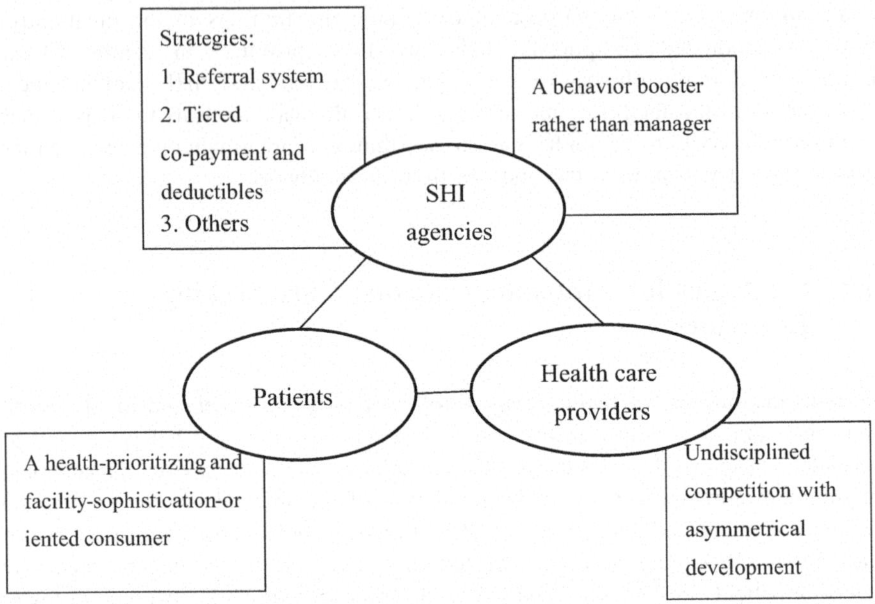

Fig. 4.3 Dysfunction of the behavior management mechanism

city-level hospitals. Subsequently, patients brought their certificates and other necessary documents to the county NCMS management office to gain official referral approval. With referral approval, the electronic information of NCMS participation for patients was transferred to the hospitals to which patients were admitted.

Patients were not allowed to go directly to hospitals at city or provincial level; if they had, they would receive low or even no reimbursement from the NCMS. From the perspective of an officer in the NCMS management office of County D, this referral system of the NCMS would frequently prevent patients from seeking care at city- or provincial-level hospitals:

> Our province regulates that patients going to hospitals outside their own counties have to get referral approval from the NCMS management office. After that, their electronic information can be transferred to hospitals. If they go to hospitals in the city or at provincial level directly and have no referral approval, they will not be reimbursed by the NCMS. This is a strategy of managing their choices of hospitals. We request them to be referred stage by stage, that is, being referred from county hospitals to hospitals at city and provincial level. We request them to be referred reasonably, which is expected to control their flow. (D20120906PZR)

Meanwhile, if patients obtained referral approval from local hospitals, their electronic SHI enrollment information could be transferred online to the hospitals at which they sought care, therefore being able to receive reimbursement instantly once discharged from hospital. Patients without referral approval were required to return to the county NCMS management office to obtain reimbursement.

I know that people being treated in our tertiary hospital can get their medical expenditures fully reimbursed once being discharged from the hospital if they obtain their referral approval within three days after they are hospitalized. Otherwise, they have to go back to the county NCMS management offices to get reimbursed. (C20120918PYS)

Except for adjusting patients' care-seeking behaviors, the referral system was believed to have extra benefits. Primary care facilities were undeveloped with an inadequate infusion of government finance. The referral system could boost the development of primary care facilities, county hospitals, and secondary hospitals by providing more reimbursement for treatments in these hospitals than in tertiary hospitals. It could also enhance the affordability of patients' medical costs. From the perspective of a doctor in a district-level secondary hospital, the regulation of the NCMS for NCMS patients obtaining referral certificates from local hospitals would encourage these patients to stay in these local hospitals.

There are some new regulations in some hospitals that patients are required to receive services in these hospitals and are forbidden to be referred to higher-level hospitals. If patients really want to go to other hospitals, they will get lower reimbursement. So we receive many NCMS patients. For instance, NCMS patients in this district have to come to our hospital to receive services. If they want to go to hospitals at a higher level, they have to seek our permission. If they go to city-level hospitals directly without our permission, their reimbursement rate will be lowered from 70% to 60%. They will lose 10% of reimbursement due to not being referred. (B20120926MYS)

Moreover, the referral system of the NCMS would prevent patients from overusing health services in tertiary hospitals and as a result, would reduce the working burden of doctors in these hospitals and guarantee the quality of health services.

NCMS patients coming to our hospital [a tertiary hospital at provincial level] are decreasing in recent several years compared with ever before. This is because policies are changing. The allocation of healthcare resources within the system was unreasonable and unbalanced in the past. Plenty of patients flew to large hospitals at city and provincial level, with few primary care facilities. To balance the profits of these organizations and to meet the needs of patients, department of health management has to take some actions. For a patient with tonsil infection, she really doesn't have to go to our tertiary hospitals. The actions taken by health management department are to deal with these situations. (A20121019ZJ)

However, urban SHI agencies did not implement this referral system. An officer in an urban SHI agency in City B said that this was because none of the state policies supported them to launch such a system, stating that neither a bidirectional referral system nor tiered copayment was able to produce the desired effect of adjusting patients' care-seeking behaviors.

With regard to the bidirectional referral system proposed by the health department, it is just propaganda. How to use referral to restrain people's choices of hospitals? It is just used by the NCMS, which regulates that patients would enjoy low reimbursement rates without referral certificates issued by primary care facilities. It is a very rigid regulation. But we urban SHI agencies cannot implement it because of no supporting state plan … Before the enactment of related state policy, we urban SHI agencies just guided patients using tiered copayment. But its effect is too weak. (B20120927SKZ)

Second, tiered copayment and deductibles. Both rural and urban SHI agencies used tiered copayment and deductibles to adjust patients' choices of hospitals. The detailed goal of these strategies was "to keep patients with minor diseases treated in village clinics (or community health stations), those with general diseases in THCs (or CHCs), and those with serious diseases in county hospitals (or district hospitals)," with those whose diseases could not be cured in primary care facilities being admitted to tertiary hospitals.

> The NCMS provides higher reimbursement to rural patients being hospitalized in THCs than in higher-level hospitals. Thus, many go to THCs to get more benefits. Patients going to hospital at the higher level decrease, because what common people care about most are substantial monetary benefits. Why not enjoy a 90 % reimbursement rate in THCs but go to county hospitals to enjoy 80 %? Only if they get severe diseases, they go to hospital at county and city level and above. The principle of the NCMS is to keep patients with minor diseases treated in village clinics, those with general diseases in THCs, and those with serious diseases in county hospitals. (D20120822CYS)

The copayment for treatment in primary care facilities was set to be very low. The reimbursement rate within the scope of the NCMS policy for treatment in THCs was as much as 90 % during our fieldwork in 2012. The actual reimbursement rate of UEBMI for treatment in primary care facilities in City B reached 70–80 %.

> The state gives priority to developing primary care and secondary hospitals, with setting low deductibles and high reimbursement rates for patients treated there. The reimbursement benefits provided in these hospitals are distanced from the benefits provided to patients in tertiary hospitals. For a hospitalized patient in primary care hospitals in our city, the actual reimbursement rate has reached nearly 80%, which means that a patient spending ¥100 pay only about ¥20 out of pocket. I think the benefits offered by UEBMI and URBMI are really substantial. In theory, health insurance is a mechanism of risk sharing. If insurance is designed to provide full reimbursement, it will be harmful as there is no restraint of patients' behaviors. Now patients hospitalized in primary care facilities can generally get 70% of their expenditures reimbursed. I think that the rate is enough with no space to increase. (B20120927SKZ)

In addition to the copayment, the deductible was set to be tiered across hospitals at different levels, with low deductibles for treatment in primary care facilities and high in tertiary hospitals. Furthermore, patients being hospitalized for the second time or later in the year would receive fewer deductibles than for the first time.

> Over 60% to nearly 70% of the funds of the UEBMI in our city flow to tertiary hospitals, and about 80% flow to secondary and tertiary hospitals, with about 20% to primary hospitals. Why do we keep adjusting our regulations of deductibles? For patients hospitalized in primary hospitals, they can enjoy ¥300 of deductibles for their first hospitalization and ¥200 for their second one. For those in tertiary hospitals, they can enjoy ¥800 of deductibles. We keep our priority of policies toward primary hospitals to induce patients with general diseases to go there. We hope those with catastrophic diseases go to hospitals at a higher level, which can reduce the stress of large hospitals in admitting patients. The aim of adjusting regulations is to guide patients' choices of hospitals. We do this partly through lowering deductibles for primary hospitals. For example, we reduced deductibles for patients hospitalized in primary hospitals from ¥400 to ¥300. (B20120924WKZ)

Low deductibles in primary care facilities were believed by a clerk in the municipal SHI agency of City C to directly decrease the OOPS of patients:

> The deductibles of UEBMI were lowered from ¥800 to ¥500 and ¥700 in primary/secondary hospitals and tertiary hospitals, respectively. The decrease of deductibles leads to the decrease of the OOPS of enrolled employees. The goal of the policy is to encourage enrollees to go to primary and secondary hospitals rather than overflowing to tertiary hospitals. If patients get serious diseases like the transplantation of a kidney, they would go to tertiary hospitals; otherwise, they can go to secondary hospitals with some general illnesses like catching a cold, appendicitis, or uterine leiomyoma. (C20120910ZJ)

Tiered copayment and deductibles of SHI were also considered to have extra benefits. A chief physician in a city-level secondary hospital in City C believed that a high reimbursement rate of NCMS in primary care facilities would adjust the unequitable allocation of healthcare resources across health facilities at different levels:

> In our country, the limited healthcare resources are overallocated in large and middle cities. To adjust this problem, the state increases the reimbursement rate of the NCMS for patients treated in THCs. This is to attract patients to go to THCs and lead them back from hospitals at city and provincial level. The aim of this regulation is good. (C20120918WYS)

Third, other strategies. SHI agencies might also use other strategies to adjust patients' choices of hospitals. For example, the municipal SHI agency of City C used tripartite negotiation to guide patients' care-seeking behaviors. It first negotiated with the CHCs and the suppliers of some drugs for treating severe chronic diseases, to reduce the prices of these drugs. It then regulated a baseline price for purchase in CHCs. If patients bought these drugs in higher-level hospitals at prices higher than the baseline price, they would not be reimbursed. It used this strategy to guide patients to buy these drugs in CHCs.

> We started the tripartite negotiation on the prices of drugs used for outpatient services of severe chronic diseases a few years ago. The inpatients hospitalized in CHCs can also enjoy these prices. We have considered expanding the range of these drugs… . If patients go to the City People's Hospital but not CHCs to buy these drugs, we plan to not reimburse them for their expenditures, as we set the discounted prices of these drugs as a baseline standard. We intend to do this to guide patients to go to CHCs. But expansion of these discounted drugs is just a vision and has not been implemented. We will probably do it in future. Now we just focus on a limited number of drugs. Moreover, we want to use this strategy to negotiate the prices of medical consumption materials. We cannot force patients to buy the discounted drugs in CHCs. But we can set a baseline price, expenses over which will not be reimbursed. It is just like Hong Kong, with those going to private doctors enjoying no benefits provided in public hospitals. Our aim is to guide them to seek care reasonably, as it is not necessary for them to spill over to CHCs without mandatory regulations. That is why we want to set a baseline price to guide them. (C20120912XDW)

As well as controlling the flow of patients to higher-level hospitals, the NCMS management office also restrained patients from flowing to other counties, because the NCMS funds were pooled at county level. This localized management of the NCMS forced patients to go to hospitals in their own counties rather than other counties; if they did not like to receive treatment in their own counties, they could go to hospitals at city and provincial level.

> One problem of the NCMS, I perceive, lies in its mandatory pooling at county level, which enforces local patients to be hospitalized in hospitals inside their own county. For example, our county and WZ County adjoin. There are several villages in WZ County neighboring our THC, with some cycling distance. Moreover, the technical level of our THC is good, therefore attracting patients in those villages to seek care here before the implementation of the NCMS. However, after its implementation, its regulation on pooling at county level forced patients to receive medical services in their own county. Hence, the patients in WZ County never came to our THC, which reduced substantially our revenue. (D20120812XWB)

4.3 The Healthcare Provider: Undisciplined Competition with Asymmetrical Development

Although SHI agencies used various strategies to guide the care-seeking behaviors of patients, tertiary hospitals were still overcrowded with patients. Healthcare resources, especially medical talents, were overallocated in the large hospitals. Meanwhile, hospitals competed in a disorderly way to attract patients. Their profit-driven incentives overrode the effect of the bidirectional referral system and tiered copayment and deductibles.

4.3.1 The Improving Facility Sophistication of Primary Care Facilities

After the new round of health reform in 2009, the government infused substantial new funding to the healthcare system, of which about 30 % was targeted at rural and primary care institutions, including county hospitals, CHCs and THCs, community health stations, and village clinics. The government did not increase its subsidies much for secondary and tertiary hospitals (Yip et al. 2010).

Apart from the infusion of government finance, the development of SHI schemes also boosted the facility sophistication of primary care facilities. In some areas, the THCs conducted privatization reform to stimulate incentives for doctors. All these factors improved the development of primary care facilities:

> It is for sure that the development of the NCMS has generally boosted THCs. Only patients with general diseases sought treatment in THCs in the past. In addition, in 2002, the THCs in our county were reformed by allowing private funding to be infused in THCs. So, the facilities in THCs have been improved a lot. This, together with the effect of the NCMS, attracts more and more patients to THCs. (D20120906PZR)

Secondary hospitals also developed fast. A doctor in a secondary mental health hospital in City C explained that it was due to the increasing social demands for health services:

> Both social demands for high quality services and the incidence of diseases are increasing. In the past, only serious mental diseases like schizophrenia were counted as mental diseases, but now people with slight psychological and mental problems also like to seek care in our mental health hospitals. Some patients hospitalized in general hospitals also suffer from problems of the stomach and other places of the body and feel that they are poorly rehabilitated. Then they want to come to our mental health hospital to receive rehabilitation services. All of these push us to buy some devices, and the services provided by us are boosted gradually. People's demands from enjoying mental health services do increase substantially. They ask directly for device tests once they come. So the director of the hospital realizes that this is a good opportunity for our development. We keep buying and updating high-tech detective as well as treatment devices. (C20120918WYS)

The development of healthcare facilities corresponded to the social demands of patients for health services as well as the reimbursement provided by SHI schemes. As a result, we found that healthcare providers focused on facility development because they realized that patients prefer to use certain medical services such as device tests. They anticipated certain behaviors of patients that are beneficial to them. They also did this because SHI as a welfare institution provides a bonus for them. Healthcare providers calculated their gains in correspondence with the behaviors of other stakeholders and institutions.

However, healthcare resources continued to be inequitably allocated. Facilities in tertiary hospitals were much more advanced than in the primary and secondary hospitals. Although the government prioritized the development of primary care facilities after 2009, this had not been done prior to then and the status quo of health resource allocation was greatly affected by these previous conditions. The facilities sophistication of primary care facilities continued to lag behind due to very little government finance in the past.

> The government infused substantial resources to hospitals at city and provincial level, but neglected the development of primary care organizations and just let them rely on themselves. Especially, the government didn't put emphasis on the development of THCs and didn't infuse many resources. So did county hospitals, which also survived by user charges rather than government investment. Therefore, most patients spill over to hospitals at city and provincial level because they have no trust in hospital at county and township level. Patients do not go there even if they get some diseases which can be treated well in county hospitals. Especially, if children catch illnesses, their parents would absolutely go to large hospitals at city level and above. (D20120906PZR)

The undeveloped facility sophistication of primary care facilities caused patients to have no trust in the healthcare quality of these facilities and affected the care-seeking behaviors of the patients. Therefore, many patients remained unwilling to seek treatment from them.

> I think that the various aspects of healthcare reform are interlocked. Patients are always criticized as irrational by going to large hospitals. But they have no choice. Health resources are overallocated in these hospitals. Patients have to go there to seek care if they want to survive. (D20120827GXH)

4.3.2 The Outdated Technical Competence of Primary Care Facilities

Apart from facility sophistication, the technical competence of doctors in primary care facilities and secondary hospitals was hardly comparable to that in tertiary hospitals. The small hospitals had techniques to treat only general and not serious diseases. This affected patients' choices of hospitals, although the charging level of health services in tertiary hospitals were usually high.

> The charging level in tertiary hospitals is too high. Except for the high deductible and copayment rate, there are many items outside the reimbursement formulary of SHI which needs payment out of pocket if patients seek care in tertiary hospitals. If they are hospitalized in tertiary Grade A hospitals, they would be charged at least over ¥10,000, out of which they have to pay a half, that is, ¥7,000-¥8,000 out of pocket. However, patients have no alternative choices, because small hospitals like ours [a CHC] can treat only some general diseases. If they catch some severe illnesses, they have to go to large hospitals. (B20121101GSL)

It is arguable whether primary care facilities should buy sophisticated equipment and recruit specialized medical professionals, as the government has set them up to provide primary care. However, it would be a long journey to improve even the training of primary care professionals such as general practitioners. In County D, some village doctors and doctors in THCs gained the certificate of general practitioner through only short training and an exam. It would not be possible to enhance their technical competence in a short time.

> To be honest, the government has really infused substantial resources to primary care facilities. It produces some desired effects, such as the establishment of infrastructure and the update of beds and even sheets on beds. The infrastructure has improved a lot, which looks okay. However, what about the doctors? Patients go to see doctors, but find that doctors are still those old and familiar faces. The quality of doctors cannot be enhanced within a short time. Moreover, the government encourages training for general practitioners. But it would take too many years. People's trust in primary care doctors is still too low. Even if we increase reimbursement for patients if they get treated by these doctors, patients do not care as their economic conditions improve a lot. (B20120927SKZ)

4.3.3 The Undisciplined Competition Between Health Facilities

The asymmetrical allocation of healthcare resources was accompanied by an ineffective referral system partly because there was no transfer system between the large and small health facilities. A doctor in a THC in County D said that hospitals compete with each other intensely. The small hospitals would not refer patients with serious diseases to the large hospitals, and vice versa. He said that "a hospital is like an independent kingdom."

> You see, in foreign countries, there are mature healthcare markets and large medical groups. Those small hospitals can be deemed local agencies of these large groups and receive guidance and management by the latter. If small hospitals received patients with catastrophic diseases, they have special contingency measures and a referral system to refer these patients to hospitals which have the ability to treat them, or the large hospitals dispatch specialists to these small hospitals. These systems are better than ours in terms of either transportation or mutual communications. However, in our country, county hospitals have almost no relationship with THCs. A hospital is like an independent kingdom. Hospitals compete with each other, even with mutual accuse and defamation. (D20120827GXH).

In particular, the lack of a sound mutual transfer system means that patients have no appropriate and effective choice of health facilities. Most interviewed patients had no idea whether a hospital had adequate technical competence to cure their disease. Under a case of medical emergency, patients and their family members might lose their equanimity. All they could do was seek hospitals and doctors by themselves, rather than effectively being referred to an appropriate hospital by local health facilities.

> My wife caught a severe disease this April when she was doing some agricultural work. She fell and lost consciousness immediately. I rushed to call 120 (the medical emergency call) to take her to the THC. She kept throwing up. The doctors in the THC were unable to detect what her problem was. Then I rushed to call the county Chinese Medicine Hospital. It took us away and then conducted some CT tests. We stayed for 3 hours in the hospital until they said that they were unable to conduct surgery for her disease; neither could the County hospital. We rushed hurriedly to the 371 Hospital in the city. Finally, the 371 Hospital conducted surgery. We were lucky to go directly to this hospital rather than the county People's Hospital after we came out of the county Chinese Medicine Hospital. Someone told me that if we went to the county People's Hospital, the symptoms would be exacerbated due to the delay in necessary treatment. If so, my wife could have died or become a patient in a persistent vegetative state. Although we spent more in the 371 Hospital than in the county hospitals, it was okay as long as my wife became well. If I didn't want to spend much at that time, my wife would become a patient in a persistent vegetative state. Actually, my mind was vacant at that time. I felt hopeless and didn't know what to do. (D20121030XGM)

Apart from the lack of a sound mutual transfer system, hospitals were profit-driven and competed for income. This was because they received few subsidies from the government and therefore had to rely on user charges to make a living. However, this may have caused patients to suffer. The mother of a patient who had been hospitalized in a secondary hospital in City B said that the hospital had no technical capability to cure her daughter's disease but just delayed and did not permit her exit from hospital, with the purpose of earning more money:

> My daughter caught aplastic anemia last year. At the outset, we didn't know exactly what disease she had. We went to the City No. 1 People's Hospital. She was hospitalized for one month and was charged over ¥30,000. But the hospitalization produced no effects. Fuck! They didn't have relevant techniques to cure this disease. They admitted my daughter just for money. During that month of hospitalization, they told us nothing and just prescribed drip infusion. They said that they would conduct a bone-marrow transplant operation. However, they had no relevant techniques but would have to invite doctors from a provincial hospital to do it. We hopelessly watched them delaying and having no action. Then I called my husband who was working in a real estate company in Shanxi Province.

He looked for some information online and saw that there was a blood disease hospital in Tianjin which ranked number 1 in the whole country. Then he came back and went with my nephew to the City Central Hospital to learn the information of that disease. A doctor in the Central Hospital suggested we go immediately to Tianjin and said that no other hospitals were able to cure this disease. Therefore, we decided to go to Tianjin to receive the cure, no matter how much money we would spend. (D20121028LTZ)

Moreover, to earn more money, some county hospitals even took advantage of the referral system of the NCMS by forbidding patients from going to higher-level hospitals. They refused to issue referral certificates for patients. Patients without referral certificates had to stay in the county hospitals; otherwise, they would receive lower or even no reimbursement of SHI if they went to higher-level hospitals.

You know, we [a city-level tertiary hospital] are good at functional surgeries. Our technical competence is at the top level in the whole province. The patient I just received is from another city in the province. Many patients from other cities come here to seek care. The revenue of our service department comes mainly from functional surgeries. Without functional surgeries, we cannot survive as some county hospitals forbid patients from being referred to hospitals at the upper level. You see, in YJ County, all patients are not allowed to be referred. If patients go to our hospital without referral, they have to receive less reimbursement and pay more out of pocket. County hospitals generally implement strict referral regulations, where their directors require doctors to keep patients staying. (B20120927WZY)

As well as the delaying when delivering treatment, and the refusal to refer patients to other hospitals, a hospital with no relevant technical competence might invite doctors from higher-level hospitals to conduct treatment. This phenomenon was common although illegal, according to relevant regulations. The invited doctors wanted to work for extra income, although this was not permitted by the hospitals they belonged to.

When I got a hernia this year, I planned to go to the THC in my township to receive surgery. However, I asked others and knew that the scale of the THC was too small. In addition, the technical capability of doctors there is so low that they could not conduct this surgery. They have to invite doctors in county hospitals to come to operate on a Sunday. My son was at home at that time and urged me to seek care as soon as possible. Therefore, I didn't want to wait until Sunday and then snatched a surgery in the Red Cross Hospital in the county. (D20121107LZY)

There were some other tactics to attract patients to receive inpatient services in a hospital. The hospital might provide some "under-the-table" benefits to doctors in primary care facilities, and correspondingly, the latter would refer patients to that hospital. For example, the THC in County D where I conducted fieldwork regulated that NCMS patients had to consume over the deposits in their household saving accounts in village clinics before they could seek outpatient services in the THC. A doctor in that THC said that this was to provide benefits to village doctors and, in turn, to encourage them to refer patients to the THC rather than county hospitals:

Our THC regulates that patients have to spend over all the deposits in their saving accounts of the NCMS in the village clinics before they can seek outpatient services in our THC. We

> do this to bring benefits to both the THC and the village doctors. In principle, village doctors are subordinate to THCs directly. The relationships between village doctors and county hospitals and the county BoH are not so close. Therefore, if we provide some benefits to village doctors, they will also return with benefits by referring patients who need to be hospitalized to us rather than to county hospitals. This can increase the revenue of THCs, which compete with other hospitals intensely. (D20120816ZHX)

4.4 The Patient: A Health-Prioritizing and Facility-Sophistication-Oriented Consumer

Patients bought healthcare services from doctors and in turn received reimbursement from SHI agencies. Patients selected health facilities according to the severity of their diseases, affordability, and other socioeconomic factors. However, human beings cherish their lives. The consciousness of valuing health more than reimbursement of the SHI made Chinese patients neglect to obtain sufficient information about healthcare quality in hospitals. In particular, with increasing health consciousness as well as economic status, Chinese patients trusted healthcare quality in the large hospitals rather than that of the small hospitals. Meanwhile, patients used a number of strategies such as seeking social relations to reduce the risks of their choices.

4.4.1 The Combined Effects of Patients' Health Consciousness and Economic Status

The health consciousness of Chinese patients was improving, with both rural and urban patients putting greater emphasis on their health than on the reimbursement benefits provided by the SHI schemes. This consciousness counteracted the effect of the strategies for adjusting the care-seeking behavior of patients used by SHI agencies. Patients preferred to receive treatment in the large hospitals, which were perceived as providing a higher quality of care, even if the small hospitals had sufficient technical capability to cure their diseases.

> Although we provide a tiered copayment system for patients treated in hospitals at different levels, it produces unsatisfactory effects. There may be many reasons. For example, people's awareness of health is improving. They value their health more than their medical spending. But we the UEBMI agency care about how much money they spend. (C20120910ZJ)

From the viewpoint of an officer in the municipal SHI agency, it was deemed normal that patients preferred to receive inpatient services or to go to large-scale hospitals. She even thought that the referral system was not a well-designed policy in that it brought the inconvenience of reimbursement to patients.

> Since 2008, the general reimbursement rate of UEBMI in our city has increased by 15%, which is the reason why the amount of inpatients rose so quickly. In my opinion, the rise of inpatients is quite normal. The blockbuster expansion of people's healthcare demands is due. People don't care much about our adjustment of the tiered reimbursement rates. Moreover, I chat with patients in hospitals sometimes and find that they are unsatisfied with the referral system. They say that they want to go to higher-level hospitals, but primary care organizations forbid it and provide no referral certificate. Therefore, they have to receive low reimbursement rates in higher-level hospitals. In this regard, the bidirectional referral brings inconvenience to them. (B20120927SKZ)

Patients' admission to large hospitals might be exacerbated, especially in the case of some conditions, such as catastrophic disease, medical emergency, child illness, and so on.

> We [a patient and her family members] spent lots of money to cure my daughter who caught aplastic anemia last year. However, we had no alternative choices as we encountered such things. If we had no money at that time, we would certainly need to receive treatment even if we borrow money from others. When we got to Tianjin to seek care, a doctor there told us that we would spend ¥200,000 to ¥300,000. Then my husband felt very stressed. But we decided to accept treatment eventually. (D20121028LTZ)

> We [a county NCMS management office] regulate distinct reimbursement rates of the NCMS, with 90% for patients hospitalized in THCs, 80% in county hospitals, 70% in hospitals at city level, and 65% in hospitals at provincial level. Regarding pure economic benefit, patients would spend less in THCs than in other hospitals. In addition, patients who want to go to hospitals at city level and above must obtain referral approval from our NCMS management office. We also tell them that they would be better going to THCs and county hospitals rather than city-level hospitals if their disease can be treated in the former hospitals. However, they care little about our suggestions. They say that no one can be responsible for them or their sick children if they are not cured. (D20120906PZR)

Patients' health consciousness and choice of health facilities were also affected by their economic condition. An officer in the NCMS management office of County D and also one in the municipal SHI agency of City B said that their measures of adjusting patients' care-seeking behaviors were offset by people's increasing economic conditions. The affordability of expensive medical services was increasing so fast that many did not care about how little of their medical costs might be reimbursed by the SHI.

> We [the municipal SHI agency of City B] enacted a tiered copayment system for patients to prevent them from spilling over to large hospitals. However, its effect is compromised. This is a problem of national policy. People are becoming increasingly rich so that they are able to afford medical services in large hospitals. Moreover, our City B is just a small city. If my family has a patient, I can even ride a bike to find a large hospital close to my house, not to mention riding a taxi. It is possible that my meal is still hot when I come back. City B, unlike those large cities such as Beijing and Shanghai, has such an advantage in transportation. And the very thing is that my family can afford this with the increasing reimbursement of the SHI. (B20120927SKZ)

> We as an NCMS management office cannot control health cost inflation in hospitals at city level. Many rural residents spill over there, because their living conditions improve. In addition, their demand for high quality services increase. They don't believe in the healthcare quality in county and township hospitals. (D20120906PZR)

4.4.2 The Facility-Sophistication-Oriented Care-Seeking Behavior

Patients tended to seek care in tertiary hospitals not only because of their improving health consciousness and economic status, but also their facility-sophistication-oriented awareness.

Patients' care-seeking behaviors were affected by the scale of hospitals. The large hospitals were believed to possess high technical capability and therefore, to be able to provide high quality services.

> Our ordinary people have a bad habit in that if we have diseases, we like to go to large hospitals. We believe in the healthcare quality, high-tech equipment, and technical competence of doctors in these hospitals. These make us rest assured. (A20120910ZJ)

Patients were easily attracted by the facility sophistication of hospitals, especially its high-tech equipment. Hospitals realized patients' demands of this kind and therefore competed to buy high-tech test devices, devices and materials for lab tests, and so on. As a result, it caused a "medical arms race" in hospitals.

> High-test devices are the major assets in any hospitals, which are worth millions of Yuan generally. For example, I am in the department of medical tests in our hospital. The earnings of our department are the main source of revenue of our hospital, receiving about one tenth of its annual revenue. All the service departments have to rely on us. The more advanced a hospital is the more devices it has. All the hospitals are competing to buy test equipment. If you don't buy them, patients will not come. Large advanced devices are the sign of hospitals. (A20121019HYJ)

The medical arms race existed not only among hospitals, but even among primary care facilities. The latter competed to purchase CT, MRI, color ultrasonography, and other high-tech machines to attract patients.

> Medical facilities in our THC lagged behind in the past. We bought the color ultrasonography and CT to attract patients a few years ago. Now patients from other townships would like to seek care in our THC. Even patients from another county such as XW County come here now. I tell them that they would not be reimbursed due to the regulations of the NCMS about pooling at county level. They don't care and say that it doesn't matter. (D20120903TLB)

Meanwhile, patients' trust in hospitals and doctors was an important concern. Chinese patients had no strong trust in technical competence and healthcare quality in small hospitals and primary care facilities. The perceived healthcare quality in health facilities affected patients' care-seeking behaviors.

> Although we provide much reimbursement for patients treated in small hospitals, patients are unwilling to go. As far as I know, this is because of patients' untrustworthiness of the healthcare quality of these hospitals. Patients' trust in hospitals and doctors is quite an important intangible asset. Now the government has also realized this problem. If people put no trust in doctors, teachers, the government, and policemen, the society will be at the edge of breakdown. (B20120920BJZ)

> Our hospital [a provincial tertiary hospital] admits many NCMS patients. Although the NCMS provides less reimbursement for patients treated in our hospitals than in hospitals at

a lower level, patients still spill over here. That is because the government sets up a tiered healthcare system. County hospitals are the best health facilities within the county, and hospitals at city level are the best health facilities within the city. However, patients still don't believe the healthcare quality of these hospitals. In addition, if they catch serious diseases, they will come here directly. (A20121019ZJ)

4.4.3 Social Relations as an Intermediary/Warrantor

Without sufficient consumer information, Chinese patients became used to relying on their social relations to find hospitals. They thought that social relations might warrant cost effectiveness of their treatment. Nearly all the patients we interviewed in the four investigated areas found hospitals via their friends or relatives. In their opinion, if they were recommended to doctors through these social relations, they were more likely to enjoy better, responsible or low-price treatment than if they sought these doctors directly.

My daughter was hospitalized in the county People's Hospital last year because of the inflammation of her tonsil. Doctor Yang, one of the doctors supervising my daughter, was my comrade-in-arms. In this hospital, there are so many doctors I am familiar with, some of whom are my relatives. Doctor Yang works in the Department of Surgery and deals with some surgical diseases like appendicitis. He was not the doctor in charge of my daughter, but attended the surgery. The doctor in charge came from the Department of Otolaryngology (ear, nose and throat), which was the only department of services capable of conducting tonsillectomy in the whole county. (D20121030LY)

My father went to the City Hospital of Infectious Diseases to receive a lung cancer surgery this year. It was recommended by a Chinese medicine practitioner in a THC. He was the friend of a doctor named Feng in the City Hospital of Infectious Diseases. Doctor Feng became the doctor in charge of my father after being hospitalized. (D20121025LZX)

The reason why I chose the Red Cross Hospital to receive a hernia surgery is because the daughter of my wife's sister was working there. I contacted her to find a doctor who could conduct surgery for me immediately. (D20121107LZY)

4.5 SHI and Its Agency: A Behavior Booster Rather Than Manager

Confronted by so many constraints from healthcare providers and patients, SHI and its agencies played a weak role in managing patients' care-seeking behaviors, causing their strategies for adjusting these behaviors to lose magnitude. Instead, the reimbursement benefits provided by SHI stimulated patients to go to higher-level hospitals rather than primary care facilities.

4.5.1 *Inefficient Referral System and Tiered Copayment and Deductibles*

Although some hospitals refused to provide referral certificates to NCMS patients for the purpose of retaining those patients and making profit, they could not restrain the flow of patients to large hospitals. With improving health consciousness and economic status, many patients cared little about the loss of their reimbursement due to the lack of referral certificates.

In addition, county NCMS management offices introduced digitalization to manage their referral system, which brought convenience to NCMS patients hospitalized outside of the county. A doctor in a secondary hospital in City B said that NCMS inpatients in that hospital could obtain their medical reimbursements immediately, by calling the NCMS management office following discharge from hospital. They did not have to go back to their own counties. However, the digitalized referral system also reduced the constraints of referral on patients' care-seeking behaviors. In this sense, the digitalized referral system had both positive and negative effects.

> NCMS patients have to show their insurance certificates and ID cards (to get reimbursement after they are discharged from this hospital). However, they enjoy more convenience than they used to. They just call the county NCMS management offices and show their number of NCMS certificates. After that, the NCMS management offices will transfer their information online. (C20120918GKZ)

Similarly, the strategy of tiered copayment and deductibles also suffered from inefficiency. Except for the constraints from healthcare providers and patients, the gaps between the reimbursement rates of hospitals at different levels were believed to be too small.

> The amounts of admissions in tertiary hospitals increases faster than ours (a secondary hospital at city level). Even if patients have a lower reimbursement rate in tertiary hospitals, the rate is just slightly lower than that in our hospitals by 10%. (B20120926MYS)

However, SHI agencies did not want to apply more radical regulations of tiered copayment and deductibles, setting the reimbursement rate in tertiary hospitals low in order to adjust patients' care-seeking behaviors. Instead, it increased the reimbursement rate for patients admitted in tertiary hospitals in accordance with that of primary care facilities and secondary hospitals. An officer in the municipal SHI agency of City B explained that it was because most patients with serious diseases were hospitalized in tertiary hospitals. One of the main goals of the state policy was to increase the affordability for these patients to avoid disease- and medical spending-induced poverty. Therefore, SHI agencies had to keep increasing the reimbursement rate for treatment in tertiary hospitals. It suffered from the conflicting priorities between the behavior management and reimbursement mechanisms.

> The tiered copayment of UEBMI doesn't achieve the desired results, as the reimbursement rate has to be kept consistent among hospitals at different levels. If the rate is raised in

primary care facilities, it is impossible to decrease the rate in tertiary hospitals because most patients with catastrophic diseases are hospitalized in tertiary hospitals. We have to raise the rate in tertiary hospitals too. In addition, the priority of government policy is given to helping the disadvantaged groups and patients with catastrophic diseases. In this regard, the principles of reimbursing more in primary care facilities and of reimbursing more for patients with catastrophic diseases are in conflict mutually, as most patients with severe diseases are in tertiary hospitals. The inclusion of new drugs, services, and materials into the UEBMI formulary, the adjustment of drug formulary, and so on, are all policy changes to benefit these patients. Moreover, the State Council promulgated the Serious Illness Insurance to reimburse more to patients spending over ¥10,000. It also aims to help these patients. (B20120927SKZ)

In this regard, the behavior management mechanism may work well only for those patients with minor diseases. To receive more reimbursement, patients with minor diseases preferred to seek doctors in primary care facilities.

I received surgery to treat my prolapse of lumbar intervertebral disc this January 15th in the Red Cross Hospital in our county. I go there because it has equivalent health quality with county hospitals but is just a THC. So I can get more reimbursement than in county hospitals. (D20121028SXT)

4.5.2 SHI and Its Agency as a Behavior Booster Rather Than Manager

The strategies of adjusting patients' care-seeking behaviors suffered from dysfunction. What was worse, the substantial reimbursements of SHI boosted patients' admission to higher-level hospitals. It was especially serious for urban patients who lived in the city where quality healthcare resources were concentrated. An SHI reimbursement manager in a tertiary hospital in City C said that even URBMI patients with minor diseases would go to tertiary hospital to seek treatment.

Different SHI schemes regulate various criteria of expenditures per admission for our hospital [a tertiary hospital], with the UEBMI over ¥8,000, the URBMI over ¥6,000, and the NCMS ¥80,00 … Most NCMS patients coming to our hospital are those with serious diseases, while those URBMI patients with even general diseases come here. NCMS patients with slight general diseases often go to THCs first, with those with more serious diseases going to county hospitals. But URBMI patients with either slight or severe diseases go to hospitals at city level, because they can get most of their expenditures reimbursed. (C20120918WKZ)

Urban patients would also choose the large hospitals because of the internet-assisted reimbursement of UEBMI and URBMI. Unlike NCMS patients who had to present their NCMS certificates to receive reimbursement, UEBMI and URBMI patients had special insurance cards for reimbursement. The insurance card was like a credit card, by which patients only needed to swipe the cards to pay for their medical expenses.

UEBMI and URBMI patients don't have to have referral approval when they are hospitalized in our hospital [a secondary hospital at city level]. But NCMS patients, unlike their UEBMI and URBMI counterparts, have to notify their county NCMS management offices to transfer their NCMS information to us. UEBMI and URBMI patients don't need to do this. They have insurance cards. When they are hospitalized, they just swipe the cards to pay their medical spending. (C20120918GKZ)

4.6 Summary of Findings

To summarize, the behavior management mechanism of SHI required SHI agencies to manage patients' care-seeking behaviors. Correspondingly, SHI agencies used various strategies to restrain patients from spilling into higher-level hospitals. However, its efforts were offset by the interaction between healthcare providers and SHI agencies and patients, as well as in the process of institutions structuring the interaction.

With regard to healthcare providers, primary and secondary health facilities tried to attract patients. They devoted their attention to the development of facilities, equipment, and devices, especially when they received increasingly more funding from the government and benefited from the development of SHI coverage. They invited doctors from higher-level hospitals to treat patients in order to make up for their undeveloped technical competence, with some of them coalescing with doctors at lower-level health facilities to obtain referred patients. Low-level health facilities also took advantage of SHI's referral system to forbid patients to go to high-level hospitals by providing no referral certificates.

Their efforts, however, were counteracted within the larger institutional surroundings. Due to a poor compensation system for hospitals, the government provided rather insufficient finance to health facilities. All healthcare providers became profit-driven, thus formulating no mutual transfer relationship across health facilities. They competed in a disorderly manner in order to attract patients. Even if patients with minor diseases flowed to tertiary hospitals, doctors there would not refer those patients to primary and secondary health facilities. In addition, healthcare resources were inequitably allocated across health facilities at different levels. Tertiary hospitals possessed the most healthcare resources and had much higher technical competence than primary and secondary health facilities. Both health facilities and technical competence in the latter two lagged behind the former.

The larger institutional surroundings also shaped the calculations and choices of patients. As healthcare resources were overallocated in tertiary hospitals, the quality of health services there were perceived to be high; patients had lower trust in the technical competence of primary and secondary hospitals. Patients were facility-sophistication-oriented in that they chose hospitals according to the scale and number of high-tech devices of the latter. Moreover, patients had increasingly high health consciousness and economic conditions, which may have induced them to further neglect the relevant high reimbursement rates if they were admitted to primary care facilities and secondary hospitals. In addition, the rapid development of SHI and the radical increase of SHI reimbursement stimulated them to seek care in large hospitals.

With these constraints, SHI agencies became powerless to adjust patients' care-seeking behaviors and to enforce the behavior management mechanism of SHI. Urban SHI agencies, due to no policy support, were unable to implement the referral system. Both urban and rural SHI agencies were unable to enlarge the gaps between the reimbursement rates among health facilities at different levels, because the government encouraged the increase of SHI reimbursement to patients with catastrophic diseases who were mostly admitted to large hospitals. In addition, the digitalized referral system and internet-assisted reimbursement brought procedural convenience of reimbursement to patients on the one hand, and stimulated patients to go to higher-level hospitals on the other hand. Patients did not have to return to their home towns to receive reimbursement if they were hospitalized in city or provincial hospitals.

Accordingly, we conclude that the SHI system was finally embedded in the larger institutional surroundings. The malfunction of behavior management was generated by the inefficient interaction between healthcare providers, patients, and SHI agencies. Furthermore, this inefficient interaction was shaped and structured its larger institutional surroundings.

Chapter 5
The Purchasing Mechanism: A Game Between Purchasers, Patients, and Doctors

In Chap. 4, we explored the behavior management mechanism of SHI. Interpreting the dysfunction of the behavior management mechanism facilitated us to understand the statistical relationship tested in Chap. 3, that is, the mediating role that people's care-seeking behaviors played in the relationship between SHI participation and OOPS. The quantitative analysis in Chap. 3 also revealed poor performance of the SHI purchasing mechanism, in that SHI participation was unable to constrain medical cost inflation but instead boosted it to a certain degree. To explain the statistical relationship between SHI participation and medical costs, we interpret the SHI purchasing mechanism in this chapter.

Advocates of SHI claimed that information asymmetry existed in the health service market. The information advantage of providers over patients could cause serious market failures (Arrow 1963). The solution was to introduce a third party—an SHI agency or insurer—to act as the agent for insurance enrollees. Theoretically, SHI agencies could act as smart buyers because they could obtain information at lower prices and had stronger bargaining power than individual patients. At the same time, an SHI agency could curb the unnecessary health demands of utilization management. Enthoven's (1988) conception of managed competition was one such formulation. No matter whether or not there was competition between insurers and providers, a third-party purchasing of health services through separating the functions of financing from the production of services was highly appreciated (Preker 2005; Robinson et al. 2005). SHI, by shifting some power from the supply to the demand side, balanced the influence of patients versus providers, which therefore was deemed by many health planners to be a magic solution to the problems of healthcare financing (Hsiao 2007).

However, it was dubious whether health insurance could play this role in third-party purchasing and cost containment, as the theory claimed. To better understand the relationship between SHI and medical costs, therefore, in this chapter we explore the everyday administration of SHI agencies and health facilities, as well as the experiences of patients. We also probe into the interaction of different stakeholders and the grand institutional surroundings that shaped and

K. Liu, *The Effects of Social Health Insurance Reform on People's Out-of-Pocket Health Expenditure in China*, DOI 10.1007/978-981-10-1777-3_5

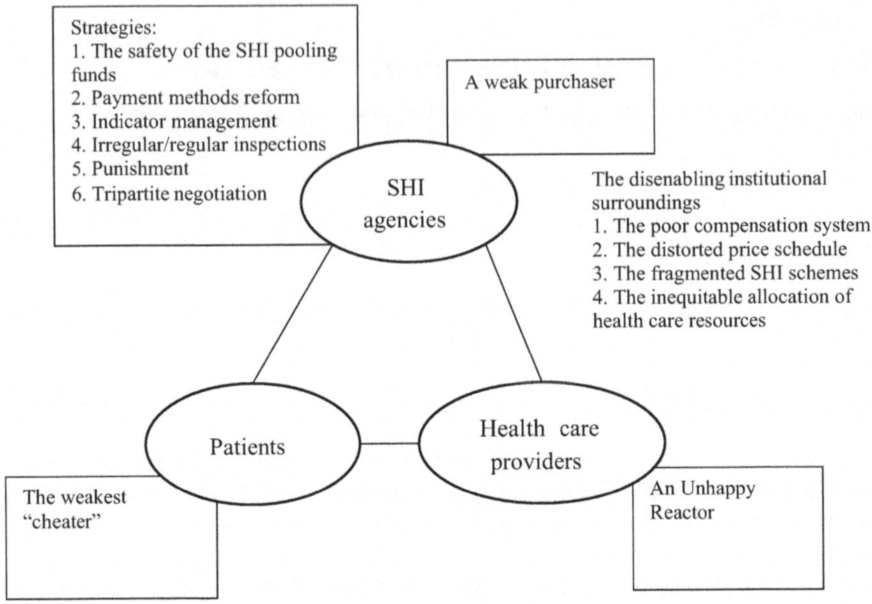

Fig. 5.1 Dysfunction of the purchasing mechanism

structured the practices of these stakeholders. In China, the largest middle- and low-income country in the world, SHI administrators, doctors, and patients faced far more complexity than those in other countries. Therefore, by examining the everyday practices of and the interactions between different stakeholders, we wished to interpret the purchasing mechanism of SHI and explain its role in the relationship between SHI participation and OOPS.

Our investigation traced the strategies that SHI agencies employed to contain cost inflation in health facilities, and evaluated the reactions of doctors and patients to these strategies. We first summarize the strategies of SHI agencies in purchasing medical services from healthcare providers as patients' representatives, and then explore the roles that SHI agencies, healthcare providers, and patients played in health cost inflation. Finally, we analyze the effects of the institutional surroundings. Using our main findings, we present in Fig. 5.1 the roles that key stakeholders played in health cost inflation.

5.1 Strategies for Purchasing

To better understand the different strategies that various SHI schemes used for healthcare cost containment, it is first necessary to review briefly the supervision structure of these schemes. The three kinds of SHI schemes, UEBMI, URBMI, and NCMS, were administered separately, each scheme being operated by localized management. The UEBMI and URBMI at municipal level were managed by municipal SHI agencies, while those at district and county level were managed by district and county SHI agencies, respectively. The NCMS was managed by a county NCMS management office. A municipal, district, or county SHI agency was a division of the municipal, district, or county bureau of human resources and social security (BHRSS), respectively. A county NCMS management office was a section or agency of the county bureau of health (BoH). At the same time, hospitals and the NCMS management office were both under the stewardship of the BoH.

We investigated the UEBMI at provincial level in City A, the UEBMI at municipal level in City B, the UEBMI and URBMI at municipal level in City C, as well as the UEBMI, URBMI, and NCMS at county level in County D. Although these SHI schemes were run by different government sections, they used quite similar strategies to purchase medical services.

We found that the safety of the SHI pooling funds was the priority and basic principle of management for all kinds of SHI schemes in the investigated areas. In addition, all SHI agencies used similar strategies of purchasing to restrain the improper prescription behaviors of doctors and the excessive demands of patients, including payment methods reform, indicator management, inspection, punishment, and tripartite negotiation. They also used these strategies to contain the inflation of medical expenditures.

First, the safety of the SHI pooling funds. Ensuring the safety of the SHI pooling funds was the first principle under repeated orders and injunctions of the governments at different levels. Most of the participants in urban and rural SHI agencies said that their most important work was to guarantee that the reimbursement expenditures did not exceed the funds held. To fulfill this task, they employed many tactics to keep a balance between the expenditure and revenue of the pooling funds. An officer in the urban SHI agency of City C emphasized the importance of ensuring the safety of the pooling funds of the UEBMI and URBMI:

> The funds of the UEBMI and URBMI are different with that of the old age insurance which is subsidized by the government finance. The funds of the UEBMI and URBMI have to be spent according to their revenues and a balance kept between expenditure and revenue. How to keep a balance? It depends on expenditures in hospitals. If the cost inflation in hospitals is higher than the increase of funds revenues, we will intervene in hospitals by telling them that we are almost in deficit. Therefore, it is very important to control the spending of the funds. There are two most important things for our urban SHI agency: one is the collection of premium, the other is the management of the funds. We would ensure at least the funds to be spent on rational things. We cannot provide reimbursement to all kinds of expenditures in hospitals. (C20120910ZJ)

A deputy director of the NCMS management office of County D said that no government sections or officers were permitted to embezzle the pooling funds. Ensuring the safety of the pooling funds was the political responsibility of the governments at different levels. In addition, SHI reimbursement plans had to be set up according to the revenue of the pooling funds.

> No one dare embezzle the funds of the NCMS which involves political responsibility and therefore draws high attention of the upper governments. The former Vice Premier WU Yi

> said that anyone who dares to embezzle the funds would be executed by shooting! Her words are scaring anyway, but do reflect the importance of the funds. The governments at all levels focus on the safety of the funds and do not dare to embezzle them. I saw from the online reports that the funds were embezzled and some governments couldn't infuse subsidies to the funds on time. These problems should not come out in theory. Generally speaking, we set up our plans of reimbursement according to the size of the funds and try to guarantee that our expenditures do not exceed the total amount of the fund revenue. Therefore, our most important tasks involve two points: one is the safety of the funds, the other is the balance between the revenue and expenditure of the funds. If we spend too much, we will have no money to reimburse patients. So, our plan on the reimbursement spending is quite important. However, the provincial government made a unique plan of the NCMS funds last year. It was too radical by increasing the reimbursement rate to 90% for THCs in all counties. The funds of many counties couldn't keep a balance. (D20120906PZR)

Some participants criticized the overemphasis of the safety of the pooling funds. For example, a doctor in the investigated THC in County D said that the importance of cost control and the safety of the funds were overwhelming and were even more important than healthcare quality.

> The goals of the NCMS policies focus too much on expenditure indicators. The government doesn't care much about healthcare quality, which is becoming increasingly poor. The attention of the governments at all levels is on medical spending. Who cares about healthcare quality if medical expenditures don't exceed the regulated extent too much? (D20120816GXH)

Second, payment methods reform. SHI agencies conducted payment methods reform by replacing retrospective payment methods, such as fee-for-services payments, partly or fully with a number of prospective payment methods, such as global budget. These prospective payment methods were used for the purpose of controlling cost inflation in health facilities.

After the launch of the new round of healthcare reform in 2009, all the investigated areas piloted the global budget and other prospective payment methods for various SHI programs. For instance, global budget was implemented for UEBMI inpatients who worked in provincial government and institutions in City A, municipal UEBMI inpatients in City B, municipal UEBMI and URBMI inpatients in City C and NCMS inpatients in County D; DRG payments was implemented for NCMS inpatients in County D; and capitation was implemented for URBMI outpatients in City C.

Among these methods, the global budget was the most commonly used. SHI agencies set the annual fixed budget for each health facility using the average expenditures of reimbursement in that facility of the past one to three years. An officer in the UEBMI management office in the municipal SHI agency of City C said that they regulated the fixed budget for each health facility by referring to many cost-related indicators. The fixed budget was stated in the contract they signed with health facilities.

> We set up fixed budgets for each hospital by referring to various types of their expenditures in the past three years, including total expenditures, inpatient admissions, the proportions of costs of Class A and Class B drugs, the proportions of drugs outside of the drug catalogue

> of the UEBMI, the proportions of drug costs and of drug costs paid out-of-pocket, the proportions of costs of test and medical consumption material, expenditures per admission, and so on. We also accounted for price inflation and reasonable increase of revenues in hospitals. After that, we conducted statistical analysis to set up indicators for the different types of expenditures mentioned above. Then we used these indicators to negotiate with hospitals. If both hospitals and us agreed with these indicators, we signed contracts to conduct the global budget. At the time of settlement at the end of the year, we paid hospitals according to their performance of monitoring these indicators. All of these strategies are aimed at controlling the total budgets in hospitals. (C20120913YM)

County NCMS management offices also used global budgets to contain cost inflation in county hospitals and THCs. However, their indictors to calculate the fixed budget for each health facility were less exact than the urban SHI agencies' indicators. Usually, they considered the total expenditures or reimbursement of each health facility without referring to more detailed cost-related indicators.

> The global budget of the NCMS is based on the average of total expenditures of each month in the past three years. For example, if our THC was reimbursed with ¥100,000 in May 2009, ¥150,000 in May 2010, and ¥200,000 in May 2011, we will get a fixed budget of ¥150,000 in May 2012. We have to monitor our spending by ourselves. If we exceed the budget, we have to reimburse patients by ourselves. If there is still surplus…we have to spend all the budgets anyway. (D20120903WSC)

The delivery of these fixed budgets to health facilities comprised several steps. First, the budget was paid prospectively rather than retrospectively. Second, only a proportion of the budget was paid, with the rest formulating a performance bond to be paid at the end of the year. Third, a certain award was provided if the hospitals did not go over budget, while a certain subsidy was provided if there was over-expenditure. These steps are reviewed one by one, as follows.

First, both the urban and rural SHI agencies replaced the retrospective payment with a prospective payment of the SHI budget. The prospective payment was enacted to satisfy the needs of health facilities in maintaining normal operations. An officer in the municipal SHI agency of City B expressed this method as "representing the provision of better services to hospitals."

> We revised the 2007 plan of the global budget of the UEBMI in 2010. Why? That was because we didn't implement prospective payment of budget to hospitals in 2007. Prospective payment is just a tool to build links with hospitals, which represents the provision of better services to hospitals by us. Hospitals always complained that they had to advance reimbursements to patients with our former retrospective payment to them. After we implemented prospective payment, the most important thing was that we changed our attitudes toward hospitals. We advanced the first 80% of the fixed budget of reimbursement to hospitals to reduce hospitals' pressure of fund turnover. This established a cooperative relationship between hospitals and our SHI agency, which led hospitals to provide better services to patients and prevented hospitals from lowering services quality…Among all the social insurance programs, it is only the health insurance that has conducted this strategy. Are there any other insurance programs being able to do this? No! They provide no prospective payment. Hospitals could be deemed a disadvantaged group in the past, but now they are in an equal position with us. Therefore, their normal operations become more and more smooth. (B20120924WKZ)

Second, the fixed budget was not fully paid in advance but partly paid, with the rate of 80 % generally being used. Officers in SHI agencies used this strategy to prevent doctors from abusing SHI funds and conducting overtreatment of patients. If the fixed budget was overused, SHI agencies could refuse to pay fully the rest of the budget (the 20 % part) or share the overexpenditure with health facilities, and may assign lower budgets to hospitals in the following year.

> The whole province conducted global budgets for the NCMS, including hospitals at provincial level. Every county calculates by itself the fixed budgets in hospitals, with different budgets for different hospitals. The calculation is conducted by the NCMS management offices. The office will advance 80% of the budget to hospitals each month, with 20% being settled at the end of the year. It tells our hospitals that the fixed budget is just that much, and hospitals have to pay by themselves if exceeding the regulated amount. We hospitals have to reimburse patients by ourselves if the budget runs out. It is impossible to stop reimbursement for the patients. If we save some budget in the current year, the NCMS management office would use certain budget surplus to award us. I cannot remember the exact percentage of the award. (D20120828GSQ)

A deputy director in the municipal SHI agency of City B deemed the partial payment of SHI funds a tool for "stimulating positive incentives" for doctors. Partial payment transferred pressure from SHI agencies to health facilities by causing the latter to worry about whether the remainder of the fixed budget would be settled.

> We have other strategies to manage hospitals. We don't provide full payment in advance, but just 80% of the budget. This partial advance payment is to prevent doctors from violating our regulations by conducting overtreatment. It pushes hospitals to correct these behaviors of doctors. If they keep overspending, their fixed budget will run out. If they don't control their expenditures, we will give them just 60% of the budget in the next month. We take this as a strategy of stimulating positive incentives. If they take efforts to control their expenditures, we give them not only 80% of the budget, but also provide them extra awards at the time of settlement at the end of the year. (B20120920BJZ)

Third, SHI agencies used a mechanism of awarding and cost sharing to monitor whether health facilities had expended their budgets. Urban SHI agencies would award hospitals the surplus funds if they had saved a certain proportion of their budget, and would provide subsidies to share the costs if there was overexpenditure.

> Our principle is providing award for surplus and subsidy for overexpenditure of the UEBMI funds in hospitals. For example, if a hospital uses ¥990,000 out of ¥1,000,000 which we assigned to them, we will use 40% of the ¥10,000 left to award this hospital. If it exceeds the assigned budget by 10%, we share a certain proportion of the overexpenditure. If the overexpenditure is 20% or 30% of the fixed budget, we will share; if 40%, it is too much and therefore we will not share. (C20120913YM)

A deputy director of the municipal SHI agency of City B said that in practice, the mechanism of awarding surplus funds was just "an illusion," because all health facilities fully expended the fixed budget assigned to them and had no surplus. Health cost inflation was so serious that urban SHI agencies were hardly able to curb medical spending in health facilities.

> In the former version of the global budget of the UEBMI in 2010, we were forbidden from using surplus UEBMI funds to award hospitals. However, we still awarded them in disguised form by transforming the surplus to the extra future budget of hospitals. Now the state permits to use the surplus to award hospitals, and we award more surplus to hospitals than ever before. Without these awards, we cannot stimulate hospitals to do self-management. We awarded hospitals surplus in disguised form in 2010. We told hospitals that if their budget was not expended, we would transform the surplus to their fixed budget in the next year. However, this statement was actually an illusion, because no hospital saved its budget. All of them said that the budget was inadequate. (B20120920BJZ)

With regard to the NCMS management offices, there was no clear policy design about the awarding and cost-sharing mechanism. Some doctors said that the NCMS management office provided an award if the health facilities did not expend their budgets, but did not provide subsidies for any overexpenditure; others said that both the award and certain cost sharing would be provided. This was mainly because the global budget in County D had only just been enacted in 2012, at the time we conducted our fieldwork. For all the participants, many detailed regulations about the global budget of the NCMS were still unknown. Two doctors in the investigated THC in County D provided opposing opinions on whether the county NCMS management office would share the overexpenditure of the THC.

> The global budget of the NCMS that was launched this May generated a great influence over our THC…To be specific, the NCMS management office provides our THC with a certain budget every month. If we exceed the regulated amount, we have to pay by ourselves; if we save some budget, the office will return part of the surplus to us. (D20120816GXH)

> If our expenditures exceed, we have to pay patients by ourselves. But there are also detailed regulations that the NCMS management office would share some if our expenditures exceed, with the hospital sharing most of the exceeding expenditures. (D20120828GSQ)

It was indicated that the aims of these various strategies that SHI agencies employed were to "reinforce the self-management capability" of health facilities or to "transfer the responsibility of management" from SHI agencies to health facilities.

Officers from SHI agencies generally complained that both the agencies and the health facilities passively managed the system with a fee-for-services payment method. An officer in the NCMS management office of County D revealed that health facilities "relied solely on the inspections by our NCMS management office" by utilizing the former fee-for-services payment.

> In the past, hospitals relied solely on the inspections by our NCMS management office. Without sound self-supervision, the fixed budget for hospitals is for sure inadequate to use. Hospitals should reduce unreasonable expenditures. (D20120906PZR)

Unlike the fee-for-services payment, the global budget stimulated health facilities "to restrain their own behaviors and to conduct self-management" and pushed doctors "to consider and save medical costs." It was deemed by an officer in the municipal SHI agency of City C a tool for "making experts supervise themselves."

> We did many works to replace passive management by our SHI agency with active self-supervision by doctors themselves. One main method is implementing the payment

methods reform by replacing the fee-for-services method with the prospective payment method. We have conducted the global budget since last July…We advance the partial budget to induce hospitals to manage themselves according to their fixed budget. If their budget runs out, it would be their own problem; if their budget is saved, they return first the surplus to us, which will be in turn awarded to them. The advantage of this method is to stimulate hospitals to restrain their own behaviors and to conduct self-management instead of only receiving supervision from our SHI agency. Hospitals can use the awards to either award doctors, to buy medical devices, or to build facilities. After we deliver the budgets to them, they use their own methods of management and supervision to deliver further the budgets to every department of services…Anyway, the self-management of hospitals would be more scientific than the supervision by us. When the directors, doctors, and even nurses of departments of services offer clinical services, they will consider the cost effectiveness and necessity of the use of drugs. They will not use the unnecessary drugs and tests…The aims of the global budget are to push doctors to consider and save medical costs without sacrificing healthcare quality ultimately. This is to make experts supervise themselves and to stimulate hospitals to conduct intra-management. (C20120910ZJ)

Third, indicator management. Both urban and rural SHI agencies used a strategy of indicator management to monitor the cost inflation of health facilities following implementation of the global budget. These indicators were extensive, ranging from expenditures per admission to the proportion of the cost of drugs outside of SHI formularies. The performance indicators were evaluated at the end of the year to decide the amount of the performance bond to be returned, which SHI agencies retained by providing health facilities with a partial budget, as mentioned earlier.

To control the use of the fixed budget and monitor cost inflation in health facilities, the NCMS management offices usually relied on indictors such as expenditures per admission and their annual growth rates, the proportion of the cost of drugs outside of the NCMS drug formulary, the hospitalization rate, and so on. The NCMS management office supervised the performance of these indicators in order to control fraudulent acquirement of NCMS funds, and prevent overtreatment and overadmission of inpatients in health facilities. Expenditure per admission and its annual growth were forbidden to exceed a regulated cut-off point.

The BoH requires that the annual growth of expenditures per admission in our hospital [a tertiary hospital at city level] must not exceed 5%. Meanwhile, different SHI agencies set various indicators of expenditures per admission for us. The expenditures for NCMS patients per admission are about ¥8,000, which was calculated based on average expenditures in our hospital last year. We are required to keep its growth within 5%. The expenditures for the UEBMI and URBMI are ¥8,000 and ¥6,000 respectively. (C20120918WKZ)

The hospitalization rate was not appointed a cut-off point but was compared with that of other hospitals, with those ranking higher being criticized by the upper authority of the BoH.

The provincial NCMS management office monitors the hospitalization rate in hospitals. Our XY Township has a population of over 30,000…Our HJ County has a population of over 300,000. The office will collect the information of the 18 local health facilities to calculate the hospitalization rate in our county in this season. It will compare further with the disease incidence rate. If the hospitalization rate is 6.2% or 7% in the whole country but 10% in our county, it will cast doubt on our normal operations. Is it due to an emergence of

> endemic diseases, or the fraudulent acquirement of the NCMS funds, or overtreatment and overadmission of inpatients in hospitals?...Our hospitalization rate must not be too high. I once went to the capital city to attend a meeting. The provincial office noticed that HX County ranked first, YY County ranked second, while our county ranked about fourteenth in terms of hospitalization rate. Our county had once ranked about top five. The aim of noticing hospitalization rates was to monitor the expenditures of hospitals and whether the NCMS funds were excessively used. (D20120830GSQ)

Urban SHI agencies used more indicators than the NCMS management offices. In addition, they conducted stricter inspection of the performance of these indicators.

> The urban SHI agency regulates many indicators for us, including a series of expenditure and healthcare quality-related indicators. The indicators regulated by the NCMS management office focus mainly on expenditures like the proportion of the cost of drugs outside of the NCMS formulary. The indicators monitored by the NCMS management office are less than those monitored by the urban SHI agency. (C20120918GKZ)

The indicators monitored by urban SHI agencies mainly included expenditures per admission, hospitalization days, the reimbursement rate for expenses within the scope of policies, the proportion of the cost of drugs outside of the SHI formularies, the ratio of the number of times of admission to the number of patients, and even a number of microindicators of clinical practices such as the criteria for infusing blood and using antibiotics. The detailed and rigorous regulations were revealed by some doctors.

> The urban SHI agency regulates several indicators for us [a secondary hospital at city level], including hospitalization days, medical expenditures of inpatient services per admission, and so on. In regard to medical expenditures of inpatient services per admission, the cut-off point of the UEBMI is ¥4,600, while that of the URBMI is ¥4,000. However, the regulated expenditures are far from adequate in our clinical services. Why? The agency regulates 65 hospitalization days for UEBMI patients and 60 for URBMI patients at the same time. However, one-day expenditures in those large hospitals are equal to the whole-month expenditures in our hospital, which is just about ¥3,000 on average. (C2012918GKZ)

> The urban SHI agency regulates more detailed indicators than the NCMS management office. For example, the former regulates the criteria for infusing blood, which we have to fulfill before we use blood. In addition, the urban SHI formularies are more standard than the NCMS ones. The NCMS formularies do not have their own standards, but always refer to the regulations of the urban SHI ones. Therefore, the indicators of the NCMS are not enforced rigorously. However, the implementation of the UEBMI and URBMI is more rigorous. Their indicators are demanding. For example, they have clear standards for the use of antibiotics. If the standards are not fulfilled, they will deem the use unnecessary or excessive. Our doctors are not quite familiar with their detailed regulations; perhaps only they are clear. But still, their supervision is more rigorous than the NCMS. (A20121019ZJ)

Highlighted among these indicators was the proportion of the cost of drugs outside of the SHI formularies. As SHI agencies established drug, health service, and medical technology/equipment formularies, many drugs and services were excluded from the formularies and had to be paid out of pocket. Urban SHI agencies monitored the proportion of the cost of drugs outside of the drug formulary directly, to control the use of drugs paid out of pocket.

In the 2010 version of the global budget of the UEBMI, we used more indicators and better settlement methods than that of 2007. We highlighted the control of the proportion of the cost of drugs outside of the formulary and the reimbursement rate for expenses within the scope of policies. We monitored the proportion of the cost of drugs outside of the UEBMI drug formulary to control the use of drugs paid out of pocket. (B20120927SKZ)

Meanwhile, SHI agencies calculated the reimbursement rates for expenses within the scope of policies to monitor indirectly the use of drugs and services outside of the formularies. An officer of the municipal SHI agency of City B demonstrated the detailed method of calculating the reimbursement rate for expenses within the scope of policies.

In the performance evaluation plan, the reimbursement rate for expenses within the scope of policies is important. It is calculated based on the expenditures minus deductibles. For example, drugs of Class A in the formulary are reimbursed with 100%, and those of Class B need patients to afford 10% or 5%. If an inpatient spends ¥10,000, the expenses within the scope of policies are ¥9,000 after subtracting a ¥1,000 deductible. If he/she is reimbursed ¥6,000, the reimbursement rate for expenses within the scope of policies would be…As our data collection is relatively complete, we will calculate the expenses within the scope of policies. The remaining ¥9,000 contains some medicines and services outside of the formulary. We will get the total expenses within the scope of policies after subtracting the cost of items outside of the formulary. After that, we divided ¥6,000 by the total expenses within the scope of polices to get the reimbursement rate for expenses within the scope of policies. Therefore, the rate is calculated rather than regulated in advance. (B20120924WKZ)

The performance of these indicators was linked directly to the return of the performance bond to health facilities. Urban SHI agencies set up a performance evaluation plan to access the performance of these indicators in health facilities. For example, the urban SHI agency of City B kept 20 % of the fixed budget assigned to health facilities as a performance bond, and delivered the remaining 80 % to health facilities in advance each month, as described above. If a hospital wanted to obtain the remaining 20 % of its budget, it had to satisfactorily control these indicators in its normal operation.

We keep 20% of the fixed budget assigned to hospitals and take it as the performance bond. We have a performance evaluation plan to evaluate in the form of scores, according to the results of which we return the performance bond to hospitals…In the performance evaluation plan, there are several essential indicators. One is the medical expenditure per admission, which is assigned with high scores. We use it not only in the performance evaluation plan, but also when calculating the fixed budget assigned to hospitals. Another is the amount of rational work, which is represented as the ratio of the times of admission to the number of patients. If the ratio is very high, we think that the hospital may separate one hospitalization into several admissions, or that healthcare quality in the hospital may decrease due to overadmission of patients. It is inappropriate with either of these two problems. Correspondingly, we will deduct a certain fixed budget rather than assigning the full budget to the hospital in the next year. These two indicators are the most essential, through which we try to cultivate the awareness of hospitals of self-management. If hospitals restrain cost inflation poorly, they will suffer from the deduction of either the performance bond in the current year or of the fixed budget assigned to them in the next year. (B20120927SKZ)

Fourth, irregular/regular inspections. SHI agencies employed both irregular and regular inspections to monitor abnormal situations in hospitals. We called it "irregular/regular inspections" due to both the content and format of inspections. With regard to the content of inspections, urban and rural SHI agencies checked and monitored health facilities from a third-party perspective in case of any kind of abnormal treatment. They were not direct managers, only inspectors. If any abnormal situations were found, such as overtreatment and/or an excessively high proportion of the cost of drugs outside of the drug formulary, SHI agencies could not use administrative orders to redress these problems but instead used other strategies, such as refusing to reimburse, or deducting a percentage of the performance bond. With regard to the format of inspections, both irregular and regular methods were used. The irregular method relied mainly on labor power, with officers in SHI agencies going on an irregular basis to health facilities to inspect the normal operations of these facilities. The latter method relied on both labor power and non-labor tools. For example, the NCMS management office of County D regularly dispatched inspectors to THCs to monitor their work, while the urban SHI agency of City C launched an SHI doctor system and a special information platform to conduct inspection.

The content of these inspections across both rural and urban SHI agencies was similar, focusing on the fraudulent acquirement of SHI funds, imposture of reimbursement eligibility, inpatients leaving health facilities without permission, excessive medical expenditure, and so on.

> The inspections by the NCMS management office focus on inpatients leaving without permission, excessive treatment for slight diseases, overtreatment, and so on. There was a doctor who prescribed six CT scans to a patient in a three-day hospitalization. He was fined ¥10,000 and forced to take self-criticism. Another focus is on fraudulent acquirement of the NCMS funds. (D20120830GSQ)

> When we [the county NCMS management office of County D] conduct inspections of hospitals, we first scrutinize the identity of patients. There are many uninsured patients borrowing NCMS certificates from others to acquire reimbursement. We also inspect the excessive prescription of drugs and diagnoses. We conducted frequent inspections of overtreatment this year. (D20120906PZR)

Among these problems, priority was given to the imposture of reimbursement eligibility, which was common in China, especially for members in one household. For instance, in one case a woman who was enrolled in the URBMI program used her husband's UEBMI certificate to buy medicine and to be admitted to hospital, although in theory the UEBMI is for urban employees. The SHI reimbursement manager at the health facility was not strict in scrutinizing eligibility in this case. In other cases, patients might counterfeit the eligibility of an SHI program to obtain reimbursement.

> We [a CHC] record the basic information of UEBMI and URBMI patients treated here. If the urban SHI agency comes to inspect, they check the information randomly. It is impossible for them to check with these patients one by one. They have a look at patients' names, addresses, diseases, contact information, and phone numbers. After that, they call these patients to confirm whether and when the latter were prescribed with drugs and what kinds of drugs were prescribed. If the patients deny, it might be a problem. The SHI agency

> would come back to hospitals to double check. If it is a real problem, the SHI agency would fine hospitals. The focus of the SHI agency's inspections is on imposture of reimbursement eligibility. (B20121101GSL)

However, SHI agencies focused on imposture of reimbursement eligibility not only because using a faked SHI certificate to acquire reimbursed was harmful to SHI funds, but also because it was easy to identify by checking the identities of patients. Other problems, like overtreatment, required professional knowledge to be detected. Detecting these sorts of problems needed much infusion of manpower and financial resources.

> We [the county SHI agency of County D] have an auditing office which has two staff members to inspect doctors' medical behaviors regularly…The most common problem is imposture of reimbursement eligibility, which often happens for retired cadres who are reimbursed based on the fee-for-services payment. Some patients have medical records where the printed names were not in accordance with their real names, or even the gender is different. We can detect these problems easily. Some elderly patients received extracorporeal shock wave lithotripsy early this year. We found that their medical records were counterfeited. (D20121030GZR)

With regard to the format of inspection, the NCMS management offices and urban SHI agencies used quite different methods of inspection. The NCMS management offices used more traditional methods by relying on labor power, conducting irregular inspections such as inspecting medical records, inventories, and receipts in health facilities, and drafting doctors from other health facilities to assist with those inspections.

> Because the officials in the county BoH are not properly trained in the medical profession, they draft doctors from county hospitals to assist with their inspections of THCs. Sometimes, the city BoH organizes a specialist group, which is drafted from the department of services in hospitals at city level, to conduct inspections. The groups may have 50 members, which are further divided into various three-person subgroups. (D20120903TLB)

As well as irregular inspections, the NCMS management offices conducted regular inspections using labor power, such as recruiting special NCMS inspectors to inspect THCs. An NCMS inspector was specially dispatched to attend a THC and monitor its normal operations.

> In regard to inspection, the county NCMS office recruits numerous NCMS inspectors and dispatches them to THCs. Most of them were recruited from THCs through a special examination. The government provides salary to them. There is one NCMS inspector who attends the NCMS reimbursement office in our THC and is not constrained by the THC. But she doesn't come frequently. She may come once a week. (D20120827GXH)

For patients admitted to city-level hospitals, the NCMS management office, as a county unit, had to audit their medical inventories and receipts instead of going directly to hospitals to conduct inspections.

> We [a tertiary hospital at city level] reimburse patients in advance once they leave hospital. After that, we send the medical inventories and receipts to the city BoH, which in turn transfers these documents to county BoH. Then county bureaus audit these documents… The NCMS funds are managed by these county bureaus, so they are responsible for

> auditing these documents. They transfer funds to us after they audit the documents. Now the NCMS funds are pooled at county level. We send the documents to the BoH regularly. The county BoH inspect us through auditing these documents. If they find some documents and items to be problematic, they may refuse to pay funds to us. (C20120918WKZ)

As the NCMS management office was a section or agency of the county BoH, the BoH, as a higher authority, might occasionally enact a number of rules to assist its inspections. For example, in 2008, the Provincial Department of Health (DoH) in our investigated province promulgated an adapted version of a "six-item ban." This administrative ban was used by county NCMS management offices to inspect individual doctors.

> The NCMS…implements a six-item ban that prohibits the embezzlement and fraudulent acquirement of NCMS funds, irrational admission of inpatients and extension of their length of stay, abuse of the formularies of services and drugs and the regulations of reimbursement, and provision of false and concealed information. If we [a secondary urban hospital in City C] violate these regulations, they will publish an administrative notice of criticism and even cancel our designated membership. (C20120918GKZ)

Similar to NCMS management offices, urban SHI agencies also inspected patients' medical records to judge overtreatment. An officer in the urban SHI agency of City C said that he had to rely on medical records, although the latter were not accurate evidence.

> When we go to conduct inspections, we rely on patients' medical records. If both a cold and the prescription of related drugs are recorded, we will deem it reasonable; if there are no records of a cold but prescription of drugs for curing a cold, we will deem it to be excessive prescription. However, medical records are written by doctors, so doctors can also argue the use of these drugs, which makes doctors seize the initiative on drug prescription. Nevertheless, we trust doctors; we trust that medical records are genuinely written. A medical record is the only indicator we can rely on to judge overtreatment. We have no alternatives. That is why many things are unclear with a fee-for-services payment. (C20120910ZJ)

However, urban SHI agencies used more innovative methods of regular inspection than NCMS management offices, such as the controlled approval of prescribing expensive drugs and medical tests, the establishment of a special information platform to facilitate inspection, and the launch of an SHI doctor system to supervise individual doctors.

> The municipal SHI agency forbids our doctors from prescribing some drugs and medical tests without its approval. We have to apply for the approval before we can prescribe them. Most of these drugs and tests are expensive. For example, if the price of an oral drug goes beyond ¥30 for a box, it needs to be approved. (B20120926ZYS)

In particular, an information platform was established by the municipal SHI agencies to facilitate inspections by employing information management, building databases, and upgrading software. An officer in the urban SHI agency of City C said that it coincided with the grand trend of "internetization, digitalization, and informatization."

> We [the municipal SHI agency of City C] have to rely on information management, building databases and upgrading software to conduct inspections. The amount of government employees [here the interviewee denoted staff members in the SHI agency] is controlled rigidly, the increase of which is quite difficult. We have to count on the improvement of inspection software…The information platform is so important that it can solve the inadequacy of inspections. Internetization, digitalization, and informatization all rely on the development of software. The admission of inpatients in the City People's Hospital in City C alone reaches hundreds. Our City C has so many hospitals and inpatients that it is impossible to audit their services one by one by labor power. The development of software could save labor power to a great extent. We can see and monitor the data on computers. For example, if someone is prescribed Roxithromycin at 11:30 a.m., I can see that and its spending simultaneously in my office. We can set some fixed parameters and risk values and establish a warning system beforehand. If hospitals spend excessively, the alarm will be raised to show the drugs or tests that are overprescribed. We will go to inspect and ask doctors after that. This is just an ideal state. We are unable to do it now. (C20120910ZJ)

Apart from innovation in technology, urban SHI agencies tried to use an SHI doctor system as innovation in policy. The SHI doctor system launched in City C was believed "to transfer the priority of management from medical services to doctors."

> We [the municipal SHI agency of City C] implement an SHI doctor system to transfer the priority of management from medical services to doctors. There have been some doctors being fined due to their violation of our regulations. That is to say that doctors are managed by both hospitals and the SHI agencies. We set up an entrance exam to recruit SHI doctors and an evaluation scoring system to supervise them. If they violate our regulations, we will deduct certain scores; if the scores are deducted to a certain degree, we will cease the eligibility of these doctors as SHI doctors or warn them. WZR, the director of our agency, went to the Ministry of Human Resources and Social Security to attend a meeting. She heard that the state may enact a nationwide uniform policy of the SHI doctor system. Moreover, the extent of SHI doctors may be expanded further to include nurses and pharmacists in hospitals and pharmacies. (C20120912XDW)

Fifth, punishment. Urban SHI agencies and NCMS management offices imposed punishment on those health facilities that violated the rules of funding safety, payment methods, indicator management, and inspections.

Most of the investigated officers from urban SHI agencies did not call this "punishment," because the relationship between urban SHI agencies and health facilities was not an administrative subordination but a contractual relationship. However, if the health facilities breached their contracts with urban SHI agencies, the latter could refuse to reimburse them. For example, a number of doctors said that if urban SHI agencies found an excessive use of drugs outside of the SHI drug formulary or high abnormality of indicators, the agencies could refuse to pay the relevant reimbursement, instead forcing the health facilities to pay reimbursement to patients.

> The county SHI agency inflicts rigorous inspections of our doctors. If we [a county hospital in County D] use many drugs outside of the SHI drug formulary, patients may complain to the SHI agency. A doctor as individual has to be responsible for it. So we have to try our best to use drugs and tests within the formularies. Although the county SHI agency has no

> detailed regulations on the proportion of the cost of drugs outside of the formulary, we have to use these drugs with the agreement of patients. If we use them without agreement, the SHI agency may audit our medical records. If we use much of them, patients may be refused reimbursement. The SHI agency forces our hospital to pay reimbursement for patients. (D20121030FYS)

If health facilities were forced to pay reimbursement, some of them might ask the doctors in charge to pay reimbursement instead. A doctor in a tertiary hospital in City A said he was very unsatisfied with such things.

> The urban SHI agency introduces more rigorous inspections than the NCMS management office. The former sets up some indicators for us. If we exceed the regulations of these indicators, we will be fined. Our doctors have to pay reimbursement ourselves instead of by our hospital. These things happen frequently these years. We are quite unsatisfied with them. (A20121019ZYS)

If a serious violation of the urban SHI scheme rules was detected in a health facility, its membership as a designated facility might cease or even be canceled. An officer in the urban SHI agency of City C said that this kind of punishment was inflicted in reality.

> If there emerged a serious violation of our rules in hospitals, we will for sure cancel their designated membership. There were some hospitals violating the rules, and we ceased their designated membership. (C20120911XDW)

A few of the strategies used by the NCMS management offices were similar to those used by the urban SHI agency, but most of them were different. As the NCMS management office was affiliated to the BoH, both administrative and economic punishment could be imposed by either the NCMS management office alone, or by the NCMS management office and BoH jointly. For overtreatment in health facilities, for example, they might inflict an economic penalty by refusing to pay reimbursement, or an administrative penalty by publishing notices of criticism. However, a deputy director of the NCMS management office of County D said that they seldom ceased designated membership as a punishment; similarly, a doctor in a CHC said that economic penalty also seldom happened. This might be because health facilities were affiliated to the BoH, with the closeness of the relationship breaking the rigidity of supervision.

> If we [the NCMS management office of County D] find serious problems existing in hospitals and THCs, we will often impose economic penalty upon them. Sometimes we just publish an administrative notice of criticism. Although the rules regulate that we can cancel their designated membership if necessary, we haven't done that indeed. (D20120906PZR)
>
> The district BoH inspects our CHC frequently. Their inspections are rigid. They are not responsible for the staffing in our CHC, rendering the inspections even more rigid. That is because they are not familiar with our doctors and therefore dare to inflict economic penalty. If we are in the same system with them, they will not. Moreover, they also cannot inflict administrative punishment because they are not in charge of the staffing in our CHC. What they can do is just economic penalty. If we violate their rules, they will deduct funding allocated to us, which is equivalent to economic penalty. But these fines are not inflicted frequently, although they evaluate us through scoring every year. (B20121101GSL)

Sixth, tripartite negotiation. Urban SHI agencies piloted tripartite negotiation to decrease the price of drugs, health services, and medical tests. Tripartite negotiation involved liaising with key stakeholders, including urban SHI agencies, health facilities, and pharmaceutical suppliers, to influence medical costs.

In City C, the municipal SHI agency negotiated with CHCs and pharmaceutical suppliers to decrease the prices of 30 kinds of medicines for serious chronic conditions. As discussed in the behavior management mechanism section of Chap. 4, the agency used this policy to guide patients with chronic conditions to CHCs to purchase drugs at low prices. This was beneficial in two ways: it either adjusted patients' care-seeking behaviors, or it contained the inflation of the cost of drugs.

> We chose some CHCs to participate in the negotiation of the prices of medicines for serious chronic conditions. We referred to their geographic distribution and chose those serving a large number of insurance enrollees and being generally recognized and accepted by enrollees…We chose about 40 CHCs in our city. Moreover, the reimbursement of the UEBMI has three categories, including reimbursement for inpatient services, reimbursement for outpatient services and serious chronic conditions, and individual account. We selected some drugs for serious chronic conditions and negotiated their prices. We first selected the most commonly used but expensive drugs that were identified and reported by the CHCs. We selected 30 types of drugs as a result. After that, we conducted an initial negotiation with the suppliers of these drugs. After negotiation, the prices of these drugs bought in the CHCs generally decreased, with 18% decrease on average and 40% for some. (C20120912XDW)

The municipal SHI agency of City C also negotiated with some hospitals, transforming them into fair-price hospitals. These hospitals provided a number of discounts for drugs and medical tests and free services for patients, especially disadvantaged patients.

> We implemented the fair-price hospital system. We promulgated regulations about the fair-price hospitals and selected some from all hospitals in the city. We provided the selected hospitals with some preferential policies by raising reimbursement rates and decreasing deductibles for patients going there. These hospitals were required to provide some discounts of drugs and medical tests and free services. Some hospitals provided 10 kinds of free services and eight kinds of discounted services. People who are poor and unable to afford expensive medical services could go to these fair-price hospitals. (C20120911XDW)

The municipal SHI agency of City B collaborated with hospitals to negotiate with pharmaceutical suppliers over the prices of several medical consumptive materials. The agency trusted hospitals to negotiate the prices of the materials with the pharmaceutical suppliers, rather than directly with the suppliers of the materials. In the opinion of the agency, hospitals had more power of negotiation than the agency had.

> We negotiated with the City People's Hospital about the prices of consumptive materials for curing hemodialysis, with which I personally am very satisfied. There are so many patients receiving hemodialysis, which is an advantage for our SHI agency. We first negotiated with the hospital which in turn made a contract with the suppliers of these materials. So it was the City People's Hospital that took advantage of its group purchasing…It had a big power of negotiation. We didn't dare to negotiate directly with the

suppliers of medical consumptive materials. We didn't dare to say that if the suppliers didn't lower the prices, we would not use the materials provided by these suppliers any more. We also didn't dare to ask hospitals to use the materials provided by the suppliers from Shanghai rather than those from Tianjin. We could not take the responsibility once medical accidents happened. However, hospitals have more advantages than us in that they are professional to select the materials. Therefore, we used effectively their advantages. We asked hospitals privately to negotiate with the suppliers to get the lowest prices. The result was good. The prices of these materials decreased from over ¥100 to over ¥90. Although the prices decreased not much, it was a remarkable breakthrough. To be honest, the expenses of the patients receiving hemodialysis are really too high. They consume one tube each time and go to hospitals twice or three times a week. What we did is good for the patients. Moreover, the awareness of hospitals in cost control is reinforced. They are actively negotiating with pharmaceutical suppliers. In the past, they were always in conflict with us. If we refused to pay their excessive spending, they would be unhappy. The doctors complained too. Now it really is progress in that they support our work. Changchun City is also conducting a good pilot in negotiation. However, most of the areas in China are still suffering. (B20120927SKZ)

In addition to the above achievements, urban SHI agencies in our investigated area used tripartite negotiation to cancel the markup on some medicines from medicine retailers, decrease the prices of medical device tests, manage patients' choices of hospitals, and so on. On the strength of the increasing scale of the SHI funds, urban SHI agencies were exploring more and more methods to boost tripartite negotiation.

5.2 The SHI Agency: A Weak Purchaser

As we demonstrated earlier, SHI agencies used multiple strategies to restrain cost inflation in health facilities. However, the quantitative analysis in Chap. 3 revealed that SHI participation had a statistically positive relationship with medical expenditures and OOPS. Why did these strategies fail to contain cost inflation? What was the role of the SHI agency in cost containment? We first examine the interaction between SHI agencies and other stakeholders in the healthcare sector.

Our fieldwork and qualitative investigation revealed that although an SHI agency employed multiple approaches to control cost inflation, it remained a weak purchaser. Three themes were revealed through our thematic analysis, including the problems of incentive, scarce resources, and unaffordable transaction costs. To be specific, an SHI agency was a weak purchaser mainly because it suffered from poor incentives containing cost inflation, had scarce resources, and was unable to afford the excessively high transaction costs.

5.2.1 Incentive Problems

Both urban and rural SHI agencies in China lacked incentives and political responsibility for containing medical cost inflation. However, they did care about the safety of SHI funds, often using crude strategies to control cost inflation instead of implementing prudent design, and effective tactics and indicators.

Overemphasis on the safety of SHI funds overrode all other concerns for managing the funds, such as cost effectiveness and reasonable spending. A financial director in the municipal SHI agency of City C explained that even a reform of the management of SHI funds was deemed to be harmful to funds' safety and was therefore forbidden by the higher authority.

> Regulations [on the safety of SHI funds] in the past years were strict. The provincial government had enacted some regulations, so our city-level government and agencies could not violate them; it was forbidden to break through the regulations of funds and to do some innovations. The requirement on the safety of SHI funds was very strict, and the policy control was rigid. (C20120917WW)

Some respondents said that even if SHI agencies conducted some cost containment, such as a reform of payment methods and inspections of the behaviors of healthcare providers, their aims were not directly to control unreasonable medical costs. Any cost containment strategies were probably implemented due to the emerging threat to the safety of SHI funds, the incidence of corruption relating to SHI funds, or the inspections by higher authorities.

> As far as I [an SHI reimbursement manager in a tertiary hospital in City C] know, the reason why the NCMS of our province enforced a global budget was because the reimbursement rate (at the beginning of this year) had been set too high…therefore nearly 40% of NCMS funds were spent in the first three months of this year; if the benefit level went on, the total funds were definitely insufficient. So, a global budget was implemented to avoid the crash of funds. Meanwhile, the reimbursement rates were lowered and the deductibles were raised. (C20120918WKZ)

In the investigated province, a serious case of corruption occurred in one of its cities three months earlier. The provincial Communist Party of China Commission for Discipline Inspection took the lead to inspect the fraudulent acquirement of NCMS funds and medical overtreatment; as a result, the county NCMS office of County D enhanced the density of inspections.

> In the past three months, we have been working hard on inspections, the repeated inspections; health facilities inspected themselves first, then we the NCMS management office inspected them, after that the municipal government would inspect them, and eventually the provincial Communist Party of China Commission for Discipline Inspection will inspect them…This year the reasonable prescription of medicine and diagnosis and the problems of overtreatment are prioritized; the inspections are highly intense. (D20120906PZR)

This safety-oriented management interplayed with central government regulations concerning the reduction of large surpluses of SHI funds. Local SHI agencies could neither overspend the funds nor keep too much surplus; thus, this reduced any incentive to contain costs. An NCMS reimbursement manager in the investigated THC in County D said,

> [When the global budget was implemented], the county BoH would reward us if our THC could keep the surplus of NCMS funds at less than 10% of all the funds assigned to us, because the most important task of the BoH is to keep the safety of NCMS funds; therefore,

keeping a little surplus is the best choice. However, if we keep too much surplus, the BoH would punish our THC. (D20120816ZHX)

Conversely, the incentive problems experienced by SHI agencies were exaggerated by a lack of top-level policy design by related higher institutions. In a country with such centralized politics as China, local authorities receive incentives for and legitimization of their actions from the regulation of higher authorities. However, neither central nor local governments enacted detailed reform strategies of SHI third-party purchasing. Some officers in the municipal SHI agencies of both City C and City B said that without top-level policy design, they had no standard by which to evaluate the costs of medical services and facilitate negotiation.

About the tripartite negotiation…the central government just mentioned through a sentence in its healthcare reform guidelines in 2009, but has not said more until now, and has not said clearly which government departments will participate in the negotiation, not even a sentence. All depends on the exploration of localities…If there is an official document providing clear requests and some guidance, it would benefit the practical work. (C20120912XDW)

I have some worries on this [negotiation on drug prices], because it will inevitably refer to a question of percentage in the future…For example, we want hospitals to reduce their profits, but how much percentage of profits? 5%, 10%, or 20%? What is the standard? Without these, our negotiation becomes quite unclear…Moreover, what is the process of negotiation? We have no standard to rely on…Personally I think it is unwise to do unclear things. (B20120927SKZ)

Without these detailed regulations, officers in SHI agencies had no strong incentive to inspect the work of healthcare providers, or to refuse to pay reimbursement to those healthcare providers who committed overtreatment or other illegal behaviors. In practice, there were seldom cases of refusing to pay reimbursement to health facilities.

We [the county SHI agency of County D] don't go frequently to inspect hospitals. Apart from the refusal of paying reimbursement to hospitals, hospitals themselves have a set of rules of self-management. If they find some doctors conducting abnormal behaviors, they will fine the doctors. But few of them enforce punishment rigorously. Moreover, although our county SHI agency also has rules of inflicting penalty, it is not easy to implement. We should refuse paying reimbursement to hospitals if the latter are found with many problems. But we have scarcely done it these years. (D20121030GZR)

Inspection and approval of medical records…we [the municipal SHI agency of City B] normally just have several officers to have a general look at them; we cannot refuse to pay reimbursement to the hospitals crudely…so refusal of payment rarely happens. (B20120924WKZ)

An NCMS inspector in the investigated THC said that although she was affiliated with the county NCMS management office and took charge of inspecting the work of the THC, she had to maintain good relationships with its director and doctors and would not report the problems she found to the county NCMS management office.

I [an NCMS inspector who was arranged in THC A to conduct inspections regularly] scarcely go to the county NCMS management office. If this THC does some unsatisfactory things, I would communicate with the director of this hospital first, telling him to resolve the problems in time. I will not report to the county NCMS office if the hospital has already resolved them; if I find some problems and then go to report them to the county office, it will not be appropriate, either to the director or doctors of this THC. (D20120904PJGY)

Correspondingly, due to both the overemphasis on fund safety and the lack of top-level policy design, SHI agencies' most used methods of cost containment were adjustment of reimbursement benefits or crude change of payment methods, rather than controlled perverse incentives for doctors and the moral hazard problem in relation to patients. Obviously, the former methods were direct and easy to implement, while the latter would not only cost more and need a larger personnel, but foresaw no obvious results. Moreover, some SHI agencies had poor management capabilities and did not establish a clear budget for future spending; therefore, they adjusted the reimbursement rates and deductibles frequently, and even set a low reimbursement level at the beginning of the budget year and conducted a second-round reimbursement at the end of budget year if there were large surplus funds.

The regulations of the NCMS in this county [County D] change quite fast, and change once every several months. This is because the management of NCMS funds is difficult; if the surplus funds is much, the policy will regulate a high reimbursement rate; if the surplus is little, the regulations will be tightened. (D20120816ZHX)

If the surplus of SHI funds is abnormal, we will adjust reimbursement regulations in time… first, increase the reimbursement rate…second, adjust deductibles and ceiling amounts… third, provide some reimbursement items for some special patients, like benefit packages for patients using hemodialysis…We use these methods to adjust the rate of surplus of SHI funds. (C20120917WW)

5.2.2 Scarce Resources

The hidden rule for the establishment of an SHI agency was the so-called "small horse pulling a large cart," which required SHI agencies to manage substantial funds of various SHI schemes with limited personnel and resources. However, the "horse" in reality was too small to be able to pull the large cart. Both urban and rural SHI agencies lacked sufficient financial resources, personnel, and facilities to restrain medical cost inflation.

The administrative funds of SHI agencies were earmarked especially by the government. However, these funds were so inadequate that SHI agencies were unable to carry out high quality management and innovations. Table 5.1 shows that the earmarked administrative funds of Chinese SHI agencies in 2010 accounted for only 1 % of SHI funds, far less than those of other countries. SHI funds were regulated to be used for fixed purposes and were forbidden from being embezzled. So SHI agencies could only expect the funds to be earmarked by the government if they intended to conduct any kind of reform. The investment by central government was insufficient, while that of local governments varied greatly. Some governments in poor areas always ran short of finances. The shortage of administrative funds directly decreased work incentives and the management capability of SHI agency administrators.

Table 5.1 Resource input of health insurance agencies in various countries

Country	Organizations/schemes	Year	No. of administrative officers (unit: 1000 persons)	No. of insured people (unit: 1000 persons)	Average no. of insured people for one insurance officer	No. of medical staff (unit: 1000 persons)	Average no. of medical staff for one insurance officer	Proportion of administrative funds to insurance funds (%)
Finland	Social Security Institute	2003	5.2	5200	1008	–	–	6.3
Ireland	Voluntary Health Insurance Board	2003	0.7	1490	2031	–	–	9.8
Australia	Health Insurance Commission	2003	4.7	20,600	4377	–	–	2.9
India	Employees' State Insurance Corporation	2003	21.8	39,500	1813	–	–	3.8
Germany	Statutory Health Insurance	2002	65.4	–	–	335	5	5.6
Canada	National Health Insurance	2000	178.7	–	–	793	4	–
United States	Commercial Health Insurance Schemes	2000	3037.7	–	–	8557	3	–
Singapore	Medisave	2000	0.6	–	–	8	13	–
China	UEBMI + URBMI	2010	422.3	432,630	10,245	8208	129	1.1
	NCMS	2010	215.5	836,000	38,800			

Sources Social Insurance Institute of Ministry of Labor and Social Security (2005); Ministry of Human Resources and Social Security (2011); Zhou (2011); Ministry of Health (2013). *Note*. As there are no published data, the number of administrative officers of the NCMS in China is an estimated value, which includes only the officers at county NCMS offices with those at provincial and municipal NCMS offices excluded. The value is an estimate based on a survey of 144 counties in China conducted by Song et al. (2008)

Except for the administrative funds, compared with other countries, personnel resources of SHI agencies in China were scarce, as Table 5.1 shows. Each SHI agency usually had tens of staff members who had to face thousands of medical workers and millions of insured people. Some officers of SHI agencies expressed their worries about scarce personnel:

> Our bureau [a municipal SHI agency] has a staff of 40, which is really inadequate. So our work pressure is high. It is impossible to make good stewardship just relying on one bureau. You see, the Municipal Central Hospital has thousands of staff members; there are three tertiary grade A hospitals and seven tertiary hospitals in our city; therefore, not to mention a staff of 40, can we manage well even if with a staff of 400? (B20120920BJZ)

Without adequate personnel, both rural and urban SHI agencies were unable to dispatch enough staff members to inspect the work of health facilities. As described above, SHI agencies still relied mainly on labor power to inspect abnormal prescription behaviors. In practice, each urban SHI agency only had one or two people being responsible for the inspection work. It was impossible to prevent the excessive prescription of drugs, medical tests, and services with so few inspectors.

> We [a county urban SHI agency] have an auditing office that has two people, one male and the other female. They go to inspect hospitals regularly. However, the male staff member is often drafted by the government to inspect other works like the prohibition of stalk burning in the harvest seasons…Our center has a staff of 16 in total. That phenomenon (medical overtreatment) cannot be prohibited completely even if all of our staff are dispatched to inspect and we inspect one hospital every one week…Our center also has a regulation on punishing hospitals [refusal of paying SHI funds], but it is hard to implement…The punishment was rarely executed, almost none in these years. (D20121030GZR)

Compared with urban SHI agencies, county NCMS management offices had more specialized inspectors. Each THC was assigned an NCMS inspector. However, it was difficult for one inspector to monitor the whole work of a THC. In addition, as demonstrated earlier, because there was no incentive to supervise overtreatment, the NCMS inspector was unwilling to be demanding of the health facilities.

> The provincial government arranges special township NCMS inspectors…However, to be honest, when they start their work, their power is too weak; [each THC] has only one or two inspectors who have to face the whole health center. This is difficult. So the inspectors play a weak role…They are arranged in hospitals. You see, as time goes by, they always stay with other people in hospitals, and then they cannot conduct their work smoothly. (D20120906PZR)

In addition, with inadequate personnel, staff members of SHI agencies were always exhausted by complicated policy implementation. This was also a characteristic of Chinese grassroots government departments, which operated under the stewardship of multiple higher authorities that required complex administrative work. A deputy director in the county NCMS management office of County D said that because of this complicated work, they were too exhausted to implement a DRGs payment reform.

> The Diagnosis-Related Groups payment was implemented only in the department of gynecology in the County People's Hospital, with a few diseases being involved, like hernia, appendicitis, and so on. Although this payment was required to be implemented mandatorily…many of the policies in our country are like this. They are enacted but cannot be enforced in locality. To be honest, our work is quite complicated and demanding. One policy just comes out, followed by another policy immediately. We are exhausted to handle so many policies. Sometimes we are incapable to enforce some policies. (D20120906PZR)

Moreover, it was not only a problem of the number of personnel, but also a problem of quality. The medical knowledge and actuarial capability or negotiation skills of the officers at SHI agencies were severely insufficient, as a number of officers in the municipal SHI agencies of both City B and City C stated.

> The management level of our bureau [the municipal SHI agency of City B] is low and cannot be geared to international standards. With regard to something like reimbursement rates, deductibles, ceiling amount, and so on, we should hire special actuaries to estimate them, but now we just let our own bursary do some crude calculation. Our management pressure is extremely high with the current pay-as-you-go SHI system. (B20120921BJZ)
> There are only a few staff members who are medical graduates, or are hired after they retire as doctors, or are seconded from hospitals to our bureau [the municipal SHI agency of City C]. But these kinds of people are really few…[Most of us] do not have strong medical expertise. If we have, we will not stay here but go to hospitals to become doctors, and then we will have good income. (C20120910ZJ)

Due to a lack of medical knowledge, officers in SHI agencies were appraised by doctors to be unqualified to judge overtreatment by doctors. Because healthcare was a highly specialized sector, SHI inspectors could hardly know whether a case of prescription and treatment was appropriate, or not.

> Although the county SHI agency and the NCMS management office inspect our work [a county hospital in County D] frequently, both are unprofessional. What they inspect most is whether patients are in bed, what their names are, and so on. They just make sure that no patient leaves hospital without permission or no doctor counterfeits medical records. Sometimes, they even just check the photos to identify patients. Is a photo taken a few years ago the same as the one taken now? Is a photo showing one's normal appearance the same as what he looks like when he is ill? Even if an uninsured patient pretends to be one having insurance, the inspectors cannot detect it. Furthermore, a patient may get a kind of disease, while his doctor may record two or three kinds of diseases. Can the inspectors find it? All of them are unqualified to detect these problems. They have no medical knowledge. What they are doing is just having a look at medical records. But medical records are written by doctors. A professional person writes something and shows it to an unprofessional person. How can the latter know what it is? Most of the inspectors have not received professional training of medical knowledge. (D20121030FYS)

As well as a lack of administrative funding and personnel, the facility arrangement, especially the information system of SHI agencies, was outdated. The information system was the main platform for SHI agencies to monitor cost inflation in health facilities and could overcome the shortage of personnel. The funding for establishing such an information system was also earmarked especially by the government. However, it was rather insufficient, too. This slowed down the establishment of information system, which further exacerbated the malfunction of SHI agencies in cost containment.

> Although our city is one of the two pilots establishing an instant tele-inspection system in our province, this is just propaganda. It cannot be expected when the establishment can be realized…Now, from the perspective of our SHI agency, the information support provided by them [the Information Center of the Municipal BHRSS of City B] is highly insufficient…we cannot even do statistical analysis with the current software. So our officers are really tired, because we have to export the data first, and then import to other software to do analysis when we need. (B20120921BJZ)

What was more, the information system collected data from health facilities, which meant that health facilities had to install data terminals. Therefore, the implementation of the information system relied on investment by both the government and the health facilities. A department head in the municipal SHI agency of City C said that neither SHI agencies nor primary health facilities and small hospitals had enough investment to install data terminals.

> Instant tele-inspection…we have not realized it yet. I heard that this software costs millions of Chinese yuan…We have not realized it mainly because of shortage of funds…The provincial Department of Human Resources and Social Security issued a policy document this year, assigning a task of requiring some cities to establish instant tele-inspection. However, they didn't earmark funds to us. Moreover, the establishment of this system also needs the investment of hospitals. It is okay for large hospitals because they have money, but primary and secondary hospitals have no such strong financial ability. (C20120910ZJ)

5.2.3 *Unaffordable Transaction Cost*

The malfunction of SHI agencies in relation to cost containment derived not only from the agencies, but also from high transaction costs faced by the agencies when coordinating between departments. SHI agencies occupied no advantage in this process, generating excessively high transaction costs due to severe information asymmetry within the medical industry and complicated multi-departmental cooperation.

Doctors had highly specialized expertise that could not easily be gained by either patients or SHI agencies. As a result, strict inspections of doctors might suffer from flaws and risks. Judging overtreatment from looking at a medical record might not be appropriate, but required of more specialized tactics. This directly increased the negotiation and transaction costs when SHI agencies inspected health facilities. An officer at the municipal SHI agency of City C gave an example:

> Several years ago, a man got one of his legs hurt and could not be treated well for a long time. Later on, when we inspected the medical records of a doctor who delivered treatment to the man, we found that the doctor prescribed for the man a kind of drug Jieeryin, a vaginal washer for women. And we found that his leg was treated after he smeared the drug. Using Jieeryin to treat external injury, do you think whether it ought to be reimbursed? (C20120910ZJ)

On the one hand, if SHI agencies did not inspect the behaviors of doctors because of information asymmetry, the supplier-induced demand would be inevitably exaggerated. On the other hand, if SHI agencies inspected the behaviors of doctors strictly, both doctors and patients would have complained, therefore inducing conflict between them because SHI agencies could not judge fully the types and severity of patients' diseases as well as the rationality of the treatment prescribed by the doctors.

Some officers of SHI agencies said that with this dilemma, the practical choice for them was to turn a blind eye and not intervene much in the behavior of doctors, because they could not judge correctly the rationale behind the prescribed treatments. However, in the meantime, this reduced their ability to contain cost.

> For the same disease, there may be different treatment plans prescribed by different doctors in different regions. We, as an SHI agency, just observe and supervise them in accordance with the policies, the mechanisms and the well running of SHI funds; if we intervene in the treatment of doctors at the micro level, it is unwise. (C20120912XDW)

Moreover, the healthcare industry and its reform involved multiple interest groups, rendering inter-departmental cooperation complicated. In tripartite negotiations, SHI agencies had to deal with multiple groups including hospitals at different levels, clinics, pharmacy stores, pharmaceutical suppliers, and so on. One respondent deemed it extremely difficult to conduct sound negotiations, because the healthcare market had its own rules with which health facilities had to comply.

> Our bureau [the municipal SHI agency of City B] started the work of negotiation last year…It was hard to break through, because there was a price alliance among hospitals. If one hospital decreased its prices, the others had to decrease too. (B20120924SKZ)

In addition, the pharmaceutical market was large, which for a small SHI agency was hard to handle. Pharmaceutical representatives and suppliers of medical materials and devices often resisted negotiating with SHI agencies over the prices of drugs, medical consumptive materials, and devices.

> We [the municipal SHI agency of City C] tried to negotiate with suppliers of medical consumptive materials. You know, patients receiving hemodialysis needed to use the special one-time hemodialysis tubes which cost ¥200. There were over 80 patients receiving hemodialysis in City C. They wanted their economic burden to be decreased. We tried to ask the suppliers to lower the price of the tubes. But they resisted negotiating with us, because they said that this would disturb the market order in this region. For example, if they sold the tubes to our City C at ¥230 while to City AY at ¥250, the whole market in this region would be disturbed. The merchants in the upper reach would also be unhappy, will not cooperate with the suppliers anymore, and will find other representatives. The suppliers said that they have to comply with their industry rules too. (C20120910ZJ)

Furthermore, SHI agencies faced great difficulties with intergovernmental department cooperation. For example, in 2010, Chengdu City in Sichuan Province launched a tripartite negotiation on medical service costs. As many as 10 government departments participated in the negotiation, including the SHI agency, the Development and Reform Commission, the BHRSS, the Bureau of Bursary, the BoH, the Bureau of Supervision, the Bureau of Audition, the Bureau of Hospital Authority, and the Bureau of Drug Administration (Su, 2012). Its urban SHI agency was unable to coordinate cooperation between so many governmental departments.

SHI agencies could not handle interdepartmental cooperation, not only because of the multiple groups involved, but also because of its low administrative rank and outdated organizational establishment. The management of SHI schemes was severely localized. A municipal SHI agency was a division of the municipal BHRSS, and a county NCMS office was a section or agency of the county BoH. Their administrative ranks were equivalent to hospitals at city level and county level, respectively. Although SHI agencies had the responsibility of managing huge amounts of SHI funds, they had no corresponding administrative rank or power. According to the current policies, they had no rights or power to negotiate the prices of drugs, medical consumptive materials, and medical services. These rights were retained by the provincial joint office for centralized pharmaceutical tender and procurement.

> There are still no explicit regulations about the tripartite negotiation. All local areas are just muddling through, but it is difficult. The pharmaceutical representatives go to talk with the provincial joint office for centralized pharmaceutical tender and procurement directly; we are a municipal bureau and do not participate in the pharmaceutical tender. (B20120921BJZ)

To facilitate healthcare reform, both central and local governments had to establish special small leading groups to coordinate the cooperation of multiple departments, which simultaneously undermined the authority and role of SHI agencies.

Some localities began to give SHI agencies greater power by promoting their organizational establishment. However, this was slow progress. An officer of the county NCMS office of County D said that the outdated organizational establishment of the office undermined their authority in supervising hospitals.

> Several years ago, the county Establishment Committee issued a policy document which aimed at transforming us [the county NCMS office of County D] from an office to an agency of the county BoH, just like the county Anti-Epidemic Station, the Center for Disease Control, the Health Supervision Institute, and hospitals. But until now our organizational establishment has not been completely like these organizations…Although our number of staff is large, the organizational establishment lags behind…We have not been equipped with the matching funds and working places, so it is hard to implement much of our work. (D20120906PZR)

5.3 The Patient: The Weakest "Cheater"

The information advantage of healthcare providers over patients meant that the latter, as individuals, became vulnerable consumers when buying medical services. To deal with this backdrop, the SHI purchasing mechanism introduced SHI agencies as third-party purchasers to buy medical services from healthcare providers in representation of patients. In theory, SHI agencies managed the behaviors of both healthcare providers and patients with the purpose of mitigating perverse incentives for providers and moral hazard of patients.

However, we found that the SHI agencies in our investigated places could not effectively control the "moral hazard" problem. Patients tended to abuse health services by taking advantage of the SHI reimbursement, even cheating SHI officers to acquire the reimbursement. But it did not mean that these patients were an advantaged group when receiving medical services and reimbursement of SHI. They were still the weakest compared with doctors, SHI agencies, and the whole healthcare system. They abused medical services not only actively but sometimes passively, which was why we called patients in China the weakest "cheater."

5.3.1 Moral Hazard

SHI participation provided patients with substantial reimbursement of their medical expenses. However, it induced the moral hazard problem of patients who might abuse medial services. A doctor in a tertiary hospital in City A said that even a patient catching a cold would go to the hospital to receive inpatient services. If the doctor refused to admit a patient with a slight disease as an inpatient, the patient could complain to the hospital. Doctors therefore admitted them to avoid complaints.

> Generally speaking, patients' economic burden was reduced after the implementation of urban SHI schemes. However, in my opinion, many inpatients don't need to be hospitalized. They are admitted for the purpose of getting reimbursement. To be honest, they waste substantial healthcare resources. They really should not be hospitalized. They consume lots of SHI funds. As a result, the business of our department of gynecology has been boosted much in these years. In the past, there was no reimbursement. Many people were unwilling to go to hospitals. Now they can be reimbursed by SHI. So even when someone gets a cold, he/she would go to receive inpatient services. If the state ceased reimbursement for him/her, how dare he/she is hospitalized with a cold? Our Chinese have such kind of mind. Some patients with slight diseases intended willfully to be hospitalized. If our doctors don't permit, they will make a complaint against us. That is very absurd! But there is no way out. If they really make a complaint to the leaders of the hospital, we have to apologize to them and admit them to be inpatients. (A20121018TYS)

In the investigated province, the reimbursement rate of the NCMS was radically increased in 2012, with 90 % provided to patients hospitalized in THCs. It stimulated many outpatients to be admitted as inpatients for the purpose of obtaining more reimbursement benefits.

> The plan of the NCMS this year is too radical, with a 90% reimbursement rate for patients hospitalized in THCs, 80% in county hospitals, 70% in hospitals at city level, and 60% in hospitals at provincial level. The whole province started this plan on 1 January, while our city B started last November. That was because the surpluses in both the NCMS pooling account and the household account were substantial last year. The government increased the reimbursement rates with the aim of stimulating people to use these sedimentary deposits. However, it led to some problems. In my opinion, the provincial government increased the reimbursement rates too much. What was more, the government was unclear about the reasonable thresholds of spending for inpatient services and hospitalization days at which patients are eligible to be reimbursed. Therefore, it had no relevant regulations and

just increased reimbursement benefits. It increased the admissions of inpatients so much that even patients with slight diseases were hospitalized. With these substantial reimbursements, many outpatients transformed themselves into inpatients. Later on, the funds of the NCMS were spent too much and were near to be in deficit. After that, the government regulated that a patient had to be hospitalized for at least three days and spend at least ¥500 before he/she is eligible to be reimbursed. (D20120828GSQ)

NCMS patients preferred inpatient to outpatient services not only due to the radical increase of the reimbursement rate for inpatient services, but due also to the structure of reimbursement for outpatient services. Except for a big gap in the reimbursement rate between inpatient and outpatient services, the ceiling amount of the pooling funds for outpatient services was just ¥200 per person. Considering the serious cost inflation of healthcare in China, we could understand that an outpatient might quickly spend ¥200 and thereafter, pay out of pocket. Therefore, it was not surprising that they wanted to abuse inpatient services.

The amount of outpatients admitted to our THC in the latter half of the year decreased. Why? Although the reimbursement rate for outpatient services increased to 55%, the rate for inpatient services rose even more and got to 90%. Now even patients with slight diseases want to be admitted as inpatients. 90% is higher than 55% anyway. In addition, the ceiling amount of pooling accounts for outpatient services is just ¥200 per person. It is very low. For example, a patient comes to receive a drip infusion. If he/she is admitted as an outpatient, he/she will receive low reimbursement and will have to pay much out of pocket. Correspondingly, he/she is eager to be admitted as an inpatient. (D20120904DJ)

Although patients preferred to abuse inpatient services, it did not mean that they would not abuse outpatient services as well. As mentioned above, SHI agencies assigned their enrollees the eligibility to receive the reimbursement from pooling funds for outpatient services, which would expire at the end of year. An officer in the urban SHI agency of City C said that even people without illnesses would buy drugs using URBMI pooling, as they thought that "it would be a loss for them" if the eligibility expired.

The pooling account of URBMI for outpatient services suffers from many problems. People don't have to have an illness, but all have the right to get at most ¥200 of medical spending reimbursed. In the autumn, people easily catch a cold. However, even if not catching a cold, they still go to clinics to buy some drugs. They think that it would be a loss for them if they don't use the quota of ¥200. (C20120910ZJ)

In addition, moral hazard was induced not only by patients but by doctors, too. In this sense, we could say that doctors and patients conspired together to acquire the reimbursement of SHI, by both parties being willing to abuse medical services. Doctors could generate income, while patients could enjoy the reimbursement of SHI.

The state will launch the Serious Illness Insurance soon this year. Our province has enacted a similar policy, in that the NCMS reimburses 80% of expenses for inpatients spending over ¥60,000, and 90% for inpatients spending over ¥100,000. The purpose of this policy is good. It aims to reduce the OOPS of patients with catastrophic diseases. However, we find that this policy causes many problems in practice. For example, if a patient has spent over ¥50,000, the doctor will suggest that the patient spends ¥10,000 more to reach the 80% cut-off point. The patient is happy to agree with the doctor. But this causes many resources to be wasted, especially the overspending of NCMS funds. This policy is ill-considered because it is based on a fee-for-services payment. If it is based on a diagnosis-related group payment, it will restrain hospitals from conducting overtreatment…Another example is the regulation of the provincial government on reimbursement rates of the NCMS. The NCMS provides a 90% reimbursement rate for patients hospitalized in THCs with a deductible of ¥200. Correspondingly, some patients with slight diseases would not go to receive out-patient services, but to receive inpatient services. This is due to the inducement of doctors on the one hand; on the other hand, it is because patients are willing to do so. The benefits of both of them are in accordance. But it causes medical expenditures to be wasted. If a patient's illness could be cured via outpatient services, admission of him/her to be an inpatient would render much expenditure unnecessary. (D20120906PZR)

In County D, the father of a student patient counterfeited an NCMS certificate to acquire reimbursement under the guidance of a doctor, even though the student was enrolled in a school health insurance program.

I am working at the Administrative Office for Industry and Commerce of a county town. My daughter caught acute tonsillitis and received a surgery of tonsil extirpate last year. I have to say that the phenomenon of counterfeit is too serious in China. When my daughter received the surgery, the doctor suggested that I borrow an NCMS certificate to get more reimbursement. She was finally charged ¥2,000 for the treatment and was reimbursed ¥900. If I didn't borrow this certificate, I would have had to pay the full expenditure of ¥2,000. My daughter was attending a medical school where she was enrolled in the school health insurance. But the reimbursement procedure of the school insurance was quite complicated and required going through many formalities. I had no choice. So I borrowed an NCMS certificate. The doctors warned me many times that I must not let others know it; otherwise, he would be fined. (D20121030LY)

5.3.2 The Weak Role of Patients Compared with that of Doctors

Although patients might abuse health services and SHI reimbursement, they remained vulnerable compared to doctors with regard to their lack of medical knowledge and passiveness in clinical practices.

SHI agencies used indicator management as one method to prevent doctors from prescribing too many drugs and medical services outside of the SHI formularies. They also regulated that doctors had to seek patients' agreement before prescribing these kinds of drugs and medical services and tests. However, doctors might not follow this guide, because most patients had no relevant awareness. Patients played a weak role in monitoring the use of drugs outside of the SHI formularies due either to information asymmetry or to their unawareness. A doctor in a county hospital in County D said that the legal awareness of most Chinese people was outdated. Patients might not complain if being prescribed many expensive drugs, because they were satisfied as long as they obtained SHI reimbursement.

The county SHI agency and the NCMS management office regulate that doctors have to seek patients' agreement if they intend to use drugs outside of the SHI formularies;

> otherwise, the expenses of patients would be refused to pay if such kind of drugs are used too much. However, the regulation plays a weak role in practice. It still depends on the awareness of patients in constraining the use of drugs outside of the formularies. If these drugs are used too much, patients who know well the rules of reimbursement may ask doctors to explain. For those who know little, they won't ask doctors and just take the amount of reimbursement they obtain for granted. No organization can inspect doctors' behaviors in a professional manner. It all depends on patients' auto feedback and complaint. But most of the patients have no idea of medical knowledge and don't investigate these things. The legal awareness of most Chinese people is outdated. They take the reimbursement provided by the SHI schemes as extra benefits. Even if they get a small amount of reimbursements, they are satisfied. (D20121030FYS)

Moreover, patients valued health more than money. This was the case especially when their illnesses were severe; therefore, some doctors asked them to buy from pharmacies expensive drugs outside of the SHI formularies. This was either because the drugs might be necessary for clinical treatment but were not included in the SHI formularies, or because buying from pharmacies could decrease the proportion of the cost of drugs outside of the formulary. Whatever the reason was, patients had to pay much out of pocket as a result.

> I [a pharmaceutical sales representative] was a doctor in a tertiary hospital at provincial level. Some expensive drugs were outside of the SHI formularies or took a large share of the proportion of drug costs if being prescribed. For example, some expensive antibiotics cost hundreds of yuan for a piece. Doctors ask patients to buy them at pharmacies by themselves. These situations are common. The department of internal medicines relies on some antibiotics, and the department of oncology relies on some antineoplastic drugs. Some of these drugs cost even tens of thousands yuan for a piece. Doctors just let patients buy by themselves. (A20121019YXZ)

Because so many drugs outside of the SHI formularies were used in health facilities or were bought from pharmacies, the magnitude of the reimbursement of SHI was hindered. Patients had to pay much out of pocket even if they received SHI reimbursement.

> My father had caught carcinoma of the colon and was hospitalized in the city No. 2 People's Hospital three years ago. The total spending was over ¥40,000. The reimburse rate was just 40%. The reimburse rates of the NCMS were generally low at that time. At the same time, many drugs were not within the scope of reimbursement. We were finally reimbursed less than ¥10,000. The doctors prescribed many kinds of nutraceutical which were not eligible for reimbursement. For example, albumin cost ¥400–¥500 for a bottle but was not eligible for reimbursement. We used several bottles. After getting reimbursement, we still spent a lot out of pocket. Most of the expensive drugs were not eligible for reimbursement. (D20121025LZX)

5.3.3 The Weak Role of Patients Compared with that of the Healthcare System

Patients had a weak position compared not only with doctors, but the whole healthcare system. They were susceptible to the changes in the regulations of SHI agencies, as shown earlier. In addition, the implementation of grand policies, the status quo of the healthcare market, and even the decision of a director in a hospital might affect patients greatly.

In the investigated township in County D, for example, the NCMS provided both a household savings account and a pooling account for outpatient services. In theory, patients could access any designated clinic or the THC. In practice, however, the household savings account of the NCMS was constrained for consumption within the village clinics of the villages in which patients lived, while the pooling account was constrained to the THC. In addition, the pooling account was permitted to be used only after the household savings account funds had been depleted.

This rule didn't come from NCMS policies, but was the personal decision of the director of the THC. When this director was interviewed, he explained that the rule aimed to maintain the business of village doctors and avoid the loss of the NCMS pooling funds, because the slow internet development in village clinics might disenable the THC to collect data from village clinics on time, causing duplicated records of the consumption of pooling funds. However, some doctors provided different viewpoints. They said that the mandatory consumption of the household savings account in village clinics was to provide profits to village doctors, which might induce village doctors to refer patients to the THC rather than other health facilities. In addition, as the county BoH regulated a rigid proportion of drug costs for each hospital, the decision of that director was also to reduce the proportion in the THC, because most rural residents used their household savings account to buy drugs.

Whatever the reason, the territorially separate consumption of different accounts for outpatient services stimulated patients to buy their own drugs. For the patients who needed to receive outpatient services in the THC, they first had to expend their household savings account through buying drugs in village clinics, even if they did not need those drugs. What was worse, NCMS participation was based on a household as a whole, which meant that the premiums (¥30 for each member) of all members in a household were put into a household savings account of the NCMS. In a large-sized household, a member had to expend hundreds of yuan before she/he was admitted to the THC as an outpatient.

An alternative choice, as revealed in the following dialogue between a patient and a doctor in THC A, was paying out of pocket:

> Doctor TYS: Do you have the NCMS certificate? Do the deposits in your household account for outpatient services run out?
>
> Patient 1: No. I haven't expended the deposits.
>
> Doctor TYS: If the deposits are not expended, you won't be reimbursed for your spending in the THC.
>
> Patient 1: That's okay if I cannot be reimbursed. But I just don't understand. I am in the same township as the THC. Why do I have to expend the deposits in my household account before I can get reimbursement?
>
> Doctor TYS: You have to spend the deposits in your village clinic before you enjoy the reimbursement from the pooling account for outpatient services.

Patient 1: I am unable to spend all the deposits of all my family members. I have several family members. The deposits of ours, if added up, are too much for me.

Doctor TYS: I can't help you. You can't enjoy reimbursement if you don't expend the deposits. Let me check your NCMS certificate first…There is still ¥101 of deposits.

Patient 1: That's okay if I really can't be reimbursed. It's fine only if my disease gets cured. That's the regulations of the government. That's good if I can get reimbursed but is okay if I can't. Haha. (D20120904TYS)

In another case, a girl in County D caught aplastic anemia and spent over ¥300,000 for her treatment. After leaving hospital, she had to continue to take an expensive drug for rehabilitation. This drug cost ¥200 per box and it was outside of the NCMS drug formulary. Her parents behaved illegally to obtain reimbursement, as the mother describes below. Her parents were "cheaters" to acquire the reimbursement illegally, but most certainly were vulnerable compared with the pharmaceutical market where the prices of drugs were inflated. They were also vulnerable compared with the poor but demanding SHI system that excluded some expensive drugs from its formularies and provided an unsound reimbursement mechanism.

My daughter caught aplastic anemia last year. She was prescribed a kind of drug after she left the hospital and had to keep taking it. She consumed five to six boxes of this drug each month. The drug was quite expensive and cost ¥200 for a box. But it was out of the reimbursement scope of the NCMS. We had to pay out of pocket. Later on, we figured out a way. Every time we sought a doctor, we asked him to write two medical records, with one for this drug and the other for other drugs. Then we went to get reimbursement using the medical records for the other drugs. For example, when we went to buy this drug, we asked doctors to record what we bought as cyclosporine. Cyclosporine was within the reimbursement scope of the NCMS. The officers in the NCMS management office didn't know these things. What we did was actually illegal. But our medical spending was really too much, but we couldn't get reimbursed if we didn't do this. We had to use this strategy. Every time, we could get the reimbursement of ¥900 out of the expenses of over ¥1,000. (D20121028LTZ)

5.4 The Doctor: An Unhappy Reactor

Doctors in China were criticized for a long time for inducing unnecessary demands on patients, prescribing excessive and expensive drugs and tests, overcharging patients, and so on. Conversely, however, they received a low basic salary and had to compromise to earn bonuses by altering their prescribing behaviors; they suffered from heavy workloads as they had to compete to attract and retain patients to generate earnings for hospitals (Yip et al. 2010). Even worse, doctors were suffering from a deteriorating reputation, as both government and social media had been suggesting a decrease in the social morality of the medical profession (Yang et al. 2008; Bloom et al. 2000); the relationship between doctors and patients was deteriorating, and doctors often became victims of terrible violence (The Lancet 2010). To summarize, Chinese doctors were doing wrong, while suffering at the same time.

To redress these problems, the government tried to formulate the SHI purchasing mechanism. The aim of this mechanism lay in stimulating doctors to provide cost-effective services with payment and inspection by SHI agencies. How did doctors react to these strategies of payment and inspection? We traced the process, by discovering the concern of doctors, their attitude and recognition toward the strategies, and in turn, their reaction to these strategies.

5.4.1 Doctors' Concern

The increased reimbursement benefits of SHI no doubt provided extra resources to improve the development of hospitals and the business of doctors. However, doctors had to be inspected and monitored by SHI agencies. Hence, there would certainly be conflicts between SHI agencies and doctors. As stated by a chief physician in a mental health hospital in City C, the SHI agency's concern was to ensure the safety of SHI funds and to control cost inflation in health facilities, while that of the doctors was to realize both economic profits and medical safety. These different concerns collided.

> What the SHI agency cares about is finishing the task of SHI and ensuring the safety of SHI funds; what the hospital director cares about is earning revenue to sustain the development of the hospital. As head of the service department in a hospital, what I care about includes two parts: one is economic profit, the other is medical safety. I rest assured that I make rational diagnoses after I prescribe patients with medical tests; otherwise, I don't. The devices for medical tests have to perform well. If I prescribe a test of color ultrasonography, the diseases of patients would be detected with a high quality mirror image of the color ultrasonography; otherwise, they will be missed. All of these are substantially important either for guaranteeing medical safety or increasing our profits. Subsequently, medical expenditure is rising. We collide with the SHI agency who forbids us from overexpenditure of SHI funds. But we exceed the budget indeed. What should we do? Let our hospital director seek solutions. (C20120918WYS)

It had to be acknowledged that the economic profits earned by doctors were for both the hospitals and the doctors themselves. The part earned by doctors could be further divided into legal and illegal profits. Doctors earned a basic salary and a bonus from hospital revenues legally, as well as off-the-book income from overtreatment and drug kickbacks, and relied on both to make a living. That was why doctors continued to prescribe so many drugs outside of the SHI formularies even if SHI agencies inflicted strict inspections on the use of these drugs.

> I [the relative of a patient in County D] have a relative who was hospitalized in the Red Cross Hospital. His attending doctor prescribed a kind of drug which was promoted by a pharmaceutical company from Xi'an City. This drug was not within the scope of reimbursement. Other drugs were within the scope. The drug was bought privately by that doctor. That doctor told him the truth directly. His total expenditures were over ¥700. According to the rule of the NCMS, a patient hospitalized in THCs can get 90% of his expenditures reimbursed. My relative should spend less than ¥100 out of pocket in theory. But he finally spent ¥300 out of pocket. The doctor just explained that one of the prescribed

drugs was bought privately. He was really bold to say it. But he also explained that the drug was with good clinical efficiency. If so, how could a patient say no? (D20121105ZSF)

5.4.2 Doctors' Attitudes

During our fieldwork, doctors expressed extreme complaints against the payment methods reform and inspections launched by SHI agencies. When asked the effects of these strategies on their work, doctors were generally dissatisfied with either the fixed budget and indicators set by SHI agencies, or the way SHI agencies, especially those in urban areas, conducted inspections.

Generally, doctors protested that the fixed budgets assigned by SHI agencies were low, that they ignored the detailed conditions of diseases, and that the proportion of the cost of drugs outside of the SHI formularies could not fulfill their clinical needs. A chief physician in a mental health hospital in City C criticized that the actions of SHI agencies were not based on sufficient investigation.

It is rational for the urban SHI agency and the BoH to restrain total medical expenditures. However, they should suit their measures to the detailed conditions of diseases. The price of curing a disease has increased from ¥1,000–¥2,000 to ¥4,000–¥5,000. Why? Because our detective and treatment devices have both increased. But the SHI agency still sets fixed expenditures for our department of mental diseases, according to the criteria for general hospitals, and allows our expenditures to increase by only 5% annually. The SHI agency is unfamiliar with our practical conditions. It should set up its plan based on sufficient investigation. One shoe cannot fit all feet. Should our mental health hospital not buy CT and MRI devices? The SHI agency should raise our budget and growth rate to some degree based on sufficient investigation. A patient may spend tens of thousands for a month in a general hospital. It would be big money if the expenditure in a general hospital increases annually by 5%. But in a small hospital like us, a patient may spend just ¥3,500 for a month. How much money it is even if the expenditure increases annually by 10% or 20%? Not to mention 5%. All mental health hospitals suffer from a poor budget. (C20120918WYS)

A doctor in a tertiary hospital in City A warned that the fixed budget and indicator management might even increase total medical costs, because it forbade the prescription of some clinically significant drugs outside of the SHI formularies, which might produce unsatisfactory clinical effects.

Much supervision by the urban SHI agency and the NCMS management office is necessary, but generally speaking, it is too much. I would not say they are trailing us, but sometimes they do affect our clinical treatment. Some drugs outside of the SHI formularies are necessary for clinical treatment but we cannot use them. Therefore, the treatment produces an unsatisfactory effect and extends further hospitalization days and increases total costs. (A20121019GYS)

As well as the fixed budget and indicator management, doctors were also unsatisfied with the way in which SHI agencies, especially in urban areas, conducted their inspections. They criticized that they were bureaucratic and overly strict, and that they did not consider the clinical practices of health facilities. They opposed SHI agencies' intervention in their clinical practices.

> The SHI agency is just a bureaucratic organization…they set up a crude fixed budget for us, impose the restriction on us [a mental health hospital in City C], but they rarely do practical investigation. This is bureaucracy…when they inspect our medical records and expenditures, they judge its appropriateness according to their regulated rules and indicators. If our expenditures overrun according to their rules, then they judge our expenditures as over-expenditures; if they regulate drug usage not exceeding 15 days and we use drugs for 16 days, they deem our prescription of drugs to be a violation of the regulations…They use these rules to check our medical records one item by one item. (C20130918GKZ)

A doctor in a mental health hospital in City C even thought that the inspections by SHI agencies were beyond their authority, in that they conducted them and imposed punishment without coordinating with the BoH, which was the department in charge of health facilities.

> The inspections by the urban SHI agency are not only overly strict, but are beyond their authority. Hospitals are set up by the BoH, but the urban SHI agency goes directly to inspect hospitals, without the permission of the BoH. In theory, the urban SHI agency merely plays a role of inspector and monitor. However, it functions as a manager in practice. In theory, it should coordinate with the officers in the BoH who supervise SHI schemes. But now, once it allots a file, we will be fined. Before it fines us, it should at least coordinate with the BoH to explain where we went wrong. If it does this, I will say that what it does is an efficient monitoring. But now its power is expanded in that it acts as a king to intervene in our clinical practices. If it has no idea of the practical operations of hospitals, then how can it intervene? It is the BoH that provides detailed guidance to treat some diseases like chronic diseases. I think that the best way is to build the cooperation between the SHI agency and the BoH and then to select a major manager. If the SHI agency is set as a major manager, it should bring in the staff of the BoH to work together and to act coordinately. Without doing that, the role of the SHI agency should be an inspector rather than a manager. But now it acts as both an inspector and a manager; it always sets impractical action guidelines for us. What it does is beyond its authority. SHI agencies in the whole country are like this. (C20120918WYS)

5.4.3 Doctors' Reactions

Before exploring doctors' reactions to the strategies of SHI agencies, it is first necessary to note that the governance of the Chinese healthcare system continued to be poor. To be specific, the distorted price schedules set high-tech medical tests with high prices, the poor compensation system caused health facilities to rely on user charges to generate their revenues, SHI third-party purchasing was not sound, and the pharmaceutical system was penetrated with drug kickbacks. Poor governance enabled doctors to use a number of countermeasures in reaction to the regulations of SHI agencies and to compensate for their income. These countermeasures included rejecting patients with catastrophic diseases, forging medical records, compensating for the loss of drug profits with prescriptions for medical tests and services, and so on. At the level of the health facilities, a health facility might abuse the subsidies provided by SHI agencies for overexpenditure and endure temporary financial hardship in one year in order to receive more budget in the next.

Doctors might use the strategy of "cream skimming" to counteract the effect of a global budget. SHI agencies assigned a fixed budget to health facilities to control the cost inflation. To avoid deficit spending, doctors might refuse to admit some patients with catastrophic diseases who would consume too much of the budget assigned to them. An SHI reimbursement manager in a tertiary hospital in City A revealed this inconvenient truth:

> A global budget is dignified in improving the self-management of hospitals. But actually it just brings social conflicts to our hospitals, replaces the harmonious doctor–patient relationship with conflict between doctors and patients, and exaggerates the conflicts. The urban SHI agency sets up its budget in advance and forces hospitals to pay if hospitals' expenditures exceed the fixed budget. But how can we pay so much money? A global budget pushes us to select patients…Now we admit patients with catastrophic diseases very selectively, because their expenditures are high. If we accept all of them, we will suffer losses; we cannot afford these losses. (A20121018GJ)

Doctors might also invent medical records to counter inspections by SHI agencies and BoH. A doctor in a county hospital in County D said hospitals may counterfeit data to make their indicators of expenditure look good.

> The society now is hard to manage. The population is dense and ill-educated. A number of the published data in the health sector are faked. For example, a county government intends to set up a county hospital as a model and therefore controls the hospital rigidly. In order to meet the inspection request, the hospital draft doctors to forge a bulk of medical records that look good. The government declares that healthcare reform produces the desired effects as the expenditures and proportion of the cost of drugs decrease in its county hospital. However, can one county hospital represent all hospitals in the county? Are the statistical results true? (D20121030FYS)

In addition, BoH seriously monitored the proportion of drug costs, and urban and rural SHI agencies monitored the proportion of the cost of drugs outside of the SHI formularies. Both of these regulations aimed to avoid the overprescription of drugs. However, in practice, doctors might increase the prescription of device tests, lab tests, surgery, and other medical services to subsidize the loss of drug profit. The increasing prescription of these items would increase total medical costs, which would then further reduce both of the proportions mentioned above. Moreover, the increasing use of these items would compensate for the income of doctors and hospitals.

> The urban SHI agency regulates the fixed proportion of the cost of drugs, with no more than 18% for all kinds of drugs and no more than 10%–15% for drugs outside of the SHI formulary…To meet the requirement of limiting the proportion of drug costs, we have to use as few drugs as possible in the normal treatments. Usually we encourage patients to buy drugs by themselves after they leave our hospital. During the treatment, we try to use multiple services, such as electronic stimulation, MTT assay, and so on…If patients are hospitalized, we use as many medical tests and treatment services as possible for them. So the proportion of drug costs in our hospital does not look so high. (C20120918GKZ)

In its normal operations, a hospital might link the prescription of medical tests and services to the income of doctors. It aims at revenue generation through the overcharge and overtreatment by doctors. A doctor in a CHC in City B said that many large hospitals permitted doctors to extract profits as extra income from each medical test.

> In the large-scale hospitals, the excessive use of medical tests like CT is really severe. This is a serious social problem. Hospitals set directly earning criteria for doctors. For instance, a doctor can extract ¥50 if providing a CT scan, ¥100 for an MRI scan, and so on. How can the excessive use of medical tests not be prevalent with these criteria? The criteria set by hospitals are really bad…It was so in the past, and is so now too. Hospitals focus on revenue generation, and therefore stimulate doctors to provide unnecessary tests. Prescribing a CT scan may bring ¥50 to a doctor and the hospital may earn more, perhaps ¥100. But the cost of a CT scan may be just about ¥10. Therefore, how would they deny doing so? There is serious corruption, from hospitals to doctors. (B20121101GSL)

At the level of the health facilities, a health facility might abuse SHI subsidies for overexpenditure. A vice director of the urban SHI agency of City B reviewed that it was the regulation of providing subsidy for overexpenditure in health facilities that aggravated the excessive medical expenditures.

> We [the municipal SHI agency of City B] replaced the 2007 regulation of no subsidy for overexpenditure with the regulation of providing subsidy for their overexpenditure in 2009. Hospitals thought that we might have much surplus of UEBMI funds when we started subsidizing them. As a result, most of the hospitals spent excessively in 2009. However, we actually had not so much surplus of funds. Therefore, we didn't provide subsidy for their overexpenditure in 2009. Hospitals were highly unhappy. Although part of their overexpenditure might be reasonable, it was very abnormal when the overexpenditure were so excessive. We didn't provide subsidies and as a result, hospitals protested against us. (B20120921BJZ)

Moreover, to obtain a substantial amount of the fixed budget from SHI agencies in future, hospitals may endure temporary financial hardship by spending excessively and paying for their own overexpenditure. Because the fixed budget assigned to health facilities was based on the expenditures in past years, health facilities spending excessively would definitely receive a bigger fixed budget in the future. This abnormal strategy induced hospitals to neglect cost control.

> If we [a secondary mental health hospital in City C] follow the strategies of other hospitals to overcharge patients, the urban SHI agency would assign us with more budget in the next year…We plan to pay for our deficit in advance by ourselves. We continue to invite specialists, to introduce high-tech treatment items, and to admit as many patients as we can. So now we are just waiting. We spend more than our revenue and keep going, and next year the SHI agency would assign us with more fixed budget. (C20130918GKZ)

To summarize, doctors and health facilities obtained different benefits from SHI agencies. To counteract the effects of the purchasing strategies of SHI agencies, doctors and health facilities used many countermeasures to transform medical costs and gain as much funding as they could for self-development. However, due to these reactions, unnecessary services were prescribed to a larger extent than ever before. Medical costs could not be satisfactorily restrained, but instead were highly inflated. A doctor in a secondary hospital in City B revealed this paradox by saying that medical expenditures just "flow from some medical items to other items." He meant that medical expenditures were transformed from spending on drugs to spending on medical tests and services.

> Medical costs have inflated quickly in recent years. For example, the major expenditures for a department of medicines are on drugs. The government now requires the decrease of the proportion of drug costs and of device test costs. But the nursing costs will rise correspondingly. The cost of some items decreases, while that of other items will definitely rise. In the past, we might not charge for some items, but we may charge now. In total, a patient's expenditures will not decrease. They will just flow from some medical items to other items. It is impossible that drug costs decrease while others stay the same. Do doctors and nurses not want to survive? All in all, the government cannot provide a full salary to doctors. Doctors have to earn by user charges to make a living. They will use all kinds of countermeasures. (B20120926MYS)

5.5 The Disenabling Institutional Surroundings

All the actors were embedded in their institutional surroundings. Although the new round of healthcare reform in 2009 gave local SHI agencies major duties to improve third-party purchasing, the grand institutional and policy surroundings disenabled their initiatives, thus creating a paradox for third-party purchasing. These institutional factors included the poor compensation system, the distorted centralized pharmaceutical tender and procurement system, the fragmented SHI schemes, and the inequitable allocation of healthcare resources.

5.5.1 The Poor Compensation System

China had been experiencing serious health cost inflation since the 1990s. Retrenching government finance was criticized to be one of the most salient risk factors because it stimulated perverse incentives for doctors. Without adequate government finance, health facilities had to rely on user charges to survive, which exacerbated supplier-induced demands. The poor compensation system reduced the magnitude of the purchasing efforts of SHI agencies. A deputy director from the NCMS management office of County D said that the state did not infuse many resources to county hospitals; therefore, the NCMS management office would not conduct strict inspections of hospitals because hospitals had to survive via user charges.

> We [the NCMS management office of County D] run up against considerable opposition to our inspections. The state gave priority to the development of primary care facilities in 2009 and infused considerable resources to THCs. After finishing the establishment of the infrastructure of THCs, the state now focuses on the development of county hospitals. The County People's Hospital and the County Chinese Medicine Hospital obtained ¥30 million to improve their facilities this year. Therefore, if our policies are unfavorable to the development of these health facilities, the latter won't enforce the policies. We cannot

complain much. These health facilities have to survive and earn income. The state didn't infuse many resources to them but still positioned them as public organizations. But actually they have not been public in nature. (D20120906PZR)

To reform the poor compensation system, the government increased health finance, starting from the early 2000s, especially following the new round of healthcare reforms in 2009. Both central and local governments increased subsidies for enrollment to SHI schemes, infrastructure development and medical staff training of primary health facilities, provision of public health services, and so on. The government targeted about 30 % of its new funding at rural and primary care institutions, including county hospitals, CHCs and THCs, community health stations, and village clinics (Yip et al. 2012). These funds were infused into infrastructure building, increases in basic salaries, public health services, substitution for drug markup, and so on. A deputy director in the municipal SHI agency praised the achievement of governmental financial infusion to rural and primary care facilities.

The three-year healthcare reform (2009–2011) has made remarkable achievement…The achievement, first, really deserves praise. The government infuses substantial resources. It planned to invest ¥840 billion, but runs over its initial budget by investing over ¥1 trillion. Where does the money flow? Our country is really large. So is the inequality between urban and rural [health facilities]. Township and community health centers, which we call primary healthcare providers, collapsed in the past. People suffered from the great inconvenience of accessing them. It needs considerable sums of money to boost them. A big part of these finance was infused to them. Their infrastructure building has almost finished during these three years. The achievement is great indeed. (B20120920BJZ)

However, the government did not increase its subsidies by much for most hospitals, with the latter continuing to rely on drug profits to survive and to charge a drug markup of 15 %. Nevertheless, more government finance was provided than ever before to build infrastructure and to increase the basic salary of hospital doctors. This finance, however, was tiny compared with the annual revenue of hospitals. A doctor in a tertiary hospital said his basic salary rose after 2009, but only by a few hundred yuan.

My basic salary, which was slightly over ¥1,000, had not increased for years. After I was promoted to chief physician, it was raised to ¥1,300. After the new healthcare reform, our basic salary rose by ¥200–¥300. As a result, my basic salary reached ¥1,600. (B20120927WZY)

Subsequently, the compensation system reform caused widespread complaint by doctors. Doctors were generally dissatisfied with either the amount of government finance or its effect on their income. During our fieldwork, there were two different types of opinions, from doctors in hospitals and from those in primary health facilities. Doctors in hospitals denied that there was any effect of the increased government finance on their income, deeming it inadequate. For example, a doctor in a tertiary hospital in City C said that most of doctors' income still came from user charges, with little from government finance.

The government takes little responsibility for us. The hospital is a nonprofit unit and should be subsidized by the government. But the government really takes little responsibility. It

> only provides finance to make up 20% of the salary for the employees of a formal establishment. The salary of those without an establishment has to be dispensed from the revenue of the hospital. We occasionally launch some free diagnosis activities. The government should provide subsidies to us, but it does not. Anyway, it takes little responsibility…If we need money, no people care. The government just ducks its responsibility. (C20120918PYS)

Doctors in primary health facilities (CHCs and community health posts in urban areas, and THCs and village clinics in rural areas) complained that there was even an adverse effect of government finance on their income. A village doctor in County D complained of his decreasing income after the new round of healthcare reform in 2009.

> The government does increase subsidies to us. However, the money is totally inadequate. If we have no other sources of income, we can hardly make a living. Moreover, the subsidies are settled after we provide services. They should be paid in advance so that we can provide services. In this society, even a peasant going outside to do construction work can earn hundreds of yuan every day. We doctors earn less than them…and we earn less than ever before. I can earn at least ¥40,000 a year in the past. Now I earn only hundreds of yuan a month. (D20120823ZYS)

Doctors generally attributed this adverse effect to a zero-drug-profit policy and strict supervision of drug prescriptions by the government. In the past, primary care facilities were permitted to add a maximum of 15 % markup for drugs. After 2009, the government promulgated an essential medicines list and enacted a zero-drug-profit policy in primary care facilities, in that primary care facilities were forbidden to either import non-essential medicines or to add drug markups, and drugs had to be sold to patients without profit. The loss of these drug profits was to be financed by government subsidies; however, the subsidies delivered to doctors in primary care facilities could not substitute for the loss of their income. In addition, the strict supervision of drug prescriptions reduced the income of doctors.

> After the cancelation of the drug markup, THCs both gained and suffered. Doctors also reacted differently. Some praised it, while most of them complained. In the past decades, hospitals sustained their development by selling drugs. The cancelation of markup reduced the revenue of hospitals. How could hospitals survive? Not to mention the government subsidy that is always insufficient and in arrears. (A20121018DYSZYS)

A doctor in the investigated THC in County D attributed the decrease of income to the source of his salary. He thought that without the drug markup, the major source of his salary shifted from drug prescription to government finance.

> The salary of our doctors came mainly from the user charges of hospitals in the past. Now it is different. The government canceled drug markup, and the revenue of hospitals decreased after that. The government correspondingly provided some subsidies to hospitals. Hereafter, the major source of our salary shifted from drug prescription to government finance. However, the budget of our county government is always in deficit and cannot deliver subsidies on time. Our income decreased after the new healthcare reform. (D20120811WSC)

To summarize, the purchasing and inspecting initiatives of SHI agencies were partly impeded by the weak or even adverse effects of government health finance on doctors' income and the revenue of hospitals. Without sufficient income and funding support, doctors were more likely to violate the regulations of SHI agencies and conduct overtreatment. The ultimate victims would most certainly be the patients.

5.5.2 The Distorted Centralized Pharmaceutical Tender and Procurement System

The purchasing initiative of SHI agencies was counteracted by the centralized tender and procurement system of drugs and medical consumptive materials and devices. A provincial joint office for centralized tender and procurement took charge of pharmaceutical tender and procurement in most provinces. This joint office consisted of many provincial departments of the government such as the Development and Reform Commission, the Department of Bursary, and so on, while the DoH was just one of its members. Unusually, the DHRSS was not a member. Each of the latter two departments could not decide the tender, procurement, and prices of medicines, let alone the rural and the urban SHI agencies that were affiliated to the two departments, respectively. Some officers in the municipal SHI agency of City B and of City C said that the current system gave no rights to SHI agencies to negotiate medical prices with pharmaceutical suppliers.

> The municipal government is forbidden from conducting the tender of drugs; only the provincial government can. The participants of provincial tender include the DoH, the Development and Reform Commission, the Commission for Discipline Inspection…it includes most of the relevant government departments, but excludes our Department of Human Resources and Social Security…This induces a problem. Pharmaceutical suppliers sell drugs to hospitals, hospitals sell these drugs to patients, the money is spent, then hospitals come to our SHI agency to let us pay the bills. (C20120910ZJs)

> Our provincial Department of Human Resources and Social Security is excluded from the tender and price setting of medicines, let alone our municipal bureau. We have no rights to participate in that process. (B20120924SKZ)

With the restriction of centralized pharmaceutical tender and procurement, SHI agencies were unable to do much about price negotiation; they could only conduct some pilots of price negotiation within the current system. For example, the municipal SHI agency of City C found that the tender and procurement policy applied only to nonprofit public hospitals where most healthcare resources were allocated. Therefore, they selected CHCs as pilots of medicine price negotiation. For another example, the officers in the municipal SHI agency in Chengdu City in Sichuan Province noticed an item in a policy document entitled "Notice on Issuing the Drug Formularies of National Basic Medical Insurance, Industrial Injury Insurance and Maternity Insurance issued by Ministry of Human Resources and Social Security." The item regulated that,

> for the complex drugs not included in the Drug Formularies but composed of the Western drugs in the Formularies, they can be deemed to be drugs of subgroup B of the Formularies

> and enjoy reimbursement if their prices are no higher than the sum prices of the composed Western drugs. Detailed rules are enacted by locality. (Guo 2011)

The officers, therefore, conducted price negotiations for these kinds of drugs (Guo 2011). However, only limited kinds of drugs were suitable for drug negotiation, with most commonly used drugs tendered and procured via the provincial joint office.

In addition, with the restriction of the centralized procurement system, SHI agencies had no rights to negotiate the prices of drugs with health facilities. A policy document regulated that "the nonprofit hospitals operated by governments at county level and above…are requested to attend the centralized procurement of drugs…It is forbidden to conduct another bargain on the prices of tender drugs" (Ministry of Health et al. 2010). An officer in the urban SHI agency of County D said that all the prices of drugs were set by the provincial Development and Reform Commission, and that both SHI agencies and hospitals were unable to negotiate the prices.

> Medical prices are set by the provincial Development and Reform Commission; hospitals just procure drugs in accordance with these prices. We have nothing to accuse hospitals of, do we? The role of our SHI agency is weak; hospitals at all levels just operate according to the prices set by the provincial Development and Reform Commission. (D20121030GZR)

The centralized pharmaceutical tender and procurement system not only deprived SHI agencies of the rights to negotiate the prices of drugs, but also in a sense exaggerated the excessively high prices of drugs. An officer from the NCMS management office of County D and an officer of the municipal SHI agency of City B both said that the prices of tender drugs were higher than that of nontender drugs.

> As reflected by the staff in some pharmacies, the tender prices of medicines are not necessarily lower than the prices of medicines imported directly by these pharmacies. This is unable to be resolved and is likely to be a national problem. (D20120906PZR)

> Several years ago, I started to do some evaluation work and therefore focused on the prices of medicines. I found that the prices were low if medicines were not tendered for; once being tendered for, the prices would rise. But hospitals are forced to use tender medicines. This is the reality. The prices of medicines become increasingly higher with the tender system. The problem is unable to be resolved. (B20120927SKZ)

An officer in the municipal SHI agency of City C provided a more detailed explanation and attributed the high prices of drugs to the spending of pharmaceutical suppliers on public relations, that is, lobbying health facilities for selling drugs. Usually, the lobby equaled bribe.

> In the process of tender, some medicine suppliers may get a bid at the same time. When they supply their medicines to hospitals, hospitals decide which suppliers' goods to use. Then these suppliers will use all kinds of tactics to let the hospitals use their goods…But the suppliers will definitely earn this public relation spending back; they will raise the prices. (C20120910ZJ)

In November 2009, the National Development and Reform Commission and two other ministries jointly issued a policy document explicitly requiring local governments to explore this negotiation mechanism (National Development and Reform Commission, Ministry of Health, & Ministry of Human Resources and Social Security 2009). However, it was still in its early stages; without sound institutional surroundings, the pilots in many places were hard to implement and were merely a formality in an inefficient way (Wei et al. 2012)

5.5.3 The Fragmented SHI Schemes

The three SHI schemes—UEBMI, URBMI, and NCMS—were run separately by different government departments; moreover, each scheme was operated by localized management. These factors interplayed to form thousands of independent SHI agencies and SHI pooling accounts across the whole country. This fragmentation of SHI schemes reduced the scale and power of SHI agencies. In addition, both the NCMS and the health facilities were supervised by the BoH, which did not like to inspect health facilities rigorously.

The separate management of SHI schemes by different government departments led to various styles of supervising SHI. The UEBMI and URBMI were managed by urban SHI agencies, which were affiliated with the DHRSS. The NCMS was managed by the NCMS office in the county BoH. A deputy director in the municipal SHI agency of City B said that the management of urban SHI schemes by the DHRSS was to "introduce a third party to prevent the BoH from acting as both a player and a referee." Here, "player" meant that the BoH was in charge of health facilities, while "referee" meant the manager of SHI schemes.

> With regard to the macro level of the top design, the SHI is divided into basic medical insurance and supplemental insurance for catastrophic disease. The basic medical insurance can be divided further into the NCMS, the UEBMI, and the URBMI. The Department of Human Resources and Social Security is in charge of the UEBMI and the URBMI, while the DoH the NCMS. Before the implementation of the UEBMI, all social health insurance programs were managed by the DoH. The healthcare reform introduced a third party to prevent the DoH from acting as both a player and a referee. The government lets the urban SHI agency manage the UEBMI and the URBMI, while still asking the DoH to manage the NCMS for rural residents. The DoH had managed health insurance for rural residents for so many years that they were unwilling to abandon it. (B20120921BJZ)

Many participants indicated that the inspections by urban SHI agencies were more rigorous than the NCMS management offices. A salient problem of the NCMS was that both hospitals and NCMS management offices were affiliated to the BoH. The BoH remained both a player and a referee in that it managed both health facilities and the NCMS management office. This close relationship reduced the magnitude of inspection and punishment by the NCMS management office and the BoH. This was acknowledged by an officer in the NCMS management office of County D.

> Although the rules regulate that we can cancel the designated membership of hospitals if necessary, we haven't done that indeed. You may think about it. Both our BoH and

hospitals are within the same system, where we set up and supervise hospitals. It is hard to ignore our relationship and to punish hospitals rigidly. It has disadvantages to let the BoH monitor itself and its affiliates. Many works can hardly be conducted rigorously. If there are no serious problems in hospitals, we will not be that demanding to supervise them. (D20120906PZR)

In addition to the metaphor of player and referee, a doctor in a secondary hospital in City C described the relationship between the BoH and hospitals as the relationship between a parent and its children. Both the metaphor of player/referee and of parent/child denoted that the BoH would not supervise hospitals strictly due to this close relationship.

The BoH and hospitals are within the same system. If hospitals make some faults, the BoH just turns a blind eye to these faults. However, if hospitals dare to make faults, they may violate regulations and even laws in future. This is the real practice. That is why the magnitude of inspections by urban SHI agencies and that by the NCMS management office differs so much…It is inefficient to supervise hospitals by the BoH. How can a parent punish his/her child rigorously? It causes many problems. (C20120918WYS)

As a result, in practice, inspections by the NCMS management offices and the BoH were said by some doctors to be irresponsible.

Generally speaking, the BoH would not come to inspect our work if the central, provincial, or municipal governments have no big action. (D20120816ZHX)

[The inspection by the BoH] is quite irresponsible! They just go around to have a general look, and then let our director host them to have a lunch. After that they will leave. (D20120904DJ)

However, with regard to the UEBMI and URBMI, the separation of the management of insurance and that of the health facilities did not automatically guarantee an efficient purchasing mechanism. Without strong incentives, sufficient resources, and the support of grand policies, the urban SHI agencies were weak purchasers, just like the NCMS management offices.

Our inspections [the county SHI agency of County D] of supplier-induced demand in hospitals are not so rigid, because hospitals are our cooperative units…For example, an inpatient should be prescribed one test of color ultrasonography but is actually prescribed two. We should audit both of the two tests in theory, because we regulate that any medical items worth over ¥80 should be approved by us. However, we don't audit them rigorously. (D20121030LKZ)

Urban SHI agencies did not inflict strict supervision of health facilities, not only because of problems with their own incentives and resources, but also because of the public relation actions of the health facilities. To lessen the tense atmosphere, health facilities might send gifts and even money to officers of the urban SHI agencies, to beg for lax inspections.

The relationship between hospitals and the urban SHI agency is important. If the relationship is good, the urban SHI agency will not care much about the problems existing in hospitals…Therefore, every hospital employs special staff members to deal with public relations with the urban SHI agency. This is the Chinese characteristic. Some hospitals send gifts and money to the officers in the urban SHI agency on every festival. Correspondingly,

> the inspections by the agency would be lax and the refusal of paying reimbursement would not happen in the next time period…The key to these things is the authority and power of the urban SHI agency that is conducting not just inspections, but also the management of hospitals. (C20120918WYS)

The management of SHI schemes generated low incentives and power for SHI supervision, because not only were they separately managed by different government departments, they also suffered from being localized. The UEBMI and URBMI at municipal level were managed by a municipal SHI agency, while those at district level and county level were managed by a district and a county SHI agency, respectively. All of these agencies were affiliated to the DHRSS. The NCMS was managed by the county NCMS office in the county BoH.

This fragmentation caused many problems. One of them was that local SHI agencies found it difficult to inspect out-of-town hospitals due to the low pooling level of SHI funds. A deputy director with the NCMS management office of County D said that the performance of the global budget payment enacted by a county NCMS management office would be undermined in hospitals at city level.

> Those [patients] going to out-of-town hospitals or hospitals at city and provincial level have to advance their medical expenditures first and then come to our office for reimbursement; we are unable to inspect those out-of-town hospitals. (D20121030GZR)

In particular, for patients admitted to hospitals at city or provincial level, their medical spending was usually much more than that of patients admitted to hospitals at county level and below. Most medical expenditures remained free from inspection simply because of the localized management of SHI schemes.

> After the enactment of the global budget, the hospital [a tertiary hospital in City B] assigns fixed budgets to every department of services. Our doctors have to admit patients referring to the amount of budget assigned to our department. However, our hospital will for sure develop and we continue to receive as many patients as we can. The regulation of the global budget doesn't have a great influence on our department of neurosurgery, because most patients from our local city suffer from slight injuries and don't come here. Our admissions are almost always patients from other cities and are generally catching severe diseases and therefore spend a lot. The rules of the global budget and the inspections by SHI agencies in other cities cannot influence our operations much. (B20120927WZY)

As well as the incentive and power problems, the fragmentation of SHI schemes could increase administrative costs for both SHI agencies and health facilities. For example, the fragmented SHI schemes induced overlapping information systems across health facilities.

> Either the BoH or the BHRSS considers their own sectional interests. It causes problems for hospitals, because hospitals have to equip two information systems for these two bureaus respectively. Now we are pursuing informatization. But one such information system costs tens of millions of yuan. Each bureau has one; what a big waste…Overlapping establishment is a big problem. From the perspective of hospitals, they said that they are also confused. They have to build data terminal equipment for each bureau, and have to set two corresponding offices to manage. Moreover, the regulations of the three SHI schemes are different, causing many problems. (B20120920BJZ)

One way to solve the fragmentation of SHI schemes was to pool SHI funds across a larger area rather than just pooling the funds at county/district level; however, this was hard to achieve. Although the central government required each locality to start pooling SHI funds at the city level, most places unified at most only the benefit package of the same SHI scheme across the city, with SHI funds remaining locally managed. As the management of SHI funds was the priority for SHI agencies, localized management of the funds caused local agencies to have no incentive and power to inspect the medical expenditures occurring in out-of-town health facilities.

> Pooling urban SHI funds at the city level was required in a policy document in 2011. But the management software in the whole city was not unified until the second half of this year; then the reimbursement rates, reimbursement procedure, ceiling amount, deductibles, and so on, were just kept uniform…However, for the SHI funds, we still just manage the municipal SHI funds now, including the SHI funds for the administrative organs, for public institutions, and for enterprises directly under the municipal government. We have not yet managed the staff at county SHI agencies. (C20120917WW)

Unifying SHI funds at city level was very hard to implement because of the interests of local government. A deputy director of the municipal SHI agency of City B said that the imbalance between fund pooling and staff management made unifying SHI funds at city level impossible. Staff members at county SHI agencies were managed by county government, and received salaries from the locality, too. Pooling funds at city level without also pooling staff management would encounter opposition from local government.

> The central government has set up the future guideline of pooling SHI schemes at city level, out of which pooling SHI funds is the most important. However, we [the municipal SHI agency of City B] cannot dampen the work incentives of the county SHI agencies. They have managed county SHI funds for so many years and have developed their own management methods. If we suddenly take their funds away but leave their staff members behind and just let the staff collect premiums for us, this would cause a problem of imbalance between rights and duties. Moreover, the salaries of these staff members are still paid by county government. So pooling their SHI funds only causes them to be displeased and puts great pressure on them. How can I work for you while receiving a salary from the county government? Local governments have their own interests. (B20120921BJZ)

5.5.4 *The Inequitable Allocation of Healthcare Resources*

The inequitable allocation of medical resources disenabled SHI agencies to choose freely the designated health facilities, therefore damaging the purchasing function. Tertiary hospitals usually occupied most of the medical resources in a city, forming a monopoly in the healthcare market. Primary and secondary hospitals had limited resources and were unable to compete with tertiary hospitals. The flow of UEBMI and URBMI funds in City B and City C were described as follows.

> Most of the funds [of UEBMI in City B] flow to six tertiary hospitals in our city, accounting for 70% of the whole funds; if secondary hospitals are included, it would account for near 80%. The primary health facilities account for the remaining 20%. (B20120924WKZ)

> The two tertiary hospitals [in City C], the Municipal People's Hospital and the Oilfield Employee's Hospital account for 60% of fund expenditures (of UEBMI and URBMI); they account for 70% of expenditures among hospitals at secondary level and above. (C20120917WW)

In addition, the power of choosing designated hospitals was not owned by SHI agencies but by an administrative section of the municipal BHRSS. This problem, together with the influence of tertiary hospitals on the healthcare market as described earlier, almost meant that SHI agencies could not exclude a tertiary hospital from its designation list even if there were illegal medical behaviors in the hospital.

5.6 Summary of Findings

To sum up, in this chapter the qualitative study explored the purchasing mechanism of SHI and the complicated interaction among different stakeholders in the purchasing process. It first found that SHI agencies used multiple strategies to control health cost inflation. The agencies put emphasis on the safety of the pooling funds of SHI programs, took efforts to keep a balance between the revenue and expenditure of the funds, and set up reimbursement plans according to the revenues. They conducted a payment methods reform to replace a retrospective fee-for-services payment method with various prospective payment methods, such as a global budget; for those who used the global budget, they paid fixed and partial budgets in advance to health facilities, awarded health facilities that saved their fixed budgets, and shared overexpenditure with the health facilities with the purpose of promoting self-management of those health facilities. They used indicator management to decide the return of a performance bond and focused on the use of drugs outside of SHI formularies, expenditures per admission, the reimbursement rate for spending within the scope of policies, the hospitalization rate, and so on. They conducted inspections of health facilities, relying on both labor power and the development of an information platform. They punished health facilities who violated their regulations by refusing to pay reimbursement and ceasing designated membership. In addition, they conducted tripartite negotiations to decrease the prices of drugs, medical tests, and services.

However, during the fieldwork we found that these purchasing strategies were undermined in the process of interaction between stakeholders, and with the dynamics of the institutional surroundings structuring and shaping the behaviors of its actors. In terms of the SHI agencies, they suffered from incentive problems to conduct cost containment, only adjusting reimbursement plans to deal with the emerging health cost inflation. This was because they assumed the political responsibility of maintaining the safety of pooling funds, which overrode the importance of cost control; at the same time, there lacked top-level design of third-party purchasing policies, leaving SHI agencies no means by which to support cost control. In particular, the NCMS management offices had low incentive because both it and the health facilities were subordinate to the BoH. SHI agencies also suffered from scarce resources in terms of administrative funds, personnel, and facility development. In addition, they could not afford the high transaction costs of supervising other stakeholders. This was because the information asymmetry between them and health facilities was so large they had low capability to inspect the behaviors of doctors. They also had low administrative ranking while having to face multiple interest groups and governmental departments in its practical operation. Furthermore, because of the inequitable allocation of healthcare resources, SHI agencies were incapable of strictly inspecting tertiary hospitals that had monopolistic positions in the healthcare market. They were constrained by the distorted price schedule of drugs and medical services and the centralized drug tender and procurement system, and had no power to negotiate the prices of drugs and medical services with pharmaceutical suppliers and health facilities. Moreover, SHI agencies were powerless because of the fragmentation of SHI schemes, which in turn was caused by the separate and localized management of those schemes. Facing these constraints, the calculated choices of SHI agencies were to turn a blind eye to the improper behaviors of doctors and to rely on adjusting reimbursement plans, which would most certainly undermine the benefits of the patients.

In terms of the healthcare providers, these had different benefit concerns to SHI agencies, with the former focusing on economic profits and medical safety while the latter on the safety of pooling funds. The institutional surroundings shaped the benefit concerns of healthcare providers in that the poor compensation system induced doctors to obtain bonuses and that the distorted price schedule brought substantial drug kickbacks to doctors. Facing the multiple cost-containment strategies of SHI agencies, healthcare providers chose to complain about SHI agencies and used a number of hidden strategies to transform the medical costs of patients, such as refusing to admitting patients with catastrophic diseases, creating fake medical records, increasing the use of device tests and medical services, as well as purposefully spending excessively to acquire a bigger budget in the following year.

With regard to the patients, the problem of moral hazard meant that they preferred to be hospitalized even with minor diseases, abused pooling funds for outpatient and inpatient services, counterfeited certificates of SHI participation to obtain reimbursement, and colluded with doctors to receive unnecessary services. Their choices were shaped either by their health consciousness or institutions. They tried to obtain reimbursement, some with illegal behaviors, due to the excessively high prices of drugs and medical services caused by the distorted price schedule, the exclusion of some expensive drugs from the SHI drug formularies, and their low capability in monitoring the use of these nonreimbursable, expensive drugs. They preferred to be hospitalized either because of their improving health consciousness of valuing health more than reimbursement, or because SHI plans provided substantially higher reimbursement for inpatient services than for outpatients. To sum up, the practical choices of patients within the special institutional surroundings were to collude with healthcare providers to “cheat” SHI agencies.

To conclude, we found that SHI, as a kind of welfare institution, operated against its slogan of purchasing because of the problematic interactions between SHI agencies, healthcare providers, and patients. These interactions were further shaped by larger, disenabling institutional surroundings. In this sense, an institution gained or lost its efficiency in the interaction of actors and in its relationship with the larger institutional surroundings.

Chapter 6
A Call for a Single Payer Model?

This study answers the question: How does social health insurance participation affect people's out-of-pocket health spending in China? This question may seem simple on the surface, but it in fact requires careful consideration. It originates from an observed paradox in China with respect to its ongoing healthcare reform: the faster SHI develops, the quicker healthcare costs and people's OOPS increase. On the one hand, China is constructing the largest SHI system in the world. Up until 2012, over 90 % of its 1.3 billion population was covered by its SHI schemes. Yet, on the other hand, the country is suffering from serious health cost inflation, causing widespread public discontent. OOPS per capita have increased by 64 % from 2006 to 2011 (Ministry of Health 2013).

To uncover the detailed mechanisms behind this paradox, this study sets out to investigate three interrelated questions: (1) What is the effect of the expanding SHI participation on individuals' OOPS in China's healthcare reform? (2) Through what kinds of institutional arrangement does the effect take place? (3) How does the institutional arrangement take effect?

Correspondingly, this study embraces a new institutionalist perspective to elaborate on the effects of welfare institutions on social outcomes. It thus develops a theoretical framework grounded on theoretical studies of the institutional arrangements of social policy, as well as empirical studies of SHI. The framework has two perspectives: of determination and of strategic interaction. The perspective of determination serves to indicate the mediating mechanisms of institutional arrangements in the relationship between welfare institutions and outcome. Three mechanisms—reimbursement, behavior management, and purchasing—are developed to substantiate the institutional arrangement of SHI. The dimension of strategic interaction explores the relationship between welfare institutions and the behaviors of individuals. It employs a calculus approach to structure the interaction between SHI agencies, healthcare providers, and patients, as well as to examine the role that SHI and other institutions play in shaping that interaction.

Furthermore, this study adopts a mixed-methods design to facilitate answers to the three research questions. A quantitative analysis draws data from a nationally

K. Liu, *The Effects of Social Health Insurance Reform on People's Out-of-Pocket Health Expenditure in China*, DOI 10.1007/978-981-10-1777-3_6

representative dataset (CHARLS). Using regression analysis with the instrumental variables method, it first analyzes the effect of SHI participation on a set of indicators of medical expenditures, relying on data from six subsamples: UEBMI outpatient and inpatient samples, URBMI outpatient and inpatient samples, and NCMS outpatient and inpatient samples. In addition, using structural equation modeling, the study analyzes the data of 1645 hospitalized patients to examine the performance of the reimbursement, the behavior management, and the purchasing mechanisms of the SHI schemes, namely, how the three mechanisms mediate the relationship between SHI participation and OOPS. Subsequently, a qualitative study explains the quantitative findings. It uses semistructured interviews to capture the interaction between different stakeholders within the three SHI schemes. The researcher conducted four months of fieldwork in three cities and one county, in a province in central China. The researcher interviewed 70 stakeholders including officers in urban and rural SHI agencies, doctors and SHI reimbursement managers in urban and rural health facilities at different levels, patients enrolled in various SHI schemes, and so on. A thematic analysis is used to distill important themes and to outline the profit chain and various interactions between stakeholders under the institutional arrangement of SHI.

6.1 Summary of Findings

The quantitative analysis finds that various SHI schemes have positive effects on the rise of medical expenditures by increasing the usage of different treatment items, prolonging days of hospitalization, and increasing total medical expenditures and patients' OOPS. It also finds that the reimbursement mechanisms of the four SHI schemes (UEBMI, URBMI, NCMS, and GMI) offer considerable benefits to insured patients. Individuals' OOPS may be cut down while they claim reimbursement from the SHI schemes to which they belong. However, the behavior management and purchasing mechanisms of SHI are dysfunctional. SHI participants prefer to choose higher-level health facilities compared with uninsured patients. Meanwhile, patients who participated in the GMI are more likely to prolong their stay in hospital than the uninsured. Patients enrolled in the UEBMI and the NCMS are more likely to use a wider range of treatment items than the uninsured. In addition, taking the mediation of the level of facility and length of stay into consideration, participation in all four schemes has a significant and positive indirect relationship with either length of stay or types of treatment items. As well, all the levels of facility, lengths of stay in health facilities, and types of treatment items have a positive relationship with OOPS. As a result, SHI participation has a weak negative effect (for the UEBMI and URBMI) or no significant effect (for the GMI and NCMS) on the OOPS of the hospitalized patients. It indicates that the malfunction of the behavior management and purchasing mechanisms of SHI undermines the reimbursement mechanism.

The qualitative analysis first looks at the behavior management mechanism to explore why it renders the reimbursement mechanism ineffective. It finds that SHI agencies use some strategies to direct patients' choices of health facilities. NCMS management offices use a referral system to restrain rural patients from spilling into tertiary hospitals. Both NCMS management offices and urban SHI agencies primarily use tiered copayment and deductibles to admit patients to primary care facilities. In addition, tripartite negotiation arrangements and localized management of SHI are used to affect individuals' care-seeking behaviors and to restrain excessive inpatient admission. However, the magnitude of these strategies is offset by the status quo of healthcare providers and patients. To be specific, healthcare resources are unevenly distributed while high quality medical professionals are usually attached to large hospitals. Meanwhile, there exists undisciplined competition among health facilities. It is more in the interests of health facilities to attract more patients and make profits than to obey the bidirectional referral system and to submit to the tiered copayment and deductibles of SHI schemes. In addition, Chinese patients are health-prioritizing and facility-sophistication-oriented consumers. As they value health over the cash paid to maintain it, the reimbursement issue is deemed secondary. With the prevailing common belief that large hospitals provide better healthcare services than primary health facilities, it is understandable that individuals flow into the large hospitals, especially when their health consciousness, as well as their economic means, improve. Without specific attendance to the profit-seeking behaviors of health facilities and the health concerns of patients, SHI and its agencies exert little influence in managing patients' care-seeking behaviors. Their strategies of adjusting these behaviors may lose magnitude. But rather, the reimbursement benefits provided by SHI may stimulate patients to go to higher-level health facilities rather than primary care facilities.

Furthermore, the qualitative analysis probes into the purchasing mechanism of SHI. It reveals that the safety of pooling funds is the prime concern of SHI agencies to manage all SHI schemes. Correspondingly, all the SHI agencies use similar strategies of purchasing to restrain the improper prescription behaviors of doctors and the demands of patients, including payment methods reform, indicator management, inspection, punishment, and tripartite negotiation. They employ these strategies to contain the inflation of medical expenditures. However, these strategies are undermined with the constraints from the SHI agency, patients, doctors, as well as their institutional surroundings. First, although SHI agencies undertake multiple strategies to control cost inflation, they remain weak purchasers as they suffer from poor incentive, scarce resources, and the inability to afford the excessively high transaction costs. Neither urban nor rural SHI agencies in China have the motivation or political responsibility to contain health cost inflation. Their sole agenda is to safeguard SHI funds, resulting in crude strategies to control cost inflation rather than the prudent design and implementation of effective methods and indicators. As well, both urban and rural SHI agencies lack sufficient financial resources, personnel, and facilities to restrain health cost inflation. The malfunction of SHI agencies of cost containment also derives from the high transaction costs faced by SHI agencies when they conduct interdepartmental coordination. SHI agencies receives no advantages in this process, generating excessively high transaction costs due to severe information asymmetry of the medical industry and complicated multi–governmental–departmental cooperation. Second, patients take advantage of the reimbursement of SHI to abuse health services. There exists the falsification of expense claims among the patients. Nevertheless, the patients remain the weakest compared with doctors, SHI agencies, and the whole healthcare system. They abuse medical services not only actively, but sometimes passively. Third, doctors have different concerns from SHI agencies. Their dual consideration is economic profit and medical safety. In face of the increasingly strict inspections by SHI agencies, doctors express extreme complaints. The poor governance of the healthcare system allows some doctors to find ways to escape the regulations of SHI agencies and to balance their income, including the rejection of patients with catastrophic diseases, forging medical records, prescribing as many medical tests and services as possible to compensate for the loss of drug profits, and so on. Moving up to the hospital level, the subsidies provided by SHI agencies for overexpenditure may be exploited to cover or overcome temporary financial hardships. Fourth, all the actions and reactions taken by SHI agencies, doctors, and patients are shaped by disenabling institutional surroundings. The poor compensation system causes the increasing government finance to generate a weak or even adverse effect on doctors' income and the revenues of health facilities. The centralized tender and procurement system of drugs and medical consumptive materials and devices disenables the purchasing initiatives of SHI agencies. The separate and localized management of different SHI schemes reduces the scale and the inspecting power of SHI agencies. Finally, the extremely inequitable allocation of healthcare resources renders SHI agencies unable to choose freely designated health facilities, thereby damaging their purchasing functions.

As a result, SHI participation has a weak negative or even no significant impact on the OOPS of hospitalized patients. This seems to contradict the principles of SHI, which aim to reduce people's OOPS and enhance their well-being. This study facilitates understanding of the question of how SHI participation affects people's OOPS.

6.2 Theoretical Implications: Elaborating on the Determinants of the Efficiency of Welfare Institutions

The new institutionalists have rediscovered the importance of institutions in social, economic, and political life. Among various schools of thought of the new institutionalists, the rational choice institutionalists argue that institutions provide the venues for interactions between actors where actors rationally weigh gain and cost by their anticipation of others' reactions toward their behaviors and choices. Different from this calculus approach, the sociological institutionalists see that institutions affect and modify behaviors by facilitating interpretation through symbols, cognitive scripts, or moral templates. Either of these two approaches puts emphasis on a holistic function of institutions and the way institutions exert influence upon behaviors and outcomes.

Different to the approaches above focusing on the unidirectional effect of institutions on behaviors of actors and in turn on outcomes, this study reveals an interplay between welfare institutions and the behaviors of actors in determining social outcomes. From a determinative perspective, it identifies three mechanisms of rather than a unified institutional arrangement of welfare institutions at the macro level; furthermore, it finds that a welfare institution may produce undesirable social outcomes because its operating mechanisms conflict with one another. From a strategic interactive perspective, the study probes into how the interactions among the stakeholders involved are influenced by the larger institutional surroundings and mechanisms thereof, and how the efficiency of welfare institutions is thus affected.

6.2.1 A Three-Way Model for the Institutional Arrangement of Welfare Institutions

From the perspective of determination, the institutional arrangement has a mediating effect on the way in which welfare institutions determine social outcomes. This study identifies three kinds of institutional arrangement: benefit provision, provision rationale, and provision mode. It demonstrates that despite the benefits provided through welfare participation, patients' dysfunctional behaviors and healthcare providers' inefficient service delivery eventually offset the effect of benefit provision. Welfare policies without mature consideration of the possible behavioral deviance of actors and the malfunctions of the mediating institutional arrangement are insufficient to ensure satisfactory social outcomes. Therefore, we have to concentrate on the mediating role that the institutional arrangement plays in the relationship between welfare institutions and social outcomes. To guarantee the efficiency of welfare delivery, welfare institutions should act not only as universal benefit provision, but as a policy instrument for adjusting the behaviors of actors and as a catalyst for improving delivery efficiency. This study proposes a three-way model for the institutional arrangement of welfare institutions in determining social outcomes, as follows.

Welfare institution as universal benefit provision. In industrial societies, nearly all people are dependent on selling their labor power as a means to life. By selling their labor, they are continually commodified as "things," to which their existence as human beings is gradually eroded, too (Esping-Andersen 1990). To counteract the adverse effects of industrialization and the labor market on human beings, social democrats advocate a conception of social rights, arguing that such rights imply an equal status of membership that allows people to claim welfare benefits (Lewis 1998; Marshall 1963). In its essence, welfare participation recognizes social status rather than private contract, submits to social justice rather than market price, and declares equal rights rather than the free bargain (Marshall 1963). This study regards universal welfare participation as the most significant approach by which to guarantee people's fundamental well-being. Welfare participation—SHI participation in this study—must be recognized as the rights of citizenship, not as the result of labor market competition.

Welfare institution as policy instrument for adjusting the behaviors of actors. Although welfare participation should be insured on a universal basis, it must not be provided unconditionally. Unconditional social rights link welfare entitlement with social outcome via the institutional arrangement of merely expanding the size and extent of welfare benefits, but without considering the mediating institutional mechanism of duties and behavior management. This study takes the welfare institution as a policy instrument to adjust the behaviors of beneficiaries. Welfare benefits should be delivered with the request for certain contributions or behaviors, such as contribution to social insurance and employment-oriented social assistance programs. The behavior management mechanism aims at transforming the citizen's role from passive recipient to active citizen. In recent years, enrollment contribution and behavior management of the welfare system has become a necessity for welfare participation in many counties. The provision of social rights with a behavioral requirement, such as work and rational care-seeking behaviors, is thus expected to have an effect on behavior management.

Welfare institution as catalyst for improving delivery efficiency. In order to deliver the intentions that lie behind social policies in ordered and predictable ways, the state must set up procedures and institutions to carry them out (Baldock et al. 2003). In the traditional argument, state provision and free market are the two most mentioned delivery models. However, both models are not perfect solutions for the conflicts between benefit provision and delivery efficiency. On the one hand, direct state provision is criticized to be inefficient and ineffective as it serves the interests of bureaucrats and professionals rather than meeting the needs of its clients (George and Wilding 1994). On the other hand, free market embraces market value rather than social rights. It is criticized to have little public accountability and to be vulnerable to risks. Since the 1970s, a "new managerialism" has emerged against the background of a mixed economy of public services; it embraces privatization, competition, and the internal market, deregulation, a commitment to customers, and contract out (Baldock et al. 2003). This study considers the role of welfare participation in the interplay between welfare provision and delivery efficiency, and advocates the establishment of a third-party purchaser in the domain of welfare services. Welfare participation should act as a catalyst for improving delivery efficiency. The re-drawing of the boundaries between state provision and free market is not simply an exercise in downsizing state or market responsibility, but introduces a third-party purchasing mechanism to ensure both benefit provision and delivery efficiency. A strong and responsible purchaser, commissioned and entrusted by the government, will purchase welfare services from the free market in representation of its beneficiaries. This kind of tripartite-related welfare participation, among third-party purchasers, service providers, and beneficiaries, may bring a positive influence on the efficiency of welfare provision. This provision model grounds itself in the re-creation of a mixed economy, as well as a civil society based on a partnership among individuals, organizations, and government (Field 1997).

6.2.2 A Strategic Interaction Perspective of Determining the Efficiency of Welfare Institutions

From the perspective of strategic interaction, the strategic interaction between actors is shaped by institutions. In addition, this study finds that despite the influence of a certain kind of welfare institution upon individual choices and behaviors, other institutions—along with the larger institutional surroundings—are nevertheless imparting effects, too, which may influence the efficiency of the welfare institution in shaping the behaviors of actors and in affecting social outcomes. Moreover, the conflicts between the internal mechanisms of a welfare institution's institutional arrangement also exert influences on the efficiency of the welfare institution.

Previous studies focus on how welfare institutions affect the behaviors of actors. Taking SHI schemes in China as an example, the reimbursement, the behavior management, and the purchasing mechanisms of these schemes certainly shape the way in which different stakeholders decide how to act, according to their benefits calculation. For instance, the referral system enforces patients to gain approval before they go to large hospitals; tiered copayment and deductibles provide patients more benefits if they choose to be hospitalized in primary care facilities; the cost-containment strategies used by SHI agencies guide both doctors and patients to consider the cost effectiveness of drugs and medical tests and services.

However, if most of the other institutions impose an action agenda in the direction of moderating a welfare institution, the efficiency of the latter will be greatly impaired. This denotes that the behaviors of actors might be influenced, by both a welfare institution and other institutions, along with the larger institutional surroundings. If the benefits gained by following some other institutions outweigh what the welfare institution is able to provide, actors may change their behaviors shaped by the welfare institution, and follow the direction of the other institutions. The efficiency of a welfare institution is hampered as a result. The relationship between welfare institutions and the behaviors of actors is not unidirectional, but bidirectional.

Taking SHI reform in China as an example, first, both the efficiency of the behavior management and of the purchasing mechanisms are disrupted by the inequitable allocation of healthcare resources, which results from higher-quality health service resources being concentrated in tertiary hospitals. Patients prefer tertiary hospitals to primary care facilities even though a higher reimbursement rate is offered when admitted to the latter, either because the health concern precedes that of the expense, or people hold strong beliefs that tertiary hospitals with substantial resources provide the best services. Without adequate resources and much policy support, primary care facilities and SHI agencies find it hard to attract patients, though they have tried and invested effort. The inequitable allocation of healthcare resources also affects the magnitude of the inspections by SHI agencies. Because tertiary hospitals hold a monopolistic position in the healthcare market, SHI agencies lose the incentives and authority to punish them or cease their designated membership, even if they observe doctors' malpractices such as prescribing medical items beyond necessity. Second, the efficiency of the SHI purchasing mechanism is offset by the poor compensation system under which health facilities become profit-driven and rely on user charges to make money. Notwithstanding the strategies that SHI agencies employ to contain the use of drugs and medical tests and services, health facilities take advantage of the weak health governance so as to draw medical profits from SHI agencies and patients. Third, the distorted price schedule undermines the efficiency of the SHI purchasing mechanism. The distorted price schedule affects the behaviors of patients, doctors, and SHI agencies. To be specific, prices of drugs inflate so much that patients who cannot pay the bills have to counterfeit certificates of SHI to gain reimbursement and to abuse the pooling funds of SHI; some doctors take kickbacks from pharmaceutical suppliers and prescribe expensive drugs and medical tests to gain off-the-table income; and SHI agencies are excluded from the procedure of price negotiation and as a result become disempowered. Fourth, the efficiency of both the purchasing and behavior management mechanisms cannot be realized within a fragmented SHI system. There are thousands of SHI agencies in the country owing to its fragmented design, resulting in every agency remaining powerless with scarce resources and low administrative ranking. They can neither negotiate with healthcare providers and other government departments, nor restrain the flow of patients to large hospitals.

Except for the bidirectional strategic inaction between welfare institutions, the behaviors of actors, and other institutions embedded in the larger institutional surroundings, this study also finds that a welfare institution may have difficulty in fulfilling its efficiency when its own mechanisms contradict one another and misguide the actors involved. Some mechanisms may even harm the welfare institution itself.

Still, taking the case of SHI in China, the quantitative analysis shows that the reimbursement mechanism of SHI may be undermined by dysfunctional behavior management and purchasing mechanisms. However, in the qualitative analysis, we find a countereffect that the reimbursement mechanism may in turn undermine the latter two mechanisms. Patients may take advantage of the SHI reimbursement system to gain admittance to large hospitals as they view their health as a primary concern over money. SHI reimbursement provided by SHI agencies, on the one hand, eases patients' financial difficulties while on the other hand, obscures the actual cost of medical services to patients. The reimbursement mechanism also induced patients and doctors to collude to use substantially unnecessary medical services, therefore undermining the purchasing mechanism. The result would become tricky if we combine both the quantitative and qualitative analysis. The magnitude of the purchasing and behavior management mechanisms undermines the reimbursement mechanism, which rebounds to hinder the purchasing and behavior management mechanisms. The reimbursement mechanism undermines itself, ultimately. It pushes patients to go to large hospitals and to use unnecessary medical items, which reduces the actual reimbursement to patients as a result.

To sum up, we use both a determinative and a strategic interactive perspective to examine the relationship between welfare institutions and social outcomes. We imply that the mechanisms of the institutional arrangement of welfare institutions play a mediating role in the process of welfare institutions generating influence on social outcomes, that the efficiency of welfare institutions and their mechanisms may be shaped and undermined by the larger institutional surroundings through the strategic interactions among actors, and that the mechanisms of institutional arrangement may be in conflict through those interactions so that the efficiency of welfare institutions in affecting social outcomes may be hampered, too.

6.3 Policy Implications: Establishing a Single Payer Model

This study reveals the operating strategies of and the constraints faced by SHI agencies, healthcare providers, and patients, as well as the complicated interactions among these stakeholders in the process of SHI reform generating effects on individuals' OOPS. It also provides a complicated profile of the flow of SHI reimbursement benefits among these stakeholders.

A weak and malfunctioned purchaser is the main cause of the dysfunctional institutional mechanisms of SHI; it can neither divert the patients' care-seeking behaviors nor adjust healthcare providers' asymmetrical development and undisciplined competition. As a result, the primary concern of this study's policy implications is how to establish a strong and responsible SHI purchaser so as to re-orient the care-seeking behaviors of patients and to encourage responsible practices of healthcare providers.

Correspondingly, this study proposes a single payer model of SHI in the hope of providing insights to China's healthcare reform. Figure 6.1 describes briefly the essential elements and relationships in the proposed model. In the figure, the oval represents the stakeholders in the healthcare reform, the solid line with single arrow denotes the unidirectional relationship between two stakeholders, the solid line with double arrows demonstrates the bidirectional relationship, and the dotted line with single arrow represents the potential unidirectional relationship. Note that the government acts as a regulator of promulgating laws, policies, and regulations and relates to all the other stakeholders in the healthcare reform. The related lines are omitted for the sake of clearance and brevity.

6.3.1 Establishing a Strong and Unified SHI Purchaser

Currently in China, SHI agencies lack incentives, resources, power, and policy support to be strong and responsible purchasers of health services. In addition, there

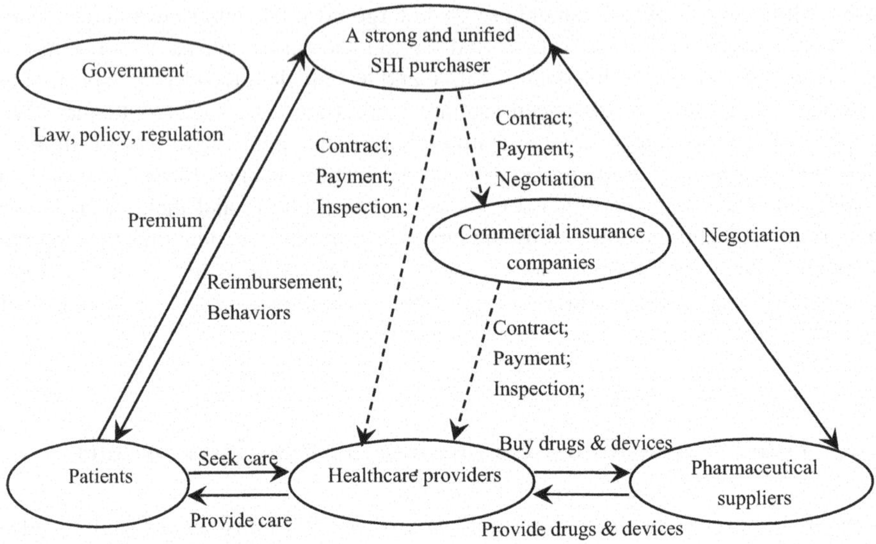

Fig. 6.1 A single payer model

are thousands of urban and rural SHI agencies nationwide owing to the separate and localized management of SHI schemes. These fragmented small-scale SHI agencies suffer from low administrative ranking, insufficient resources, and other problems in managing patients' and doctors' behaviors. The fragmentation of SHI schemes also generates high transaction costs, which SHI agencies cannot afford. Wagstaff (2007) contends that a health insurance system may not necessarily be more efficient than a tax-financed health system, because the separation of providers and insurance agencies increases the interagency transaction costs. Unless the money saved by the insurance agency is higher than the transaction costs, health insurance is no better choice. Therefore, the first step for practical healthcare reform is to establish gradually a strong and unified SHI purchaser, that is, a single payer of SHI.

Policy reform in its initial stage is to deal with the fragmented SHI schemes. To date, the UEBMI and URBMI are run by the Ministry of Human Resources and Social Security, while the NCMS is run by the Ministry of Health. Each scheme is further managed by local departments within the two ministries. This fragmented model restrains the behavior management and the purchasing practices of local agencies and is unfavorable to the safety of SHI funds. Policy makers should pool gradually the SHI funds at the higher-level SHI agencies, revoking the privilege of management from the county NCMS management offices and the county, district, and municipal SHI agencies. The ultimate goal is to formulate a nationally unified SHI purchaser. This purchaser takes charge of collecting and pooling the premiums contributed by enrollees, employers, and central and local governments. The safety of the pooling funds is more likely to be ensured than it is now, with unified policies and regulations and a large risk-pooling account. The separate SHI schemes should also be unified into one scheme, but with differentiated participation criteria and benefit levels. People with different occupations, income levels, residential areas, migrant status, disease incidence risks, and so on, could select the suitable participation criteria. Meanwhile, the single SHI purchaser should adjust for the socioeconomic characteristics of these participants to ensure the equity of benefit redistribution.

Meanwhile, the single payer may mobilize as many resources as possible to raise further the benefits of reimbursement. Looking at the concurrent mixed-premium contribution system, that is, the premium of the UEBMI being paid by the employer and the individual and that of the URBMI and the NCMS paid by the government and the individual, these contributors—especially the government—should act together to raise the reimbursement rate still further for the future unified SHI scheme. This could be done either by paying higher premiums or by adjusting the reimbursement formularies to incorporate more cost-effective drugs and services. However, we must be cautious of the allocation of responsibility for this process. The contribution rate of the employer and employee to social insurance (old age, medical, unemployment, workers' compensation, and maternity), which accounts for about 40 % of wages in China, has been held to be too high (Zhou 2012). Therefore, further scientific and rigorous investigation of this issue is warranted.

Meanwhile, the single payer may transform the current SHI agencies into its local agencies. It may allow mutual competition between these agencies. These agencies could compete to enroll participants and to set designated hospitals and clinics. They will gain profits from their performance in enrolling more participants and pushing healthcare providers to implement cost-effective services.

Some areas have piloted this single payer model although it is neither a nationally unified model nor a model encouraging mutual competition between local agencies. Some cities, such as Tianjin, Chengdu, and Hangzhou, have combined the NCMS and URBMI to formulate an Urban–Rural Resident Basic Medical Insurance (URRBMI). Some of them have offered hierarchical criteria of enrollment contributions and benefit levels in this scheme. For example, Chengdu City in Sichuan Province enacted the URRBMI in 2008. The scheme provides a choice of three levels of premium contribution for different income groups: annual ¥100, ¥200, and ¥300 per person. It also offers a subsidy to low-income groups. People would enjoy different levels of benefits according to their contributions (Chengdu Government 2008).

6.3.2 *Ensuring the Responsibility of the Unified Purchaser*

The establishment of a unified SHI purchaser would generate a monopsonistic insurance market. However, it does not guarantee automatically an active third-party purchasing of health services. The Achilles' heel, whether for a monopsonistic or a competitive insurance market, is the incentive problem for the third-party purchaser (Maynard 1994; Van de Ven et al. 1994). An SHI agency, although managing substantial SHI funding, may not act as a prudent purchaser in representation of the insured, as our qualitative investigation shows. It is important to ensure that the single payer is a responsible and smart third-party purchaser rather than a bureaucratic organization.

The most important reason for the incentive problem of SHI agencies lies in the rigid management of SHI funds. As the steward of insurance funds, SHI agencies are responsible for the safety of the management of the funds, with central government stressing repeatedly the importance of their safety (Central Committee of Communist Party of China and State Council 2009; Ministry of Human Resource and Social Security 2011; State Council 2010). Thus, these regulations shift the work priority of SHI agencies from ensuring the efficient use of SHI funds to a rigid management of the funds. They also cause passive management of SHI agencies, because the agencies cannot generate revenue from the surplus of SHI funds. Meanwhile, most SHI agencies in China suffer from inadequate resources to conduct further reform. If they save much of the surplus of SHI funds with efficient management, they are not allowed to use the surplus to improve either their organization establishment or the salary of staff. As a result, it seems that the SHI agency is less a smart buyer than a crude bureaucracy. Its usual cost-containment methods lie not in supervising adverse incentives for doctors and managing the medical utilization of patients, but frequently adjusting reimbursement plans and crudely enforcing payment methods reform. Therefore, patients become the ultimate victims.

In addition, to make SHI funds sustainable, the current SHI agencies would rather generate too much surplus. Subsequently, there are overly high surplus rates of pooling funds in many places, which may render the reimbursement level insufficient to reduce the financial risks of patients (Liu 2011). According to the official statistics, in 2008, the annual and cumulative surplus rates of NCMS funds were 15.6 and 25.4 %, respectively; those of URBMI funds were 52.8 and 82.7 %, respectively; and those of UEBMI funds were 30.0 % and even 114.5 %, respectively (China National Health Development Research Center 2009; Ministry of Health 2010; Ministry of Human Resources and Social Security 2009). An overly high surplus rate of insurance funds, although conducive to the safety of those funds, may decrease the benefit level of SHI and correspondingly, yield weak or even adverse effects on the decrease of OOPS. The problem has to be solved before the SHI purchaser can be a responsible purchaser.

The policy reform should focus on the efficient use of SHI funds. The unified purchaser should still take the responsibility of ensuring the safety of SHI funds, but could use SHI funds with more autonomy. It could use innovative management to ensure the safety of SHI funds. After that, it could gain profits from their management; it may use the surplus of SHI funds to award health facilities, patients, and itself, and it may also use the surplus to develop more innovative management. The flexible use of SHI funds is expected to ensure the responsibility of the SHI purchaser.

6.3.3 Formulating an Active SHI Governance System

To date, weak and fragmented SHI agencies are unable to manage the care-seeking behaviors of patients, to adjust the asymmetrical development of the healthcare market, to solve the undisciplined competition among health facilities, and to negotiate the prices of drugs and medical services. With a strong, responsible and unified SHI purchaser, the SHI governance system should be reformulated.

The policy reform should include the SHI purchaser in the centralized tender and procurement system of drugs and medical consumptive materials and devices. The single purchaser should be allowed to negotiate with pharmaceutical suppliers over the prices of drugs, medical consumptive materials, and devices and services.

The policy reform should also boost the negotiation between the SHI purchaser and healthcare providers. It involves two potential purchasing models. The purchaser can either entrust its local agencies and dispatch SHI officers into health facilities directly to conduct inspections, or entrust commercial insurance companies to conduct payment, inspections, and negotiation. With regard to the first method, the local SHI agencies act as a policy implementer and are supervised by the SHI purchaser. In addition, the local agencies sign contracts, pay, inspect, and negotiate with healthcare providers. This method is favorable to ensure the effective implementation of SHI policies and to save transaction costs between the SHI purchaser and its local agencies. However, it may still suffer from the incentive problem, as local SHI agencies may lack professional staff and incentives to contain health cost inflation. The second method may solve these drawbacks as it is embedded in a competitive market of health insurance. The single purchaser first selects commercial insurance companies as designated units and signs further contracts with them. The purchaser uses prospective payment methods to pay these companies and entrusts them to buy healthcare services from healthcare providers in representation of enrollees. These companies sign further contracts, pay, inspect, and negotiate with healthcare providers to buy cost-effective health services. With the spontaneous power of free market, these companies are profit-driven and own strong incentives to control health cost inflation. However, this method may also suffer from some drawbacks, as these profit-driven companies may give priority to cost control rather than healthcare quality, or may conspire with healthcare providers to abuse SHI funds. The drawbacks of both of the methods are great challenges for the single SHI purchaser. Therefore, it is still not clear whether competition or monopoly in the SHI sector should be held, as neither could guarantee automatically a prudent third-party purchaser. It leaves space for further studies. Meanwhile, it is a serious challenge to reinvent the current SHI agencies, which are bureaucratic organizations in nature. More empirical studies are required to examine whether the current SHI agencies are appropriate to act as local agencies of a single SHI payer.

Furthermore, the policy reform should use the behavior management and the purchasing mechanisms of SHI to facilitate the equitable and sound development of health facilities. Primary health facilities, as gatekeepers in the health service system, are very important for the sustainability of SHI. However, they suffer from inadequate resources due to the extreme overallocation of healthcare resources to tertiary hospitals, undisciplined competition among health facilities, as well as the lack of appropriate medical information for consumers in China (Xu and Van de Ven 2012; Zhang and Kanbur 2005). Therefore, it is not enough to rely merely on the regulation of referral mechanisms and the benefit package of tiered copayment and deductibles to guide patients to be admitted to primary care facilities. The single purchaser may set a mandatory rule that SHI enrollees have to select a primary health facility as their first diagnosis facility. Patients who want to go to higher-level health facilities have to be referred by doctors in the primary health facilities. Meanwhile, the purchaser may encourage the negotiation between primary and higher-level health facilities. Primary health facilities may select and sign contracts with higher-level health facilities as their cooperative organizations. The SHI purchaser may encourage them to formulate large medical care groups in the future. Meanwhile, the purchaser has to be responsible for the formulation of sound consumer choices. Strategic promotion of medical information should be conducted to guide consumer choices of healthcare facilities and services. This will facilitate the bidirectional referral system to be implemented between rural and urban areas, among facilities at different levels, and across regions.

It should be noted that these efforts, emphasizing the broader reform of China's healthcare system, call for joint actions among various government departments and between the state and its people. The effective working of the purchasing mechanism depends on the transformation of healthcare governance toward a contract model, with the purpose of maintaining a power balance among healthcare providers, purchasers, and regulators (Preker 2005). Therefore, the government's role as a regulator in promoting these joint actions has to be taken into consideration. Meanwhile, the government should quit its traditional roles as both health service provider and SHI purchaser. This will facilitate a formulation of a mixed economy or a contract model in the healthcare sector.

Moreover, the establishment of a single and smart buyer has a long way to go, especially in developing countries where resources are seriously short and infrastructure are outdated. It is not merely an issue of resource input, as other factors including the incentive problem, high transaction costs, and disenabling institutional surroundings may together produce effects that make the infusion of healthcare investment a wasted effort. More efforts should be devoted to investigating the determinants of the efficiency of the SHI system as well as the interaction between the SHI system, other institutions, and the relevant stakeholders.

6.4 Limitations of the Study

It is important to acknowledge the limitations of this study. One of the limitations is that is suffers from a problematic integration of the quantitative and qualitative parts of the mixed-methods design, although the design itself has been criticized to be problematic in nature. To be specific, the quantitative study generates three mechanisms of the institutional arrangement. It further reveals that the reimbursement mechanism functions well, but is undermined by the dysfunctions of the behavior management and purchasing mechanisms. However, our qualitative study uncovers that even the reimbursement mechanism is problematic. It may undermine the other two mechanisms, too, and even itself. The two parts do not exist in an integrated way. Although we try to use both determinative and strategic interactive perspectives to bridge the gaps, there is still much room to improve the integration.

With regard to the quantitative study, there are several methodological limitations. First, as the CHARLS focuses on people at mid-age and above, the average age of the samples is higher than that of the population as a whole. Second, our investigation is cross-sectional, so the causal relationship cannot be guaranteed although we use an instrumental variables method to try to avoid the endogeneity problem when analyzing the relationship between SHI participation and a series of medical expenditure indicators. Third, the variable types of treatment items when using structural equation modeling may not accurately reflect the cost of treatment. Fourth, when using structural equation modeling, we are unable to control for a number of possible confounding variables, such as regional differences and the type and severity of diseases, which may influence both SHI participation and OOPS.

Regarding the qualitative study, we suffer from problems of both sampling and presentation of our findings. Although we identify three stakeholders, including SHI agencies, healthcare providers, and patients, other stakeholders, such as officials in the Department of Finance, the Office of Drug Tender and Procurement, and so on, should also be included to investigate the role that the government plays in the interaction of stakeholders. However, we failed to reach them owing to contact problems. In addition, we try to organize the manuscript in a clear way by considering different stakeholders one by one and summarizing their interactions simultaneously. However, this style causes overlapping information.

6.5 Conclusion

To conclude, this study embraces a new institutionalist approach and uses both determinative and strategic interactive perspectives to examine and explore China's rapidly expanding SHI programs and their institutional arrangements. It provides a rich understanding of the role that the institutional arrangement of SHI plays in influencing the relationship between SHI participation and OOPS, and of the interactions between stakeholders, the SHI system, and other institutions in affecting the efficiencies of these institutional arrangements.

To be specific, the behavior management and purchasing mechanisms of SHI perform poorly, undermining the function of the reimbursement mechanism and mitigating the impact of SHI participation on OOPS. This is because patients who participate in SHI schemes tend to abuse medical services and spill over to the large hospitals; this is also because doctors take advantage of the reimbursement of SHI to compete in a disordered way to attract patients, to conduct overtreatment to earn their living, and to generate profits for health facilities. With the constraints of incentives, resources, transaction costs, and the institutional surroundings, SHI agencies become weak purchasers.

This study is expected to contribute to both theory and policy in the following ways. It investigates the role of institutional arrangements in responding to a number of long-standing debates about welfare institutions and outcomes. It argues that a welfare institution must be taken as a policy instrument for adjusting the behaviors of actors and as a catalyst for improving delivery efficiency, in addition to universal benefit provision. It also reveals that welfare institutions and their mechanisms may be shaped and undermined by the larger institutional surroundings and the conflicts among the mechanisms through the strategic interactions between actors. Finally, this study combines quantitative and qualitative evidence to propose a single payer model. This model provides a profile of how to establish a strong and unified SHI purchaser, to ensure the responsibility of the purchaser, and to formulate an active SHI governance system. It is expected to provide insights into China's ambitious healthcare reform.

Appendix A

See Tables A.1, A.2, A.3, A.4, A.5 and A.6.

K. Liu, *The Effects of Social Health Insurance Reform on People's Out-of-Pocket Health Expenditure in China*, DOI 10.1007/978-981-10-1777-3

Table A.1 Results of regression analysis for UEBMI outpatient subsample: method 1

	Device test		Lab test		Drip infusion		Injection		Share of OOPS drug cost		Total cost		OOPS	
	Probit	IV	Probit	IV	Probit	IV	Probit	IV	OLS	IV	OLS	IV	OLS	IV
UEBMI	0.26***	0.99*	0.82**	1.02*	0.24	−0.12	−0.49*	−0.35	−0.38***	−0.15	2498.89**	3170.53**	678.21	941.53
Age	0.01*	−0.02*	−0.01	−0.02	0.00	0.00	0.00	0.00	0.00	0.00*	14.97	13.36	10.69	10.29
Male	0.18	0.21	−0.02	−0.01	0.03	0.14	0.17	0.22	0.05	0.04	−93.83	−119.60	−246.22	−258.32
Education	0.09*	−0.18	−0.11	−0.11	−0.03	0.01	−0.09	−0.08	0.00	−0.01	−616.89*	−700.28**	−113.89	−145.79
Urban	0.24	0.05	−0.09	−0.14	0.00	0.18	0.60**	0.55*	−0.08	−0.20**	497.27	249.85	201.47	95.06
Facility location	0.09***	0.31**	0.20*	0.18	−0.15	−0.16	0.07	0.07	−0.06**	−0.06**	546.04*	548.44*	240.95	242.05
Self-reported health	0.15*	0.32*	0.59***	0.58**	0.28*	0.19	0.17	0.22	0.02	0.06	484.98	612.16	323.35	385.83
Chronic	0.06	−0.07	−0.02	−0.02	−0.08	−0.06	−0.09	−0.09	0.00	−0.01	27.05	−16.95	−45.88	−67.00
Functional limitation	0.03	0.03	−0.02	−0.02	0.05*	0.06*	0.02	0.01	0.01	0.01	60.57	59.79	27.71	27.68
Per capita household income	0.01	0.00	0.01	0.01	0.00	0.00	0.00	0.00	0.00	0.00	0.88	−4.39	−2.02	−4.32
Per capita household wealth	0.00	0.00	0.00	0.00	0.00	0.00	0.00	0.00	0.00	0.00	0.32	0.30	−0.26	−0.26

Note. ***$p < 0.001$; **$p < 0.01$; *$p < 0.05$

Table A.2 Results of regression analysis for URBMI outpatient subsample: method 1

	Device test		Lab test		Drip infusion		Injection		Share of OOPS drug cost		Total cost		OOPS	
	Probit	IV	Probit	IV	Probit	IV	Probit	IV	OLS	IV	OLS	IV	OLS	IV
URBMI	1.05**	0.55	0.67*	0.46	0.34	−0.01	−0.35	−0.72	−0.46***	−0.65*	718.02*	−171.54	117.63	−828.35
Age	−0.02	−0.02	−0.01	−0.02	0.02	0.02	0.00	−0.01	−0.01	−0.01	15.29	24.16*	13.01	18.56
Male	−0.19	−0.18	−0.10	−0.12	−0.04	0.02	0.22	−0.04	0.10	0.10	43.29	104.10	53.22	76.98
Education	−0.24	−0.27	−0.10	−0.09	0.00	0.01	−0.08	−0.06	−0.01	0.01	−21.77	39.18	−14.36	70.18
Urban	−0.25	−0.20	−0.28	−0.20	−0.24	−0.09	0.55*	0.68*	−0.09	−0.07	63.63	314.82	87.12	342.49
Facility location	0.58***	0.55***	0.40**	0.42**	−0.25*	−0.31**	0.07	0.04	−0.05	−0.06	395.09***	325.62**	316.25**	275.68**
Self-reported health	0.35	0.32	0.54**	0.56*	0.33*	0.33*	0.22	0.11	−0.05	−0.06	−120.21	−100.81	−0.36	−0.05
Chronic	−0.21*	−0.18	−0.08	−0.07	−0.10	−0.07	−0.09	−0.10	0.02	0.02	48.83	78.70	27.76	52.74
Functional limitation	0.02	0.03	0.01	0.00	0.08*	0.07*	0.01	0.01	0.01	0.02	54.04	59.37	15.66	25.45
Per capita household income	0.01	0.03	0.02	0.03	0.00	0.00	0.00	0.04	0.00	0.01	13.30	27.40	13.31	29.28
Per capita household wealth	0.00	0.00	0.00	0.00	0.00	0.00	0.00	0.00	0.00	0.00	−0.38	−0.35	−0.44	−0.39

Note. $^{***}p < 0.001$; $^{**}p < 0.01$; $^{*}p < 0.05$.

Table A.3 Results of regression analysis for NCMS outpatient subsample: method 1

	Device test		Lab test		Drip infusion		Injection		Share of OOPS drug cost		Total cost		OOPS	
	Probit	IV	Probit	IV	Probit	IV	Probit	IV	OLS	IV	OLS	IV	OLS	IV
NCMS	0.38*	0.60	0.38*	0.47	0.48***	0.39	−0.22	−0.06	−0.27***	−0.23*	854.70	1717.30	519.16	1265.28
Age	−0.01	−0.01	0.00	0.00	0.01*	0.01	0.00	0.00	0.00	0.00	−77.25**	−75.27*	−66.46**	−64.79**
Male	0.15	0.16	0.09	0.08	0.09	0.09	−0.02	−0.04	0.06	0.05	385.48	349.46	303.04	272.52
Education	−0.08	−0.08	0.12	0.13	−0.03	−0.03	0.03	0.04	−0.02	−0.02	−188.09	−159.33	−188.53	−164.79
Urban	0.19	0.21	0.19	0.21	−0.03	−0.04	0.14	0.17	0.00	0.01	855.09	992.37	736.37	853.37
Facility location	0.58***	0.59***	0.43***	0.44***	−0.10*	−0.11*	0.01	0.02	−0.01	0.00	1055.28***	1099.91***	840.83**	878.82**
Self-reported health	0.09	0.10	0.15	0.15	0.03	0.02	0.08	0.08	−0.01	−0.01	133.02	150.10	95.76	109.82
Chronic	−0.07	−0.06	0.02	0.02	0.01	0.01	−0.03	−0.03	0.02*	0.02*	−515.35**	−510.03**	−401.79*	−397.00*
Functional limitation	0.03	0.02	0.02	0.02	0.03**	0.04**	0.01	0.01	−0.01	−0.01	337.57***	325.09***	271.75***	261.01***
Per capita household income	0.00	0.00	0.00	0.00	0.00	0.00	0.00	0.01	0.00	0.00	−13.72	−19.01	−11.63	−16.16
Per capita household wealth	0.00	0.00	0.00	0.00	0.00	0.00	0.00	0.00	0.00	0.00	4.39	4.80	3.36	3.72

Note. $^{***}p < 0.001$; $^{**}p < 0.01$; $^{*}p < 0.05$.

Table A.4 Results of regression analysis for UEBMI inpatient subsample: method 1

	Device test		Lab test		Drip infusion		Injection		Surgery	
	Probit	IV	Probit	IV	Probit	IV	Probit	IV	Probit	IV
UEBMI	0.44*	0.81*	0.65**	1.63***	−0.23	−0.10	0.51**	0.62	0.00	0.22
Age	0.00	0.00	0.00	0.00	0.01	0.01	0.01	0.01	−0.02*	−0.02*
Male	0.18	0.13	0.08	−0.06	−0.01	−0.08	0.13	0.08	−0.14	−0.17
Education	−0.17*	−0.20**	0.01	−0.09	−0.12	−0.14	0.07	0.06	−0.01	−0.03
Urban	0.23	0.09	0.04	−0.32	0.23	0.20	−0.02	−0.02	0.28	0.20
Facility location	0.14*	0.14*	0.12	0.13	−0.13	−0.12	0.15*	0.15*	0.08	0.09
Self-reported health	0.10	0.08	0.21	0.20	−0.14	−0.10	0.03	0.03	−0.26*	−0.28*
Chronic	0.02	0.01	0.06	0.03	0.07	0.06	0.03	0.03	−0.12*	−0.13**
Functional limitation	0.00	−0.01	−0.02	−0.02	−0.02	−0.03	0.02	0.01	0.04*	0.05*
Per capita household income	0.00	0.00	0.01	0.00	0.02	0.01	0.00	0.00	0.00	0.00
Per capita household wealth	0.00	0.00	0.00	0.00	0.00	0.00	0.00	0.00	0.00	0.00

	Share of OOPS drug cost		Length of stay		Total cost		OOPS	
	OLS	IV	OLS	IV	OLS	IV	OLS	IV
UEBMI	−0.34***	−0.18	3.09	6.59	2734.53	9550.25**	−3106.19*	3064.25
Age	0.00	0.00	−0.05	−0.07	−24.76	−63.17	−91.03	−125.94*
Male	−0.02	−0.04	2.37	1.88	−16.42	−901.26	−131.27	−924.80
Education	0.05*	0.04	−0.95	−1.31*	46.70	−645.17	24.96	−584.75
Urban	0.00	−0.06	4.78**	3.29	4402.64**	1743.34	4020.29**	1544.47
Facility location	−0.02	−0.01	1.20*	1.28*	2363.02***	2560.06***	1700.27***	1846.99***
Self-reported health	0.04	0.03	1.35	1.32	2283.04*	2315.15*	1887.62*	1853.16*
Chronic	0.00	0.00	0.05	−0.04	−463.12	−638.46	−383.47	−546.55

(continued)

Table A.4 (continued)

	Share of OOPS drug cost		Length of stay		Total cost		OOPS	
	OLS	IV	OLS	IV	OLS	IV	OLS	IV
Functional limitation	0.00	0.00	0.19	0.22	194.68	224.17	99.41	135.69
Per capita household income	0.00	0.00	0.00	−0.03	65.24	−1.06	29.19	−26.99
Per capita household wealth	0.00	0.00	0.00	0.00	9.41	7.61	3.47	1.56

Note. ***$p < 0.001$; **$p < 0.01$; *$p < 0.05$.

Table A.5 Results of regression analysis for URBMI inpatient subsample: method 1

	Device test		Lab test		Drip infusion		Injection		Surgery	
	Probit	IV	Probit	IV	Probit	IV	Probit	IV	Probit	IV
URBMI	0.41	1.60*	0.54*	1.85*	−0.19	−0.45	0.13	1.58*	−0.22	0.99
Age	0.00	0.00	−0.01	−0.01	0.00	0.00	0.00	0.00	−0.03**	−0.04**
Male	−0.12	−0.33	0.25	0.08	0.19	0.10	−0.12	−0.26	−0.04	−0.11
Education	−0.09	−0.14	0.06	0.04	−0.05	−0.03	0.15	0.15	0.06	−0.01
Urban	0.09	−0.11	0.06	−0.14	−0.07	−0.04	0.05	−0.19	0.37	0.14
Facility location	0.19*	0.25*	0.12	0.20*	−0.29**	−0.30*	0.12	0.23*	0.04	0.11
Self-reported health	0.18	0.14	0.14	0.11	−0.08	−0.09	−0.05	−0.11	−0.16	−0.17
Chronic	−0.07	−0.08	0.03	0.01	0.05	0.05	0.03	0.03	−0.09	−0.11
Functional limitation	−0.01	−0.03	0.02	0.01	−0.03	−0.02	0.04	0.03	0.05*	0.04
Per capita household income	0.03*	0.03	0.04**	0.04*	0.08**	0.07**	0.01	0.01	0.01	0.01
Per capita household wealth	0.00	0.00	0.00	0.00	0.00	0.00	0.00	0.00	0.00	0.00

	Share of OOPS drug cost		Length of stay		Total cost		OOPS	
	OLS	IV	OLS	IV	OLS	IV	OLS	IV
URBMI	−0.17*	−0.18	1.03	3.11	−515.08	5660.53	−3925.81*	3665.75
Age	0.00	0.00	−0.18*	−0.18*	−169.92*	−159.76*	−149.91*	−150.22*
Male	−0.02	−0.02	2.27	1.71	979.77	44.20	1003.38	119.91
Education	0.06*	0.08*	−1.34	−1.56	−207.12	−144.32	−388.70	−442.29
Urban	−0.02	0.01	4.46*	3.96	3634.71*	2020.35	4045.30**	2051.36
Facility location	−0.06	−0.04	1.01	1.18	1260.15*	1615.87*	1472.91*	1829.78**
Self-reported health	0.01	0.01	1.05	1.09	1412.43	1016.85	1996.34*	1605.01
Chronic	0.01	0.01	0.46	0.51	−7.32	70.35	−352.36	−303.73

(continued)

Table A.5 (continued)

	Share of OOPS drug cost		Length of stay		Total cost		OOPS	
	OLS	IV	OLS	IV	OLS	IV	OLS	IV
Functional limitation	0.00	0.00	0.33	0.32	200.26	195.00	40.98	38.61
Per capita household income	0.00	0.00	−0.05	−0.06	64.84	53.85	51.49	35.24
Per capita household wealth	0.00*	0.00	0.00	0.00	11.44	8.21	7.50	3.31

Note. ***$p < 0.001$; **$p < 0.01$; *$p < 0.05$.

Table A.6 Results of regression analysis for NCMS inpatient subsample: method 1

	Device test		Lab test		Drip infusion		Injection		Surgery	
	Probit	IV	Probit	IV	Probit	IV	Probit	IV	Probit	IV
NCMS	0.16	−0.61	0.25*	−0.61	0.23	0.44	0.19	−0.23	0.11	−0.61
Age	0.00	0.00	0.00	0.00	0.01	0.01	0.00	0.00	−0.02***	−0.02***
Male	0.05	0.07	0.07	0.09	0.06	0.06	0.08	0.08	0.06	0.09
Education	−0.08	−0.09	0.01	0.00	−0.01	−0.01	0.08	0.07	−0.04	−0.04
Urban	−0.02	−0.08	−0.07	−0.13	0.16	0.19	−0.02	−0.05	0.00	−0.07
Facility location	0.29***	0.27***	0.25***	0.23***	−0.20**	−0.20**	0.24***	0.23***	0.23***	0.21***
Self-reported health	0.04	0.03	0.06	0.06	−0.01	−0.01	−0.03	−0.03	−0.08	−0.08
Chronic	−0.02	−0.02	0.05	0.04	0.07*	0.07	0.02	0.02	−0.11**	−0.11***
Functional limitation	0.00	0.00	0.00	0.00	−0.01	0.00	0.02*	0.02	0.00	0.00
Per capita household income	0.01	0.01	0.04***	0.04***	0.01	0.01	0.00	0.00	0.00	0.00
Per capita household wealth	0.00	0.00	0.00	0.00	0.00*	0.00*	0.00	0.00	0.00	0.00

	Share of OOPS drug cost		Length of stay		Total cost		OOPS	
	OLS	IV	OLS	IV	OLS	IV	OLS	IV
NCMS	−0.23***	−0.20*	0.09	−1.16	2236.33*	−634.65	268.55	−2200.93
Age	0.00	0.00	−0.09*	−0.09*	−32.82	−36.35	−109.23**	−113.18**
Male	−0.06*	−0.06*	1.70*	1.72*	1934.66*	2021.48*	1641.12*	1724.78*
Education	0.03	0.03	−0.93*	−0.95*	209.15	146.77	108.97	53.39
Urban	−0.01	0.00	1.70*	1.57*	2552.76**	2282.18*	2763.13**	2524.25**
Facility location	0.00	0.00	1.75***	1.70***	3600.55***	3510.40***	3046.61***	2962.76***
Self-reported health	0.03	0.02	1.40**	1.42**	1582.91**	1600.79**	1140.07*	1155.92*
Chronic	0.01	0.01	−0.32	−0.31	−612.61*	−619.84*	−706.40**	−714.52**
Functional limitation	0.00	0.00	0.26**	0.26**	176.58	175.61	315.22**	315.17**

(continued)

Table A.6 (continued)

	Share of OOPS drug cost		Length of stay		Total cost		OOPS	
	OLS	IV	OLS	IV	OLS	IV	OLS	IV
Per capita household income	0.00	0.00	−0.02	−0.02	3.19	6.58	−8.75	−4.87
Per capita household wealth	0.00*	0.00*	0.01	0.01	19.20*	18.08*	17.16*	15.97
	Share of OOPS drug cost		Length of stay		Total cost		OOPS	
	OLS	IV	OLS	IV	OLS	IV	OLS	IV
NCMS	−0.23***	−0.20*	0.09	−1.16	2236.33*	−634.65	268.55	−2200.93
Age	0.00	0.00	−0.09*	−0.09*	−32.82	−36.35	−109.23**	−113.18**
Male	−0.06*	−0.06*	1.70*	1.72*	1934.66*	2021.48*	1641.12*	1724.78*
Education	0.03	0.03	−0.93*	−0.95*	209.15	146.77	108.97	53.39
Urban	−0.01	0.00	1.70*	1.57*	2552.76**	2282.18*	2763.13**	2524.25**
Facility location	0.00	0.00	1.75***	1.70***	3600.55***	3510.40***	3046.61***	2962.76***
Self-reported health	0.03	0.02	1.40**	1.42**	1582.91**	1600.79**	1140.07*	1155.92*
Chronic	0.01	0.01	−0.32	−0.31	−612.61*	−619.84*	−706.40**	−714.52**
Functional limitation	0.00	0.00	0.26**	0.26**	176.58	175.61	315.22**	315.17**
Per capita household income	0.00	0.00	−0.02	−0.02	3.19	6.58	−8.75	−4.87
Per capita household wealth	0.00*	0.00*	0.01	0.01	19.20*	18.08*	17.16*	15.97

Note ***$p < 0.001$; **$p < 0.01$; *$p < 0.05$.

Appendix B

See Table B.1.

Table B.1 Interviewees in this study

Date	Location	Institution	Interviewee	Occupation
8/10/2012	County D	THC A	GSQ	Director of the THC
8/11/2012	County D	Department of Surgery, THC A	GXH	Doctor
8/11/2012	County D	Department of Internal Medicine, THC A	WSC	Doctor
8/12/2012	County D	Department of Otolaryngology, THC A	XWB	Doctor
8/13/2012	County D	Department of Surgery, THC A	WY	Doctor
8/14/2012	County D	Department of Surgery, THC A	GXH	Doctor
8/14/2012	County D	Department of Internal Medicine, THC A	ZHC	Doctor
8/15/2012	County D	County BoH	YJZ	Deputy Director
8/16/2012	County D	Department of Surgery, THC A	GXH	Doctor
8/16/2012	County D	NCMS Reimbursement Office, THC A	ZHX	NCMS Reimbursement Officer
8/17/2012	County D	NCMS Reimbursement Office, THC A	ZHX	NCMS Reimbursement Officer
8/21/2012	County D	Department of Public Health, THC A	FX	Doctor
8/22/2012	Village D, County D	Village Clinic	CYS	Village Doctor
8/23/2012	County D	Financial Affairs Office, THC A	CKJ	Accountant
8/23/2012	County D	Department of Internal Medicine, THC A	ZX	Doctor

(continued)

K. Liu, *The Effects of Social Health Insurance Reform on People's Out-of-Pocket Health Expenditure in China*, DOI 10.1007/978-981-10-1777-3

Table B.1 (continued)

Date	Location	Institution	Interviewee	Occupation
8/23/2012	Village X, County D	Village Clinic	ZZYS	Village Doctor
8/24/2012	Village L, County D	Village Clinic	LYS	Village Doctor
8/24/2012	Village S, County D	Village Clinic	SYS	Village Doctor
8/24/2012	Village Z, County D	Village Clinic	ZYS	Village Doctor
8/27/2012	County D	Department of Surgery, THC A	GXH	Doctor
8/27/2012	County D	Department of Surgery, THC A	GXH	Doctor
8/27/2012	County D	Department of Surgery, THC A	WY	Doctor
8/28/2012	Village B, County D	Village Clinic	FYS	Village Doctor
8/28/2012	County D	THC A	GSQ	Director of the THC
8/28/2012	County D	NCMS Reimbursement Office, THC A	ZHX	NCMS Reimbursement Officer
8/30/2012	County D	THC A	GSQ	Director of the THC
9/3/2012	County D	Department of Surgery, THC A	TLB	Doctor
9/3/2012	County D	Department of Internal Medicine, THC A	WSC	Doctor
9/3/2012	County D	Department of Internal Medicine, THC A	WSC	Doctor
9/3/2012	County D	Department of Surgery, THC A	WY	Doctor
9/4/2012	County D	NCMS Reimbursement Office, THC A	DJ	NCMS Reimbursement Officer
9/4/2012	County D	Department of Ophthalmology, THC A	DYS	Doctor
9/4/2012	County D	NCMS Management Office, County BoH	PJGY	NCMS Inspector
9/4/2012	County D	Department of Surgery, THC A	TYS	Doctor
9/5/2012	County D	THC A	GSQ	Director of the THC
9/5/2012	County D	Department of Surgery, THC A	GXH	Doctor
9/5/2012	County D	Department of Otolaryngology, THC A	XWB	Doctor
9/6/2012	County D	NCMS Management Office, County BoH	PZR	Deputy Director

(continued)

Table B.1 (continued)

Date	Location	Institution	Interviewee	Occupation
9/10/2012	City C	UEBMI Management Office, Municipal Department of SHI Administration	ZJ	Department Chief
9/11/2012	City C	Municipal Department of SHI Administration	XDW	Deputy Director
9/12/2012	City C	URBMI Management Office, Municipal Department of SHI Administration	LM	Clerk
9/12/2012	City C	Municipal Department of SHI Administration	XDW	Deputy Director
9/13/2012	City C	UEBMI Management Office, Municipal Department of SHI Administration	YM	Clerk
9/17/2012	City C	URBMI Management Office, Municipal Department of SHI Administration	BSP	Department Chief
9/17/2012	City C	Financial Affairs Office, Municipal Department of SHI Administration	WW	Department Chief
9/18/2012	City C	NCMS Reimbursement Office, City C No. 6 Hospital	GKZ	NCMS Reimbursement Officer
9/18/2012	City C	Department of Mental Health, City C No. 6 People's Hospital	WYS	Chief Physician
9/18/2012	City C	Department of Electrocardiography, City C No. 1 People's Hospital	PYS	Doctor
9/18/2012	City C	NCMS Reimbursement Office, City C No. 1 People's Hospital	WKZ	NCMS Reimbursement Officer
9/20/2012	City B	Municipal Department of SHI Administration	BJZ	Deputy Director
9/20/2012	City B	Department of Planning, Municipal Department of SHI Administration	CKZ	Clerk
9/20/2012	City B	Department of Planning, Municipal Department of SHI Administration	WKZ	Department Chief
9/21/2012	City B	Municipal Department of SHI Administration	BJZ	Deputy Director

(continued)

Table B.1 (continued)

Date	Location	Institution	Interviewee	Occupation
9/24/2012	City B	Department of Medical Affairs Management, Municipal Department of SHI Administration	SKZ	Department Chief
9/24/2012	City B	Department of Planning, Municipal Department of SHI Administration	WKZ	Department Chief
9/26/2012	City B	Department of Intervention, XH Hospital	MYS	Doctor
9/26/2012	City B	Department of Intervention, XH Hospital	ZYS	Doctor
9/27/2012	City B	Department of Neurosurgery, JFJ Hospital	WZY	Doctor
10/18/2012	City A	Department of Otolaryngology, City A Central Hospital	DYS, ZYZ	DYS: Chief Physician; ZYZ: Deputy Director of the Hospital
10/18/2012	City A	UEBMI Reimbursement Office, City A Central Hospital	GJ	UEBMI Reimbursement Officer
10/18/2012	City A	Department of Gynecology, City A Central Hospital	TTYS	Doctor
10/19/2012	City A	UEBMI Reimbursement Office, City A Chinese Medicine Hospital	GZR	Deputy Office Head
10/19/2012	City A	Department of Emergency Surgery, City A Chinese Medicine Hospital	GYS	Doctor
10/19/2012	City A	Department of Emergency Surgery, City A Chinese Medicine Hospital	PYS	Doctor
10/19/2012	City A	Department of Respiration Medicine, The First Affiliated Hospital of ZZ University	ZJYS	Doctor
10/19/2012	City A	Department of Neurology, The First Affiliated Hospital of ZZ University	JYS	Doctor
10/19/2012	City A	Department of Hepatobiliary Surgery, The First Affiliated Hospital of ZZ University	ZYS	Doctor
10/19/2012	City A	X Pharmaceutical Company	YXZ	Pharmaceutical Sales Representative
10/19/2012	City A	Lab Test Center, City A Central Hospital	HYJ	Doctor

(continued)

Table B.1 (continued)

Date	Location	Institution	Interviewee	Occupation
10/24/2012	Village D, County D	Local Household	LJG	Patient
10/25/2012	Village D, County D	Local Household	LZX	Patient
10/27/2012	Village D, County D	Local Household	LZF	Patient
10/28/2012	Village D, County D	Local Household	LTZ	Patient
10/28/2012	Village D, County D	Local Household	SXT	Patient
10/30/2012	County D	Department of Emergency, County D People's Hospital	FXS	Doctor
10/30/2012	County D	County Center of SHI Administration	GZR; LKZ	GZR: Deputy Director; LKZ: Clerk of the Department of Premium Collection
10/30/2012	County D	Local Household	LY	Patient
10/30/2012	Village X, County D	Local Household	XGM	Patient
11/1/2012	City B	CHC	GSL	Doctor
11/1/2012	City B	CHC	GSL	Doctor
11/1/2012	City B	CHC	GSL	Doctor
11/5/2012	Village X, County D	Local Household	ZSF	Patient
11/7/2012	Village D, County D	Local Household	LXC	Patient
11/7/2012	Village D, County D	Local Household	LZY	Patient
11/13/2012	County D	Local Household	GSY	Patient
11/13/2012	Village D, County D	Local Household	LXC	Patient
11/20/2012	City A	Local Household	HNS	Patient
11/21/2012	City A	Local Household	GYL	Patient

Appendix C

Interviewing Guides

Version 1: For the Doctors

1. Sociodemographic background: age, gender, name of health facility, and service department to which the participant is affiliated, and professional position.
2. The reimbursement mechanism of SHI
   (a) Which kinds of patients do you admit most? UEBMI, URBMI, or NCMS patients?
   (b) How do these SHI schemes affect people's admission in the health facility?
   (c) How do these SHI schemes affect the development of the health facility and the service department you are affiliated to?
   (d) What is the difference in the reimbursement rates between these SHI schemes? How are their reimbursement rates different?
   (e) What is the difference between the actual and policy-regulated reimbursement rates for each scheme? Why are the rates different?
3. The behavior management mechanism of SHI
   (a) What strategies do different SHI schemes use to adjust people's choices of health facilities? Do they produce the desired effect? Why?
   (b) How do people react to these regulations?
   (c) How do doctors react to these regulations?
   (d) Are there any other factors affecting people's choices of health facilities?
4. The purchasing mechanism of SHI
   (a) What strategies do different SHI schemes use to restrain health cost inflation in health facilities? Do they produce the desired effect? Why?
   (b) How do people react to these regulations?
   (c) How do doctors react to these regulations?
   (d) Are there any other factors affecting health cost inflation in health facilities?
5. The interplay between the reimbursement, behavior management, and purchasing mechanism of SHI

K. Liu, *The Effects of Social Health Insurance Reform on People's Out-of-Pocket Health Expenditure in China*, DOI 10.1007/978-981-10-1777-3

(a) Generally speaking, how do different SHI schemes affect people's out-of-pocket expenditures?
(b) How do people's choices of health facilities affect their reimbursements of SHI?
(c) How do people's choices of health facilities affect their total medical expenditures and treatment items?
(d) How do the fee-charging, treatment items and medical expenditures in health facilities affect people's reimbursements of SHI?

6. The grand institutional surroundings

(a) Generally speaking, how do you think of the health care reform in our country?
(b) Which parts of the health care system boost cost inflation much?
(c) How do these parts affect the development of SHI?

Version 2: For the Patients

1. Sociodemographic background: age, gender, family economic condition, name of the disease that the participant caught, experiences of care seeking.
2. The reimbursement mechanism of SHI

(a) Which kinds of SHI schemes do you participate in? UEBMI, URBMI, or NCMS?
(b) How much did you spend for your disease? How much did you get reimbursed by the SHI scheme? How much did you spend out of pocket?
(c) Are you satisfied with the reimbursement of SHI? How do you think?

3. The behavior management mechanism of SHI

(a) Which health facility were you hospitalized in? What is the grade of this health facility?
(b) Why did you go to this health facility rather than others?
(c) Were there any regulations of SHI affecting your choice of health facilities? Why were they affecting or not your choices?

4. The purchasing mechanism of SHI

(a) How do you think of your spending in the health facility?
(b) How many days did you live in the health facility? What kinds of medical services did you receive?
(c) How do you think of the medical services you received in the health facility? Were these services required by you or prescribed by doctors?
(d) How do you think of the general fee-charging in health facilities?

5. The interplay between the reimbursement, behavior management, and purchasing mechanisms of SHI

(a) Generally speaking, how do think of the effect of the SHI scheme on your out-of-pocket expenditures?

(b) How does your choice of health facility affect the reimbursements of SHI?
(c) How does your choice of health facility affect your total medical expenditures and treatment items?
(d) How do the fee-charging and treatment items affect your medical expenditures and out-of-pocket expenditures in the health facility?

6. The grand institutional surroundings

(a) Can you talk about your opinions on the health care in our country?
(b) How do you think of the development of SHI in our country?

Version 3: For the Officers in SHI Agencies

1. Sociodemographic background: age, gender, name of the SHI agency and office to which the participant is affiliated, and administrative position.
2. The reimbursement mechanism of SHI

(a) What kinds of SHI schemes does this agency manage? UEBMI, URBMI, or NCMS?
(b) Can you talk about the coverage of the SHI scheme in this area?
(c) Can you talk about the reimbursement plan of the SHI scheme?
(d) How does the SHI scheme affect people's admission in health facilities?
(e) How does the SHI scheme affect the development of health facilities?
(f) What is the difference in the reimbursement rates between this SHI scheme and others? Why are their reimbursement rates different?
(g) What is the difference between the actual and policy-regulated reimbursement rates for this SHI scheme? Why are the rates different?

3. The behavior management mechanism of SHI

(a) What strategies does your SHI agency use to adjust people's choices of health facilities? Do they produce the desired effect? Why?
(b) How do people react to these regulations?
(c) How do doctors react to these regulations?
(d) Are there any other factors affecting people's choices of health facilities?

4. The purchasing mechanism of SHI

(a) What strategies does your SHI agency use to restrain health cost inflation in health facilities? Do they produce the desired effect? Why?
(b) How do people react to these regulations?
(c) How do doctors react to these regulations?
(d) Are there any institutional factors affecting the enforcement of the strategies?

5. The interplay between the reimbursement, behavior management and purchasing mechanism of SHI

(a) Generally speaking, how does the SHI scheme affect people's out-of-pocket expenditures?

(b) How do people's choices of health facilities affect their reimbursements of SHI?
(c) How do people's choices of health facilities affect their total medical expenditures and treatment items?
(d) How do the fee-charging, treatment items, and medical expenditures in health facilities affect people's reimbursements of SHI?

6. The grand institutional surroundings

(a) Generally speaking, how do you think of the health care reform in our country?
(b) Which parts of the healthcare system boost cost inflation much?
(c) How do these parts affect the development of SHI and the work at your agency?

Appendix D

Consent Form

Dear Participant,

My name is LIU Kai. I am currently a doctoral student of the Department of Social Work at The Chinese University of Hong Kong. I am conducting a research entitled "Effects of Social Health Insurance Reform on People's Out-of-Pocket Health Expenditure in China: The Mediating Role of Institutional Arrangement". This research aims to collect your opinions and advices on China's Social Health Insurance and its reform.

I need to conduct a one-hour interview with you. But your participation is entirely voluntary. And you have the right to terminate the study at any time.

The interview will be conducted according to an interviewing guide. With your agreement, our talk will be recoded with audiotape. The true answer by you would be highly helpful to this study.

The interview will do no harm to you. All the information collected is just used for scientific research. Your name as well as the name of your working unit will be kept anonymous. The information collected from you will be kept confidential.

If you have any questions, you can ask me now or later.

LIU Kai
PhD Candidate
Department of Social Work
The Chinese University of Hong Kong

K. Liu, *The Effects of Social Health Insurance Reform on People's Out-of-Pocket Health Expenditure in China*, DOI 10.1007/978-981-10-1777-3

Consent Form

I agree to be in a study about investigating the institutional arrangement of social health insurance in China. This study was explained clearly by Mr. LIU Kai, the investigator of this study. The only people who will know about what I say will be Mr. LIU. Writing my name on this page means that I consent voluntarily to be a participant in this study.

______________	______________
Signature of Participant	Signature of Researcher
______________	______________
Date	Date

References

Agnew, R. (1991). A longitudinal test of social control theory and delinquency. *Journal of Research in Crime and Delinquency, 28*, 126–156.

Alcock, P. (1989). Why citizenship and welfare rights offer new hope for new welfare in Britain. *Critical Social Policy, 19*(2), 32–43.

Arbuckle, J. L. (2011). *Amos 20 user's guide*. Chicago, IL: SPSS.

Arrow, K. J. (1963). Uncertainty and the welfare economics of medical care. *The American Economic Review, 53*, 941–973.

Baldock, J., Manning, N., & Vickerstaff, S. (Eds.). (2003). *Social policy* (2nd ed.). Oxford, England: Oxford University Press.

Baron, R. M., & Kenny, D. A. (1986). The moderator–mediator variable distinction in social psychological research: Conceptual, strategic and statistical considerations. *Journal of Personality and Social Psychology, 51*, 1173–1182.

Bentler, P. M. (1990). Comparative fit indexes in structural models. *Psychological Bulletin, 107*, 238–246.

Berger, P., & Luckmann, T. (1966). *The social construction of reality*. New York, NY: Anchor.

Bloom, G., Han, L., & Li, X. (2000). *How health workers earn a living in China* (IDS Working Paper No. 108). Brighton, England: Institute of Development Studies, The University of Sussex.

Bollen, K. A. (1989). A new incremental fit index for general structural models. *Sociological Methods and Research, 17*, 303–316.

Bourdieu, P., & Wacquant, L. J. D. (1992). *An invitation to reflexive sociology*. Cambridge, England: Polity Press.

Boyatzis, R. E. (1998). *Transforming qualitative information: Thematic analysis and code development*. Thousand Oaks, CA: Sage Publications.

Braun, V., & Clarke, V. (2006). Using thematic analysis in psychology. *Qualitative research in psychology, 3*(2), 77–101.

Burch, H. A. (1999). *Social welfare policy analysis and choices*. New York, NY: Haworth Press.

Campbell, J. L. (1998). Institutional analysis and the role of ideas in political economy. *Theory and Society, 27*, 377–409.

Central Committee of Communist Party of China and State Council. (2009, March 17). Opinions of central committee of communist party of china and state council on deepening the healthcare system reform. Retrieved from http://www.gov.cn/jrzg/2009-04/06/content_1278721.htm (in Chinese).

Chengdu Government. (2008). The temporary measures of Chengdu urban-rural resident basic medical insurance. Retrieved from http://www.chengdu.gov.cn/

Chen, X., Chen, C., Zhang, Y., Yuan, R., & Ye, J. (2011). The effect of health insurance reform on the number of cataract surgeries in Chongqing, China. *BMC Health Services Research, 11*, 67–70.

K. Liu, *The Effects of Social Health Insurance Reform on People's Out-of-Pocket Health Expenditure in China*, DOI 10.1007/978-981-10-1777-3

Chen, Y., & Jin, G. Z. (2012). Does health insurance coverage lead to better health and educational outcomes? Evidence from rural China. *Journal of Health Economics, 31*(1), 1.

China National Health Development Research Center (2009). *Report on China's total health expenditure 2008*. Retrieved from http://www.nhei.cn/KS_4/ks_001/yjbg/

Clark, A. M. (1998). The qualitative-quantitative debate: Moving from positivism and confrontation to post-positivism and reconciliation. *Journal of Advanced Nursing, 27*, 1242–1249.

Cook, T. D., & Campbell, D. T. (1979). *Quasi-experimentation: Design and analysis issues for field settings*. Boston, MA: Houghton Mifflin.

Creswell, J. W. (1994). *Research design: Quantitative and qualitative approaches*. Thousand Oaks, CA: Sage.

Deacon, A. (2002). *Perspectives on welfare: Ideas, ideologies and policy debates*. Buckingham; PA: Open University Press.

Dean, H. (2001). Welfare rights and the "workfare" state. *Benefits, 30*, 1–4.

Denzin, N. K., & Lincoln, Y. S. (2011). Introduction: The discipline and practice of qualitative research. In N. K. Denzin & Y. S. Lincoln (Eds.), *The Sage handbook of qualitative research* (4th ed.). Thousand Oaks, CA: Sage.

DiMaggio, P. J., & Powell, W. W. (1983). The iron cage revisited: Institutional isomorphism and collective rationality. *American Sociological Review, 48*(2), 147–160.

Dwyer, P. (2000). *Welfare rights and responsibilities: Contesting social citizenship*. Bristol, England: Policy Press.

Dwyer, P. (2010). *Understanding social citizenship: Themes and perspectives for policy and practice* (2nd ed.). Bristol, England; Portland, OR: Policy Press.

Eggleston, K., Li, L., Meng, Q. Y., Lindelow, M., & Wagstaff, A. (2008). Health services delivery in China: A literature review. *Health Economics, 17*, 149–165.

Elster, J., & Hylland, A. (Eds.). (1986). *Foundations of social choice theory*. Cambridge, England: Cambridge University Press.

Enthoven, A. C. (1988). *Theory and practice of managed competition in healthcare finance*. Amsterdam, The Netherlands: North-Holland.

Esping-Andersen, G. (1990). *The three worlds of welfare capitalism*. Cambridge, England: Polity Press.

Etzioni, A. (1997). *The new golden rule*. London, England: Profile Books.

Field, F. (1997, September 24). *Welfare: The third way*. Speech at Victoria and Albert Museum, London, England.

Figueras, J., Robinson, R., & Jakubowshi, E. (Eds.). (2005). *Purchasing to improve health systems performance*. Maidenhead, England: Open University Press.

Finlay, L. (2002). Negotiating the swamp: The opportunity and challenge of reflexivity in research practice. *Qualitative Research, 2*(2), 209–230.

General Office of State Council (2003). State council circular on transmitting the suggestions on establishing the new cooperative medical scheme by ministry of health and other ministries. Retrieved from http://www.gov.cn/zwgk/2005-08/12/content_21850.htm

George, V., & Wilding, P. (1994). *Welfare and ideology*. New York, NY: Harvester Wheatsheaf.

Gilbert, N., & Terrell, P. (2002). *Dimensions of social welfare policy* (5th ed.). Boston, MA: Pearson Allyn and Bacon.

Gilbert, N., & Terrell, P. (2013). *Dimensions of social welfare policy* (8th ed.). Boston, MA: Pearson Allyn and Bacon.

Greene, J. C., Caracelli, V. J., & Graham, W. F. (1989). Toward a conceptual framework for mixed-method evaluation designs. *Educational Evaluation and Policy Analysis, 11*(3), 255–274.

Gu, D., Dupre, M. E., Warner, D. F., & Zeng, Y. (2009). Changing health status and health expectancies among older adults in China: Gender differences from 1992 to 2002. *Social Science and Medicine, 68*, 2170–2179.

Gu, X. (2008). *Towards universal coverage of healthcare insurance: The strategies and tactics of Chinese new healthcare reform*. Beijing, China: China Labor and Social Security Press.

Gu, X. (2009). Towards universal coverage: China's new healthcare insurance reforms. In D. L. Yang, & L. T. Zhao (Eds.), *China's reforms at 30: Challenges and prospects*. Singapore; Hackensack, NJ: World Scientific.

Gu, X. (2010). *Universal coverage of healthcare insurance in China: New frontiers*. Beijing: Social Sciences Academic Press (China).

Gu, X., & Fang, L. (2004). Between willingness and coercion: An analysis of institutional embedding and development of cooperative medical schemes in China's countryside. *Sociological Research, 5*, 1–18.

Gu, X., Gao, M., & Yao, Y. (2006). *China's healthcare reforms: A pathological analysis*. Beijing, China: Social Sciences Academic Press (China).

Guba, E. G. (1981). Criteria for assessing the trustworthiness of naturalistic inquiries. *Educational Technology Research and Development, 29*(2), 75–91.

Guba, E. G. (1990). The alternative paradigm dialog. In E. G. Guba (Ed.), *The paradigm dialog* (pp. 17–27). Newbury Park, CA: Sage Publications.

Guba, E. G., & Lincoln, Y. S. (2005). Paradigmatic controversies, contradictions, and emerging confluences. In N. K. Denzin & Y. S. Lincoln (Eds.), *The Sage handbook of qualitative research* (3rd ed., pp. 191–215). Thousand Oaks, CA: Sage.

Guo, J. (2011). The preliminary exploration of the negotiation mechanism of medical insurance in China. *China Social Security, 10*, 11–14. (in Chinese).

Hagist, C., & Kotlikoff, L. J. (2009). Who's going broke? Comparing growth in public healthcare expenditure in ten OECD countries. *Hacienda Publica Espanola, 188*, 55–72.

Hall, P. A., & Taylor, R. C. R. (1996). Political science and the three new institutionalisms. *Political Studies, 44*(5), 936–957.

Hanson, N. R. (1958). *Patterns of discovery*. Cambridge, England: Cambridge University Press.

Harrison, M. L. (1995). *Housing, "race", social policy and empowerment*. Aldershot, England: Avebury.

Holmbeck, G. N. (1997). Toward terminological, conceptual, and statistical clarity in the study of mediators and moderators: Examples from the child-clinical and pediatric psychology literatures. *Journal of Consulting and Clinical Psychology, 65*, 599–610.

Horizon China Research and Consultation Group. (2010, February 25). How Chinese people view new healthcare reform. Retrieved from http://www.ftchinese.com/story/001031441 (in Chinese).

Hsiao, W. C. (2007). Design and implementation of social health insurance. In W. C. Hsiao & R. P. Shaw (Eds.), *Social health insurance for developing nations* (pp. 21–42). Washington, DC: The World Bank.

Hsiao, W. C. (2008). When incentives and professionalism collide. *Health Affairs, 27*(4), 949–951.

Hsiao, W. C., & Shaw, R. P. (2007). Introduction, context, and theory. In W. C. Hsiao & R. P. Shaw (Eds.), *Social health insurance for developing nations* (pp. 1–20). Washington, DC: The World Bank.

Idler, E., & Benyamini, Y. (1997). Self-rated health and mortality: A review of twenty-seven community studies. *Journal of Health and Social Behavior, 38*, 21–37.

Jiang, Q., Jiang, Z., Zhao, M., Tao, J., Ling, C., & Cherry, N. (2011). Evaluation of a pilot cooperative medical scheme in rural China: Impact on gender patterns of healthcare utilization and prescription practices. *BMC Public Health, 11*, 50–59.

Johnson, R. B., Onwuegbuzie, A. J., & Turner, L. A. (2007). Toward a definition of mixed methods research. *Journal of Mixed Methods Research, 1*(2), 112–133.

Jung, J., & Liu, J. (2012). *Does health insurance decrease health expenditure risk in developing countries? The case of China* (Working Paper No. 2011–04). Department of Economics, Towson University, MD.

Kline, R. B. (2005). *Principles and practice of structural equation modeling* (2nd ed.). New York, NY: Guilford Press.

Kuhn, T. S. (1962). *The structure of scientific revolutions*. Chicago, IL: University of Chicago Press.

Lawton, M. P., & Brody, E. M. (1969). Assessment of older people: Self-maintaining and instrumental activities of daily living. *Gerontologist, 9*(3), 179–186.

Le Grand, J. (1993). Paying for or providing welfare? In N. Deakin & R. Page (Eds.), *The costs of welfare* (pp. 87–106). Aldershot, England: Avebury.

Lei, X., & Lin, W. (2009). The new cooperative medical scheme in rural China: Does more coverage mean more service and better health? *Health Economics, 18*, S25.

Lewis, G. (1998). Citizenship. In G. Hughes (Ed.), *Imagining welfare futures*. London, England: Routledge/Open University Press.

Li, L. (2009). *Improving health in China*. Beijing, China: Peking University Press.

Lister, R. (2003). *Citizenship: Feminist perspectives* (2nd ed.). Basingstoke, England: Palgrave Macmillan.

Liu, D., & Tsegao, D. (2011). *The New Cooperative Medical Scheme (NCMS) and its implications for access to healthcare and medical expenditure: Evidence from rural China* (ZEF Discussion Papers on Development Policy No. 155). Bonn, Germany: Center for Development Research.

Liu, G. G., Guan, H. J., & Pan, J. (2011). *How medical costs changed with the role of urban resident basic medical insurance program?*. Beijing: Peking University, China Centre for Health Economic Research.

Liu, G. G., & Zhao, Z. (2006). Urban employee health insurance reform and the impact on out-of-pocket payment in China. *International Journal of Health Planning and Management, 21*(3), 211–228.

Liu, J. Q. (2011). Dynamics of social health insurance development: Examining the determinants of Chinese basic health insurance coverage with panel data. *Social Science and Medicine, 73*, 550–558.

Liu, X., Tang, S., Yu, B., Phuong, N. K., Yan, F., Thien, D. D., et al. (2012). Can rural health insurance improve equity in healthcare utilization? A comparison between China and Vietnam. *International Journal for Equity in Health, 11*(1), 10–18.

Liu, X. Z., & Mills, A. (1999). Evaluating payment mechanisms: How can we measure unnecessary care? *Health Policy and Planning, 14*(4), 409–413.

Long, Q., Zhang, T., Xu, L., Tang, S., & Hemminki, E. (2010). Utilisation of maternal healthcare in western rural China under a new rural health insurance system (New Co-operative Medical System). *Tropical Medicine and International Health, 15*(10), 1210–1217.

Lu, C., Liu, Y., & Shen, J. (2011). Does China's rural cooperative medical system achieve its goals? Evidence from the China health surveillance baseline survey in 2001. *Contemporary Economic Policy, 30*(1), 93–112.

MacKinnon, D. P., Krull, J. L., & Lockwood, C. M. (2000). Equivalence of the mediation, confounding and suppression effect. *Prevention Science, 1*(14), 173–181.

MacKinnon, D. P., Lockwood, C. M., Hoffman, J. M., West, S. G., & Sheets, V. (2002). A comparison of methods to test the significance of the mediated effect. *Psychological Methods, 7*, 83–104.

March, J. G., & Olsen, J. P. (1984). The new institutionalism: Organizational factors in political life. *The American Political Science Review, 78*(3), 734–749.

Marshall, T. H. (1963). Citizenship and social class. In T. H. Marshall (Ed.), *Sociology at the crossroads*. London, England: Heinemann.

Maynard, A. (1994). Can competition enhance efficiency in healthcare? Lessons from the reform of the U.K. National Health Service. *Social Science and Medicine, 39*, 1433–1445.

Mead, L. (1986). *Beyond entitlement: The social obligations of citizenship*. New York, NY: Free Press.

Meng, Q. (2008). *Provider payment reforms in China: An updated review (World Bank AAA Report)*. Washington, DC: World Bank.

Meng, Q., Xu, L., Zhang, Y., Qian, J., Cai, M., Xin, Y., et al. (2012). Trends in access to health services and financial protection in China between 2003 and 2011: A cross-sectional study. *Lancet, 379*, 805–814.

Ministry of Health (2000–2013). China Health Statistical Yearbook 2000–2013. Retrieved from: http://www.moh.gov.cn/

Ministry of Health (2012). *The development of the new cooperative medical scheme in China* (Material 2 of the Press Conference of the State Council Information Office). Available at http://www.moh.gov.cn/mohbgt/s3582/201209/55893.shtml (in Chinese).

Ministry of Health, Correcting Industrial Illegitimate Practice Office of the State Council, National Development and Reform Commission, Ministry of Supervision, Ministry of Finance, State Administration for Industry and Commerce, & State Food and Drug Administration (2010). *Notice on issuing the work norms of centralized procurement of drugs for healthcare organizations.* Available at http://www.sda.gov.cn/WS01/CL0056/51391.html (in Chinese).

Ministry of Human Resource and Social Security (2000–2011). *China labor statistical yearbook 2000–2011*. Retrieved from: http://www.mohrss.gov.cn/

Ministry of Human Resource and Social Security. (2011, May 31). *Ministry of human resource and social security suggestions on implementing further the payment methods reform of social health insurance.* Retrieved from http://www.gov.cn/gongbao/content/2011/content_2004738.htm (in Chinese).

Ministry of Human Resources and Social Security. (2011). *National social security agencies in 2010.* Available at http://www.gov.cn/gzdt/2011-08/10/content_1923002.htm (in Chinese).

Morse, J. M. (2010). Procedures and practice of mixed method design: Maintaining control, rigor, and complexity. In A. Tashakkori & C. Teddlie (Eds.), *Sage handbook of mixed methods in social and behavioral research* (2nd ed., pp. 339–352). Thousand Oaks, CA: Sage Publications.

Murray, C. (1996). *Charles Murray and the underclass*. London, England: IEA.

National Bureau of Statistics of China. (2011). *China statistical yearbook 2011*. Retrieved from http://www.stats.gov.cn/

National Development and Reform Commission, Ministry of Health, & Ministry of Human Resources and Social Security. (2009). *Notice on issuing the recommendations of reforming medicine and medical service price formation mechanism.* Retrieved from http://www.sdpc.gov.cn/zcfb/zcfbtz/2009tz/t20091123_314758.htm.

Offe, C. (1982). Some contradictions of the modern welfare state. *Critical Social Policy, 2*(5), 7–16.

Ozawa, S., & Pongpirul, K. (2014). 10 best resources on … mixed methods research in health systems. *Health Policy and Planning, 29*, 323–327.

Peters, B. G. (1999). *Institutional theory in political science: The "new institutionalism"*. London, England; New York, NY: Pinter.

Phillips, D. C. (1990). Subjectivity and objectivity: An objective inquiry. In E. W. Eisner & A. Peshkin (Eds.), *Qualitative inquiry in education: The continuing debate*. New York, NY: Teachers College Press.

Popper, K. R. (1959). *The logic of scientific discovery*. New York, NY: Basic Books.

Popper, K. R. (1962). *Conjectures and refutations: The growth of scientific knowledge*. New York, NY: Basic Books.

Preker, A. S. (2005). Managing scarcity through strategic purchasing of healthcare. In A. S. Preker & J. C. Langenbrunner (Eds.), *Spending wisely: Buying health services for the poor* (pp. 23–46). Washington, DC: The World Bank.

Ratcliffe, J. (1983). *The rise of scientific philosophy*. Berkeley, CA; Los Angeles, LA: University of California Press.

Redden, C. J. (2002). *Healthcare, entitlement, and citizenship*. Toronto, Canada: University of Toronto Press.

Robinson, R., Jakubowski, E., & Figueras, J. (2005). Introduction. In J. Figueras, R. Robinson, & E. Jakubowshi (Eds.), *Purchasing to improve health systems performance* (pp. 3–10). Maidenhead, England: Open University Press.

Ron, A., Abel-smith, B., & Tamburi, G. (1990). *Health insurance in developing countries: The social security approach.* Geneva, Switzerland: International Labor Organization.

Schumacher, K. L., & Gortner, S. R. (1992). (Mis)conceptions and reconceptions about traditional science. *Advances in Nursing Science, 14*(4), 1–11.

Scott, W. R. (1994). Institutions and organizations: Towards a theoretical synthesis. In W. R. Scott & J. W. Meyer (Eds.), *Institutional environments and organizations: Structural complexity and individualism.* Thousand Oaks, CA: Sage.

Shepsle, K., & Weingast, B. (1987). The institutional foundations of committee power. *American Political Science Review, 81*, 85–104.

Shi, F., Zhu, W., Zhang, W., Zhang, W. P., & Liu, H. M. (2011). Trends in inpatient utilization and expenditure for the new cooperative medical scheme in a city (in Chinese). *J Med Forum, 32*, 107–109.

Shi, W., Chongsuvivatwong, V., Geater, A., Zhang, J., Zhang, H., & Brombal, D. (2010). The influence of the rural health security schemes on health utilization and household impoverishment in rural China: Data from a household survey of Western and Central China. *International Journal for Equity in Health, 9*, 7–17.

Small, M. L. (2011). How to conduct a mixed methods study: Recent trends in a rapidly growing literature. *Annual Review of Sociology, 37*, 57–86.

Sobel, M. E. (1987). Direct and indirect effects in linear structural equation models. *Sociological Methods and Research, 16*(1), 155–176.

Social Insurance Institute of Ministry of Labor and Social Security. (2005). *Research on the administrative funds of foreign health insurance agencies.* Retrieved from http://www.calss.net.cn/ (in Chinese).

Song, D., Zhao, D., Yang, Z., Liu, Y., & Wang, Z. (2008). Current situation and countermeasures of new cooperative medical scheme managerial and executive system construction. *Chinese Health Economics, 2*, 39–42. (in Chinese).

Stabile, M., & Thomson, S. (2013). *The changing role of government in financing healthcare: An international perspective* (Working Paper No. 19439). Cambridge, MA: National Bureau of Economic Research. Retrieved from http://www.nber.org/papers/w19439.

State Council (1998). *State council decision on establishing the urban employee basic medical insurance.* Retrieved from http://www.gov.cn/banshi/2005-08/04/content_20256.htm

State Council (2007). *State council guiding suggestions on piloting the urban residents basic medical insurance scheme.* Retrieved from http://www.gov.cn/zwgk/2007-07/24/content_695118.htm

State Council (2010). *State Council suggestions on the trial implementation of social insurance funds budget.* Retrieved from http://www.gov.cn/zwgk/2010-01/06/content_1504494.htm

Steiger, J. H. (1990). Structural model evaluation and modification: An interval estimation approach. *Multivariate Behavioral Research, 25*, 173–180.

Stewart, J. (2009). *The MacArthur scale of social environment notebook.* Retrieved from http://www.macses.ucsf.edu /Research/socialenviron/default.php

Su, W. (2012). Performance analysis of medical insurance negotiation in Chengdu. *China Health Insurance, 10*, 27–29. (in Chinese).

Sun, Q., Liu, X., Meng, Q., Tang, S., Yu, B., & Tolhurst, R. (2009). Evaluating the financial protection of patients with chronic disease by health insurance in rural China. *International Journal for Equity in Health, 8.*

Sun, X., Jackson, S., Carmichael, G., & Sleigh, A. C. (2009). Catastrophic medical payment and financial protection in rural China: Evidence from the new cooperative medical scheme in Shandong province. *Health Economics, 18*(1), 103–119.

Sun, X., Sleigh, A. C., Carmichael, G. A., & Jackson, S. (2010). Health payment-induced poverty under China's new cooperative medical scheme in rural Shandong. *Health Policy and Planning, 25*(5), 419–426.

Taylor, G. (2007). *Ideology and welfare*. New York, NY: Palgrave Macmillan.

The Healthcare Reform Office of the State Council (2012). *A summary report of deepening the reform of the national healthcare and medicine system.* Retrieved from http://www.gov.cn/jrzg/2012-06/25/content_2169562.htm

Lancet, The. (2010). Chinese doctors are under threat. *The Lancet, 376*, 657.

Titmuss, R. M. (1963). *Essays on the welfare state* (2nd ed.). London, England: Allen & Unwin.

Turner, B. S. (1993). *Citizenship and social theory*. London, England: Sage.

Twine, F. (1994). *Citizenship and social rights: The interdependence of self and society*. London, England: Sage.

Van de Ven, W. P. M. M., Schut, F. T., & Rutten, F. F. H. (1994). Forming and reforming the market for third-party purchasing of healthcare. *Social Science and Medicine, 39*, 1405–1412.

Wagstaff, A. (2007). *Social health insurance reexamined* (World Bank Policy Research Working Paper No. 4111). Retrieved from https://openknowledge.worldbank.org/bitstream/handle/10986/6886/wps4111.pdf?sequence=1

Wagstaff, A., & Lindelow, M. (2008). Can insurance increase financial risk? The curious case of health insurance in China. *Journal of Health Economics, 27*, 990–1005.

Wagstaff, A., Lindelow, M., Jun, G., Ling, X., & Juncheng, Q. (2009). Extending health insurance to the rural population: An impact evaluation of China's new cooperative medical scheme. *Journal of Health Economics, 28*(1), 1–19.

Wang, H., Yip, W., Zhang, L., & Hsiao, W. C. (2009). The impact of rural mutual healthcare on health status: Evaluation of a social experiment in rural China. *Health Economics, 18*(SUPPL. 2), S65–S82.

Wang, H., Yip, W., Zhang, L., Wang, L., & Hsiao, W. C. (2005). Community-based health insurance in poor rural China: The distribution of net benefits. *Health Policy and Planning, 20* (6), 366–374.

Wang, S. (2005). State policy orientation, extractive capacity and the equality of healthcare in urban China. *Social Sciences in China, 6*, 101–120.

Wei, Z., Song, J., Zhang, J., & Guan, X. (2012). Systematic reflection on the negotiation mechanism of the social medical insurance drug. *China Health insurance, 8*, 53–56. (in Chinese).

Wendt, A. (1987). The agent-structure problem in international relations theory. *International Organization, 41*(3), 335–370.

Wong, C. K., Lo, V. L., & Tang, K. L. (2006). *China's urban healthcare reform: From state protection to individual responsibility*. Lanham, MD: Lexington Books.

Wong, C. K., & Walker, A. (1998). The enlightenment of the conceptual transition of western social policy on the development of Chinese welfare systems. *Sociological Research, 5*, 44–50. (in Chinese).

World Health Organization (2014). *Global Health Expenditure Database*. Retrieved from http://apps.who.int/nha/database/Select/Indicators/en.

Xiao, S., Yan, H., Shen, Y., Dang, S., Hemminki, E., Wang, D., et al. (2010). Utilization of delivery care among rural women in China: Does the health insurance make a difference? A cross-sectional study. *BMC Public Health, 10*(1), 695–701.

Xiong, J., Xia, X., Cheng, X., & Li, Y. (2012). A SEM-based study on influence factors of hospital choice. *Chinese Health Services Management, 2*, 84–87. (in Chinese).

Xu, W., & Van de Ven, W. P. M. M. (2009). Purchasing healthcare in China: Competing or non-competing third-party purchasers? *Health Policy, 92*, 305–312.

Xu, W., & Van de Ven, W. P. M. M. (2012). The level of consumer information about health insurance in Nanjing, China. *The International Journal of Health Planning and Management*, doi:10.1002/hpm.2138

Yang, T., Lu, J. H., & Wu, M. C. (2008). Chinese doctors' salaries. *The Lancet, 371*, 1576–1577.

Yi, H., Zhang, L., Singer, K., Rozelle, S., & Atlas, S. (2009). Health insurance and catastrophic illness: A report on the new cooperative medical system in rural China. *Health Economics, 18* (SUPPL. 2), S119–S127.

Yip, W. C., & Hanson, K. (2009). Purchasing healthcare in China: Experiences, opportunities and challengers. In D. Chernichovsky & K. Hanson (Eds.), *Innovations in health system finance in developing and transitional economies*. Emerald/JAI: Bingley, England.

Yip, W. C., & Hsiao, W. C. (2008). The Chinese health system at a crossroads. *Health Affairs, 27* (2), 460–468.

Yip, W. C., & Hsiao, W. C. (2009). Non-evidence-based policy: How effective is China's new cooperative medical scheme in reducing medical impoverishment? *Social Science and Medicine, 68*(2), 201–209.

Yip, W. C., & Hsiao, W. C. (2014). Harnessing the privatisation of China's fragmented health-care delivery. *The Lancet, 384*, 805–818.

Yip, W. C., Hsiao, W. C., Chen, W., Hu, S., Ma, J., & Maynard, A. (2012). Early appraisal of China's huge and complex health-care reforms. *The Lancet, 379*, 833–842.

Yip, W., Hsiao, W., Meng, Q., Chen, W., & Sun, X. (2010). Realignment of incentives for health-care providers in China. *The Lancet, 375*, 1120–1130.

You, X., & Kobayashi, Y. (2009). The new cooperative medical scheme in China. *Health Policy, 91*(1), 1–9.

Zhang, L., Cheng, X., Tolhurst, R., Tang, S., & Liu, X. (2010). How effectively can the new cooperative medical scheme reduce catastrophic health expenditure for the poor and non-poor in rural China? *Tropical Medicine and International Health, 15*(4), 468–475.

Zhang, X., & Kanbur, R. (2005). Spatial inequality in education and healthcare in China. *China Economic Review, 16*(2), 189–204.

Zhao, Y. H., Strauss, J., Yang, G. H., Giles, J., Hu, P. F., Hu, Y. S., et al. (2013, February). *China health and retirement longitudinal study: 2011–2012 national baseline users' guide*. Retrieved from http://charls.ccer.edu.cn

Zhou, B., Yang, L., Sun, Q., Gu, H., & Wang, B. (2008). Social health insurance and drug spending among cancer inpatients in China. *Health Affairs, 27*(4), 1020–1027.

Zhou, S. (2011). *Research on negotiation mechanism of social health insurance in China* (Doctoral thesis). Huazhong University of Science and Technology (pp. 58–59). Retrieved from http://cdmd.cnki.com.cn/Article/CDMD-10487-1011110328.htm (in Chinese).

Zhou, Y. Y. (2012, November 29). *Bai Chong-en: The contribution rate of social insurance is too high, which is bad for the process of urbanization*. Retrieved from http://m.caijing.com.cn/economy/2012-11-29/112321426.html (in Chinese).

Zhou, Z., Gao, J., Zhou, Z., & Yang, X. (2012). Measuring the benefit equity in China's basic health insurance schemes. *HealthMED, 6*(1), 47–52.

Index

K. Liu, *The Effects of Social Health Insurance Reform on People's Out-of-Pocket Health Expenditure in China*, DOI 10.1007/978-981-10-1777-3

The manufacturer's authorised representative in the EU is Springer Nature Customer Service Centre GmbH, Europaplatz 3, 69115 Heidelberg, Germany. If you have any concerns regarding our products, please contact ProductSafety@springernature.com

Printed and bound by CPI Group (UK) Ltd, Croydon, CR0 4YY
25/09/2026
02222896-0002